"*Ants in My Pants* is a joyful re...
you into her magical and varied adventures in countries many of us have never visited. Her courage and plucky spirit shine through the myriad of stories that grew to define her as a woman. Funny, self-deprecating, and inspiring—you won't be able to put it down."

Deb Stratas, author of *The Kingston Twins Series*

"*Ants in My Pants* takes us up the heart-stopping heights of Mt. Kilimanjaro, diving with sharks, crossing sand dunes by camel, roughing it in rural communities without running water, celebrating the trials and triumphs of every-day people, and sailing to cold, distant corners of a world seldom seen by most. Joyce's fascinating anecdotes left me gripping my chair, gasping with laughter and holding my breath; her dedication to education and health care may have been the jumping-off point for her travels, but it's her immense bravery, in the face of some rather precarious situations, that is nothing short of awe-inspiring.

"Accomplishing the extraordinary as a single white woman in countries dominated by ruthless, intimidating men, Joyce is a true heroine. These are not the travels of your typical all-inclusive kind of vacationer but, instead, the kind of exploits that will keep you turning pages long after you should have turned out the lights."

Jeanette Manning, coauthor of *Walking Away from Hate: Our Journey through Extremism*

"Put on your hiking boots, grab your backpack and join the author as she travels the world, intent on seeing new places and meeting people of other nationalities and cultures. Her curiosity and adventurous nature are sometimes met with unexpected and sometimes dangerous situations, and she manages to keep her cool and learn from them while keeping the reader in mind by sharing with us the emotional challenges at each decision point. So, enjoy the adventure by keeping an open mind, and you may find yourself making plans for an adventure of your own."

Connie Campbell, RN, CPHQ, who worked for seventeen years in Saudi Arabia

"Wow! A fascinating voyage through many countries with a personal twist. Joyce's adventures across seven continents kept me reading almost non-stop."

Richard R. Pyves,
author of *Night Madness* and *Courage, Sacrifice, and Betrayal*

"Travel, community, and health—three things the world can use more of—all wrapped into this wonderful life story. From providing aid to needing some assistance on her adventures, Joyce shares her passion, kindness, and courage. A fun and exciting read!"

Matthew Anderson, President and Chief Executive
Officer, Ontario Health, Toronto, Canada

"There's no stopping Joyce Perrin and that is a gift for anyone reading her memoir. Every adventure is offered in her warm and inviting style so that you feel just like you're along for the journey. And what a journey. Climb Mt. Kilimanjaro to arrive at sunrise, feel the heat of a red sand dune beneath your feet, pop a freshly picked date into your mouth—no matter where Joyce takes you in the world, there are delights to discover, and people and places to know."

Ruth E. Walker, author and editor

"When I opened the first page, we were strangers. Then, Joyce took my hand and led me through the beautifully written stories of her adventurous life and we became forever-friends. I could not put the book down."

Judy Lund-Bell, attorney, pilot, and
author of *Flying with a Dragon on Our Tail*

"A delightful chronicle of a life well lived. It is so much more than a brave woman with "ants in her pants." It is a purposeful adventure, and I was moved as much by the impact the writer had on the people on her journey as I was with the travel itself. If you want to make a change in your life, explore another culture or just have a good armchair adventure, this book is for you!"

Dorothy Payne, MSc, Health and Wellness Promotion

Ants in My Pants

SHADED AREAS INDICATE COUNTRIES VISITED

The Countries I've Visited

This system divides the world into seven geographic continents: Asia, Africa, North America, South America, Antarctica, Europe, and Australia/Oceania. I include Countries and Territories that I have traveled, some extensively and others for a short time.

Countries of Africa:

- Algeria
- Benin
- Botswana
- Burkina Faso
- Burundi
- Cabo Verde/Cape Verde
- Comoros
- Egypt (transcontinental - generally considered African)
- Equatorial Guinea
- Eritrea
- Eswatini (formerly Swaziland)
- Ethiopia
- Gabon
- Gambia, The
- Ghana
- Guinea
- Guinea-Bissau
- Ivory Coast/Republic of Côte d'Ivoire
- Kenya
- Lesotho
- Libya
- Madagascar
- Malawi
- Mali
- Mauritania
- Mauritius
- Morocco
- Mozambique
- Namibia
- Nigeria
- Rwanda
- Senegal
- Seychelles
- Sierra Leone
- South Africa
- Sudan
- Tanzania
- Togo
- Tunisia
- Uganda
- Zambia
- Zimbabwe

Territories of Africa:

- Canary Islands (Spain)
- French Southern and Antarctic Lands (France)
- Madeira (Portugal)
- Reunion (France)

Countries of Asia:

- Bahrain
- Bhutan
- Brunei
- Cambodia
- China
- Cyprus (transcontinental - generally considered European)
- Egypt (transcontinental - generally considered African)

- Georgia (transcontinental - generally considered Asian)
- India
- Indonesia
- Israel (U. N. member, though partially unrecognized)
- Japan
- Jordan
- Kazakhstan (transcontinental - generally considered Asian)
- Kuwait
- Kyrgyzstan
- Laos
- Lebanon
- Malaysia
- Maldives
- Mongolia
- Myanmar (formerly Burma)
- Nepal
- Oman
- Pakistan
- Palestine (limited recognition)
- Philippines
- Qatar
- Russia (transcontinental - generally considered European)
- Saudi Arabia
- Singapore
- South Korea (Republic of Korea)
- Sri Lanka
- Syria
- Thailand
- Turkey (transcontinental - generally considered European)
- Turkmenistan
- United Arab Emirates
- Uzbekistan
- Vietnam
- Yemen

Territories of Asia:
- Hong Kong (China - Special Administrative Region)
- Macau (China - Special Administrative Region)
- Taiwan (limited recognition - claimed by China)

Countries of Europe:
- Austria
- Azerbaijan (transcontinental - generally considered Asian)
- Belarus
- Belgium
- Bosnia and Herzegovina
- Bulgaria
- Croatia
- Cyprus (generally considered European)
- Czechia/Czech Republic
- Denmark
- Estonia
- Finland
- France
- Georgia (transcontinental - generally considered Asian)
- Germany
- Greece
- Hungary
- Iceland
- Ireland
- Italy
- Kazakhstan (transcontinental - generally considered Asian)
- Latvia
- Liechtenstein
- Luxembourg
- Malta
- Moldova

- Monaco
- Netherlands
- Norway
- Poland
- Portugal
- Romania
- Russia (transcontinental - generally considered European)
- Spain
- Sweden
- Switzerland
- Turkey (transcontinental - generally considered European)
- Ukraine
- United Kingdom
- Vatican City (Holy See)

Territories of Europe:
- Gibraltar (UK)
- Northern Cyprus (not recognized, claimed by Cyprus)
- Northern Ireland (UK)
- Svalbard (Norway)

Countries of North America:
- Antigua and Barbuda
- Bahamas
- Barbados
- Belize
- Canada
- Costa Rica
- Cuba
- Dominican Republic
- Grenada
- Guatemala
- Honduras
- Jamaica
- Mexico

- Nicaragua
- Panama
- Saint Kitts and Nevis
- Saint Lucia
- Saint Vincent and the Grenadines
- Trinidad and Tobago
- United States of America

Territories of North America:
- Anguilla (UK)
- Aruba (Netherlands)
- Bermuda (UK)
- Bonaire (Netherlands)
- British Virgin Islands (UK)
- Cayman Islands (UK)
- Greenland (Denmark)
- Guadeloupe (France)
- Martinique (France)
- Puerto Rico (USA)
- Turks and Caicos (UK)
- USA Virgin Islands (USA)

Australia and Countries of Oceania:
- Australia
- Fiji
- New Zealand
- Palau
- Papua New Guinea
- Vanuatu

Territories of Oceania:
- Easter Island (Chile)
- Galapagos Islands (Ecuador)

Countries of South America:

- Argentina
- Bolivia
- Brazil
- Chile
- Colombia
- Ecuador
- Guyana
- Paraguay
- Peru
- Suriname
- Uruguay
- Venezuela

Territories of South America:

- Falkland Islands (UK)
- French Guinea (France)

Territories of Antarctica:

- Vernadsky Station (Ukraine/UK)
- Scott Base - Ross Island (New Zealand)
- Zucchelli - Terra Nova Bay (Italy)
- McMurdo - Ross Island (USA)
- Macquarie - Macquarie Island (Australia)

Source: https://worldpopulationreview.com/country-rankings/

list-of-countries-by-continent

ONE WOMAN'S UNEXPECTED ADVENTURES ACROSS SEVEN CONTINENTS

JOYCE E. PERRIN

CANADA

Gaps in travel dates appear because those adventures did not make this book. All the stories are real and as remembered. Many of the names have been changed to protect privacy. To view more accounts of the author's world travels and to contact the author, visit www.JoycePerrin.com.

Hardcover: 978-1-7388688-1-0
Paperback: 978-1-7388688-3-4
Kindle: 978-1-7388688-5-8
Audiobook: 978-1-7388688-4-1

Production by Concierge Marketing Inc., www.conciergemarketing.com

Printed in Canada
10 9 8 7 6 5 4 3 2 1

Life is what you make it, it can be a true joy!
May you fulfill your dreams and follow your
passion no matter your age.
Dedicated to all who have nourished my soul
and lent a helping hand throughout
my rich life experiences.

Contents

Introduction

I love to explore new vistas. Curiosity and thirst for knowledge are my passions. My professional expertise is in administration, quality improvement policies, and delivery systems used in hospitals and healthcare organizations in different countries.

Growing up in a loving family in Edmonton, Alberta, in western Canada, I came from pioneer stock. On my father's side, my grandfather, Dr. Peter Aylen, was a physician with the Royal Canadian Mounted Police, patrolling through southern Alberta on horseback. Later, he opened his medical practice in Fort Saskatchewan, near Edmonton, caring for the community and farming the land.

My mother's grandfather, the Honorable John Norquay, a Métis, was an early Premier of the midwestern Canadian province of Manitoba. Mount Norquay, a mountain in Banff, Alberta, was named in his honor. We were proud to be Métis (a person of mixed Indigenous and Euro-American ancestry).

Gran, my mom's mother, lived with us in Edmonton. She was the chef in our kitchen, and the corners of her mouth would turn up in a smile as she cooked. Her eyes sparkled, and her open arms welcomed anyone into her domain. She was a hugger. Her black and white hair was pulled back into a bun with rarely a strand out of place. Her earlobes drooped from the weight of her earrings, made from gold panned from the North Saskatchewan River. When she wasn't cooking, a cigarette would hang from her mouth, her hand cupped under her chin, ready to catch the ash before it hit the floor.

One of my happiest childhood memories was Gran's brown bread. Molasses and cracked brown grains of whole wheat mixed into the dough gave the bread a unique bouquet I have never forgotten. Gran always perfectly timed my arrival home from school. As I burst through the door, the rich aroma of fresh bread would fill my nostrils. The bread would still be warm, waiting to be sliced. I would slather on the soft butter and watch it melt into the bread, ready to take my first bite. Soon the loaf would disappear before it had even cooled. I have included the recipe on my website. I invite you to try it.

As a young athlete, I challenged my body in synchronized swimming and figure skating. In high school I was the head cheerleader, a winner, and a leader. As a Girl Guide patrol leader, I was curious, always learning, amassing badges, and took my patrol on trips to the Coca-Cola factory, dairy farms, and museums. I achieved the Gold Cord, the highest award in Guiding.

My horizons expanded when I was seventeen. I had the opportunity to learn about people who lived in other parts of the world when I was chosen as one of ten Girl Guides to represent Canada at an International Girl Guide Camp in Sweden. I met Lady Olave Baden-Powell, the founder of the movement, and was mesmerized by her ability to create such a meaningful worldwide organization. Someone took our photo, and I captioned it, "The Most Interesting Person I Have Ever Met."

While at camp and meeting guides from many countries, I solidified my love of exploration and curiosity about other cultures. I was captivated by how other people lived, how they dressed, what they ate, and where they went to school. Then and there, not only did I want to travel the world, but I wanted to live in other countries, to understand people and their cultures. That summer set my destiny in motion.

After I graduated from high school, I headed off to the University of Alberta to study nursing. It was a fantastic time in my life; I joined the women's Pi Beta Phi Fraternity (some are called Sororities). I was a swimmer and won several synchronized swimming championships. I also served as vice president of the Student Union and thrived, greeting international visitors from other universities. In 1958 I graduated with a bachelor of science degree in nursing and received the Dr. A. C. McGugan Prize in Nursing and the Florence E. Dodd Award for the outstanding woman graduate. Dreams of traveling still filled my mind, but I chose to marry instead.

Together with my husband, we raised three wonderful children, living and working in the United States and Canada. Life was busy. I was a nursing supervisor in a local hospital in Hamilton, Ontario; Boston; and Chicago. In Michigan I was a consultant with the Visiting Nurse Association. When we returned to Canada, I headed back to school and achieved my diploma in hospital administration (now considered a master's degree level). I was one of two women in the class. My experiences and education led to my becoming a hospital CEO. But my dreams of seeing more of the world were never too far from my mind.

By the time I could start living those dreams, Ed and I had gone our separate ways and all my children were grown and married. The opportunity to explore the world came in my late fifties when I left a senior healthcare executive job in Canada to take on a new professional role in an Arab country. I was excited to begin exploring, connecting with people, sharing meals, and listening to their life stories.

I sold my condo and stored my belongings, never unpacking them until nearly twenty-four years later. From 1993 to 2016

I traveled to as many places as I could, only returning to Canada now and again to visit family. As one granddaughter said in a school essay, "My gran is homeless."

My journey began in 1993 in Saudi Arabia, leading the quality improvement department at two separate hospital organizations. Later, I consulted for the World Health Organization and volunteered for the United Nations Development Program and the International Executive Service Corps, and then cofounded a hospice program in Panama.

I climbed Mount Kilimanjaro, swam with the sharks and turtles in the Galapagos Islands, and trekked through the jungles in Uganda to see the gorillas in their natural habitat. I explored Machu Picchu, shared coffee with Arabs in the desert, and stayed with some wonderful people in their homes in countries such as New Zealand, Australia, Zambia, Tanzania, Namibia, Lesotho, and South Africa. Each experience touched my soul. The only trip I missed was cruising through the Northwest Passage in the Arctic because first it was ice bound, then closed during COVID, and now my health is an issue.

What follows are my impressions after twenty-three years of exploring 156 countries and 31 territories, working with wonderful people, staying with welcoming families, and spreading love.

Chapter 1

Where Was I Going?
Traveling into the Unknown

My eyes fixated on the rough sea below. It would be so easy for me to climb over the railing and be gone. The water would swallow me up in seconds. There was no one else around and no one would look for me until morning.

The water broke against the *SS Britanis* as it forced its way through the roiling sea along the Chilean coast. The boat's fight against the onslaught of water matched my fight against dark thoughts and self-doubt about my life. I had resigned from my job. I had sold my condo. I had put all my treasures into storage, and I had updated my will. Everything was in order. Who would miss me?

Each day my thoughts got worse. I had gambled with my future. I had resigned from my Canadian senior healthcare executive position without the certainty of another job. What was I thinking? At night I cried about the first Saudi Arabian job I had applied for that had slipped through my fingers. Although the human resources department verbally offered me the job, disaster struck, and the company froze hiring before they processed my final papers. The job had been perfect. The salary would have embellished my bank account, and the generous vacation time would have given me a chance to explore the world. The Saudi Arabian recruiter had told me about a second opportunity, so I had applied and set off on this cruise while I waited to hear.

I was traveling solo on this fifty-two-day cruise, circumnavigating South America. My long-term vision was to be a modern-day explorer, traveling to a minimum of one hundred countries and the seven continents, fulfilling my childhood dream.

There was no one to share it with.

I was proud of my three children, who had graduated from university and married. I was a fifty-seven-year-old divorced woman, leaving my home in Canada behind. It was difficult. I felt alone, discarded, unwanted.

Days passed and my evening strolls along the deck became more frequent. I focused on the water, often charcoal black with no moon or stars. I felt the waves pull me closer. Their color mirrored my mood. Each day I waited to hear about my new job application, and each day I looked for the telegram, but no news came.

We had departed from Miami and transited the Panama Canal. Little did I know I would settle in Panama in my midseventies. The weeks continued to fly by as we visited Panama, Costa Rica, Chile, Argentina, Uruguay, Brazil, Devil's Island off the coast of French Guiana, Venezuela, Barbados, and St. Thomas. All the guests were gifted with china plates showing highlights of our cruise. My mood was changing, and life was good.

Then one night, I received a telegram during dinner. I stared at it and realized this piece of paper contained my whole future. My hands shook as I tore open the envelope.

"Wow, I'm off to Saudi Arabia starting January 1, 1993, as director of quality assurance at Security Forces Hospital in Riyadh!"

I couldn't help but yell, waving the telegram above my head in triumph. Someone at our table called for champagne, and we celebrated into the small hours of the morning.

I had gambled, and I had won!

My souvenir plate, which I still use while entertaining, always promotes conversations about adventures to share.

Chapter 2

What Have I Done?
Saudi Arabia Seems Dangerous

It was January 1 and I stood at the top of the second-floor escalator at the King Khalid International Airport in Riyadh, Saudi Arabia. I stopped breathing. Not because of the glitter of gold and silver everywhere, but because of the AK-47 machine gun pointing directly at my chest.

I automatically placed my hand protectively over my racing heart. My gasp caused a passerby, in a long black covering with a black veil, to turn quickly, stare, then move on. An AK-47 was not what I wanted to see, especially when the soldier trained it on me. Our eyes locked, the soldier's and mine. I felt oppressed. I wanted to run back to the plane and return to my familiar safe home in Canada.

Now the soldier was pointing his gun somewhere else. Other soldiers holding guns were doing the same. Were they on alert, or was this the norm? I had no idea. My legs were ready to run out of the airport and fast.

The plastic cover of my passport stuck to my hand as I pushed it under the glass barrier and glanced at the Saudi immigration officer. His eyes, unfriendly, pierced through me, increasing my anxiety as I waited. He stamped my passport, shoved it back, and pointed to the right. I turned and followed the crowd.

I felt lost in this large, spotless airport. I ached to see a friendly smile, but everyone hurried by. So many soldiers pointed their guns, as if to fire, but at what or at whom? Clearly, they were ready for an aggressor. Their stance alarmed and intimidated me. I kept my eyes down, not wanting to draw attention to myself, but it was an absolute impossibility in my Western clothes with my pale white skin, blue eyes, and blonde hair. I felt utterly exposed as I scurried through the hallways.

Where were the customs officers? I clutched my bags tighter. Breathe in. One, two, three, four. Let it out. One, two, three, four. People continued to move about, but it was unnervingly quiet. Was this the usual situation? I stopped before the entrance to customs, then immediately realized I was staring directly at another soldier. His eyes met mine for a second. I focused on my suitcases, turned thoughtlessly, pulling my bags behind me.

I cleared customs without mishap and stepped outside. The hot, dry air hit me like a slap in the face. The traffic was chaotic. Men yelled in a language that made no sense. Horns honked. The exhaust emitted from the vehicles added to the smell and heaviness of the air.

The Security Forces Hospital had sent a young woman by the name of Connie to welcome me. She held up a large sign with my name written on it. I greeted her with my first Arabic words, "Assalamu alaykum," meaning "peace be upon you."

She returned the greeting and handed me a black abaya and a scarf.

"Put the abaya on now and wear it whenever you are not in your apartment, in the women's-only compound, or at the hospital. Cover your hair with the scarf."

Soon my abaya, a full-length black cloak, and the scarf, became my constant companions. I would have preferred to keep them in a dresser drawer but knew it was the custom to wear them.

After settling into my private comfortably furnished one-bedroom apartment, I ventured out on my own to walk around the neighborhood, checking out the shops and peering into the restaurants.

My mind was filled with apprehension and excitement at the same time. Would I be able to thrive in this society? People had told me about the culture, and I had read all the books. Now I was here and experiencing it for myself. There were so many rules.

At this time, Saudi Arabia was a closed country and you had to be invited by a sponsoring organization to work there. But that meant surrendering your passport, which was something I had to do the next day. It was going to be gut-wrenching. The hospital would keep my passport, and I could not leave without their approval.

I knew managing my new life would be challenging. A year would be a long, long time to tolerate these restrictions. I kept shaking my head, thinking about the freedoms I had left behind in Canada.

There were so many regulations here; opportunities to test my boundaries would emerge frequently. Independent and determined, I often pushed the limits.

"We all push the limits," an American employee at a Saudi hospital had told me on the plane. "Learn the consequences, but more importantly, do not get caught."

Night began to fall, and I headed back to the compound and the comfort of my bed. Pulling the covers over my head, I curled up into a ball and hugged myself to sleep.

Chapter 3

Now That I'm Here – How I Made Myself at Home in an Arab Country

Saudi Arabia occupies most of the Arabian Peninsula and is a wealthy Islamic country due to its oil-based economy. It houses the site of the origin of Islam and the holiest city, Mecca, and countless mosques dot the countryside.

Geographically the country encompasses both the world's largest sand desert and largest oasis. Saudi Arabia is bordered by the Arabian Sea on the east, the Red Sea on the west, Yemen, Qatar, Oman, and the United Arab Emirates on the south and Jordan, Iraq, and Kuwait to the north.

The country emerged during the ruling Al Saud dynasty founded in the mid-1700s. Bedouin traders had ridden camels and horses as they traveled the silk routes, with Saudi Arabia as a well-known stop. Affluence produced by an oil-funded economy in the mid-1930s created lavish palaces and cities, many carved out of the desert. In the early 1990s when I was there, the wealthy continued to live in stark contrast to the traditional lifestyles of farmers and workers.

There was a lot to do as I started my new job. The endless paperwork, filling out forms and rearranging my banking took endless trips between multiple offices. I enjoyed introducing myself to department heads and soon found my way around the hospital. My new team, two American nurses, both named Connie, and a

Filipino assistant, Eppie, helped me to adjust to the dry heat so I didn't get dehydrated. It surprised me that a liter of water cost more than a liter of gasoline.

Getting dressed each day was easy. I chose either a black or navy ankle-length skirt, a jacket, and a blouse. Wearing these uniforms saved dollars on my clothes budget.

Our quality assurance team's objectives were to work with staff throughout the hospital to improve patient care by collecting data, evaluating processes, reducing duplication, and training people on standards and procedures. We also assessed risk and looked for areas to prevent accidents.

Our team provided training sessions for many departments on topics such as taking meeting minutes, establishing a consistent format for hospital records, and streamlining departmental processes throughout the hospital. Also, we delivered lectures as the hospital worked toward the American Joint Commission standards and supported departments during implementation.

Whenever there was an incident report involving patient care, I participated in meetings with the medical director and other members of the medical staff to evaluate the situation. Some meetings were stressful. Decisions could have far-reaching consequences.

Departments would suggest projects to improve care or effectiveness, and our department was ready to help. For example, together with the staff who were responsible for the patient admission process, we systematically examined the procedure from beginning to end. We used diagrams and flowcharts. Cultural, racial, and ethical issues were considered. Staff helped to develop and implement the solutions by eliminating steps and reducing admission time.

Often at the end of the day, I headed to the fitness center at the compound to de-stress from the day's discussions. Here I chatted with other colleagues and made new friends. The complex had a pool, which I loved. Keeping fit helped me stay in shape and avoid adding a few pounds.

I slowly started to feel at home, decorating my apartment with baskets and colorful rugs I purchased at the local markets. Work settled into a routine, and new friends from different parts of the world began crossing my path.

Chapter 4

My Introduction to Ramadan

In the ninth lunar cycle of each year, Muslims worldwide celebrate Ramadan for religious contemplation and ritual. First, they fast from dawn to dusk; then, after sundown, their night becomes their day, and they party with family and friends.

Only a month and a half after arriving, the hospital memo laid out the rules non-Muslims had to follow during Ramadan, including respecting Muslims' feelings and abstaining from eating, drinking, or smoking in the streets, shopping areas, and public places during the daylight hours. The rules were clear. I adhered to them throughout Ramadan.

During Ramadan, at my regular meetings, my boss's nostrils would flare as he rejected my proposals. He continually yawned, and his eyelids were at half-mast. The meetings were short, and his negative decisions were final. I soon understood a critical lesson: Ramadan was not the time to ask for special considerations or discuss contentious issues. Next year, I would get approvals for projects before or after Ramadan.

Our office continued to work full-time. However, in departments staffed by Saudis, the days were soundless as they worked shortened hours. The stillness engulfed other departments in an eerie atmosphere. The days, especially near the end of Ramadan, became oppressive because fasting staff lacked energy.

In contrast, the Saudis filled their nights with parties, prayers, shopping, and bountiful feasts. I liked the joyful atmosphere of the evening, especially while shopping. However, I constantly scanned for the mutaween, the Saudi religious police, who were out in full force. They increased their activity in the evening during Ramadan and relished confronting women. As a result, my tension grew as the evenings ticked on.

Many stores were closed during the day for Ramadan but stayed open late into the night. Late one night, while shopping at the gold market, trying on eighteen-karat Italian-made gold earrings, I removed my headscarf to look at myself in a mirror. The stillness was broken when a mutawa slapped his cane against the entrance to the shop.

He pointed his club at me and barked in broken English, "Cover your hair." Thank goodness the mutawa was not allowed to come inside the stores.

I stiffened. I was upset about being shouted at while trying on the earrings. I rubbed my sweaty forehead and the back of my neck with my left hand. I quickly purchased the earrings, then walked out, wearing my headscarf. The mutawa was nowhere in sight; however, the experience left me shaken and ruined my evening. I had intended to do more shopping for a gold necklace, but instead I grabbed a taxi home. Memories of the store and the jarring crack of the cane against the wall and his loud, piercing words, "Cover your hair," stayed with me for many years.

On another occasion, my Saudi friend Sultana, whom I had met at a businesswomen's luncheon, and I sat chatting and laughing in a restaurant, as we inhaled the aroma of spice from our full-bodied Saudi coffee. The restaurant lights reflected on her lustrous long black hair. She spoke English and our conversations flowed easily.

"Sultana, over the months I've made some Saudi friends, but I find them private people. They're like coconuts: hard to crack, but sweet inside." I reached over and held her hand. "Thanks for your friendship. You mean a lot to me."

"Many foreigners come and go. It takes personal energy to get to know people," said Sultana.

"Oh, I understand. I've had the same experience at the compound."

Sultana looked up, her brown eyes almost the same color as my coffee. "I'm inviting you to my party during Ramadan," she said.

"Thank you so much. I'd love to come."

"My driver will pick you up at 10:45 p.m. and drive you home. I'll send the invitation shortly."

I hugged her as she left and felt profoundly grateful for her genuine friendship.

I dressed carefully the night of the party, wearing my new earrings, a heavy eighteen-karat Kings Link gold chain resting against my long-sleeved navy tunic top, with a matching long skirt, black shoes, and purse.

When Sultana welcomed me at the door, I handed her a bouquet of roses. She smelled them, then gave them to an attendant, nodded, then smiled. Sultana lived in a large two-story beige-colored house with three garages, located in the compound for the Ministry of Finance employees, where her husband worked.

An attendant directed me to the exquisitely decorated ladies' section of her home, a spacious living room, dining room, and hall area. Men were not allowed to be in the women's area. Many antique pieces were from Europe. However, the statement piece immediately drew my eye. It was a breathtaking ivory-inlaid desk from India.

Massive windows, draped in rich, intricate jewel-toned brocade surrounded groupings of comfortable chairs and overstuffed sofas. The floors were polished marble and strewn with magnificent handwoven Iranian rugs, adding to the exquisite ambiance.

Sultana had displayed enormous bouquets of fresh flowers, their fragrance wafting into every room. I felt my face blush as I thought of handing her my small posy of roses. Her designer-decorated rooms projected a feeling of peace and tranquility; I felt comfortable and genuinely welcomed.

Sultana pointed to the Impressionistic-style paintings, which were from England, Europe, and the US. I didn't recognize the artists, but I connected with the pictures. One of the paintings depicted children playing on a grassy lawn. It reminded me of my children when they were younger and immediately brought back memories of summers on our own lawn.

I was the only Westerner at the party. The other guests were from Saudi Arabia, and I was pleased the ladies were happy to talk to me to practice their English. They were wearing designer dresses. I sighed with relief; I had dressed appropriately.

The attendants, wearing attractive pink uniforms, offered food and drinks throughout the evening. Later, we moved into the large dining room where we sat around the table. We were served delicious Saudi food: tabbouleh, hummus, grilled meat kebabs, and samosas. The variety and abundance of food tantalized my taste buds. There were many choices to sample, and I filled my plate.

Bowls of a local spice mixture called za'atar caused my nose to twitch. The mixture contained Middle Eastern herbs such as thyme, oregano, basil, and savory, that we sprinkled on warmed flatbread. I savored the aroma and spices.

As we ate, I relaxed and enjoyed friendly conversations with other guests. Although I had started taking Arabic lessons, it was challenging to carry on a conversation. The ladies loved to hear about my life in Canada. They could not imagine driving a car or being responsible for buying groceries, cooking, housekeeping, looking after children, and working too.

Most wealthy Saudi women had household help to prepare food, clean, and do housework. In addition, several of the women enjoyed having a driver. However, they resented the custom of being accompanied outside the house by a male relative, as written in the male guardianship law in Saudi Arabia. Some Saudi women were challenging the male guardianship order and hoped the law would give full authority to women to get a passport and other papers without requiring a male guardian's approval. They shared their concerns with me freely.

For dessert, Sultana served a sweet pastry filled with different nuts and dried fruit including apricots, dates, and raisins, which was delicious. Finally, the servers offered the sweet mint tea, served in small demitasse glass cups and saucers. The tea tasted syrupy. Saudis liked their tea this way. When it was time to leave, Sultana and I hugged, and her driver drove me home. I smiled, satisfied and sleepy, as I crawled into bed after 2:30 a.m.

Later that week, inspired by my memorable evening with Sultana, I scoured the local spice market, searching for a za'atar mixture of thyme, oregano, basil, and savory. There were so many stalls. Every booth had its own unique za'atar combination, and some added basil, marjoram, sesame seeds, and salt to the mixture. Some women added sumac as well.

One stall caught my attention. Using hand gestures to make myself understood, a heavy-set lady smiled and placed a sample of each of her five za'atar mixtures into my palm to taste. Her dark brown eyes scrutinized my face as I savored each one.

I turned away, with the intent to taste the za'atar at other booths, but she clutched my arm and looked into my eyes and said, "Fatima," pointing to her chest.

I continued tasting at the other stalls but returned to Fatima and bought one of her blends. That evening at home, I savored zeit oo za'atar (meaning oil with za'atar). First, I tore off a chunk of warm, fresh flatbread and drizzled it with high-quality olive oil. Then I dipped the bread into the za'atar. I closed my eyes and smiled as some of the olive oil escaped down my chin and murmured, "Eat and repeat often, Joyce Perrin." It was mouth-watering, both comforting and complex in its flavor, and the flatbread disappeared in a flash.

Years later, I was lucky enough to once again savor the distinct flavor of zeit oo za'atar in a restaurant in Toronto. Memories of Fatima and the spice market swirled around me; her wise brown eyes and her special blend returned to me as if it were yesterday.

Toward the end of Ramadan, the side effect of the final days of the usually twenty-nine-day event began to appear. The smell of people's bodies, as their tissues broke down due to fasting, produced a potent odor, and conversations were terse. It takes dedicated commitment, willpower, and fortitude to fast every day for a month, and I admire the people who have the resolve to complete it each year.

At the end of Ramadan, people celebrated the Muslim festival Eid al-Fitr with parties, feasting, and gift giving. To my delight, several Saudi friends gave me boxes of Medjool dates, often called the King of Dates, for an Eid al-Fitr gift. The chocolatiers stuffed the dates with marzipan, dipped them in chocolate, and sprinkled them with chopped pistachio and walnuts. I was a wholehearted fan of marzipan, chocolate, dates, and nuts. The elegantly wrapped boxes were almost too beautiful to open, but, of course, I did. And despite my best efforts to ration them over several weeks, I failed spectacularly, because I am only human.

After this celebration the tension seemed to disappear, and life returned to a peaceful rhythm.

Chapter 5

Earning My Advanced Scuba Certificate and Meeting a Shark

Exhilaration was in the air. I was taking a little break from my job in Riyadh and flying to Jeddah for a scuba diving and snorkeling weekend. Jeddah, a major city in the western territory of Saudi Arabia, is in the Hijaz Mountains and lies on the Red Sea.

At the dockside, our group noisily grabbed our gear and boarded the boat. The cloudless sky and 86°F (30°C) temperature added to my pleasure. Once we cast off, we motored out for about thirty minutes before dropping anchor in the deep water.

I found a secure place on the dive boat to stash my bag, then changed into my bathing garb and squeezed into my blue Lycra bodysuit, to protect me from the sun and sharp coral. I covered my hair with a cap, yanked on my booties to keep my feet from getting cut, put on my snorkel and mask, and plunged into the water.

I floated face down in the salt water; the waves gently pushed me toward the beach. This world was peaceful, and I treasured the solitude. Instead of thinking about work, I could concentrate on the fish below. The reef was teeming. Brilliantly colored marine life moved in all directions, as the softly waving green ferns and massive red fan corals provided a picturesque backdrop. Time ceased to exist as I drifted back toward the shore. I hailed the transport motorboat and had it drop me in the water, near our anchored dive boat, to repeat the process.

The day passed, drifting, observing, and listening to the fish as they crunched the coral. My cares vanished. I studied the plastic card with pictures and names of the tropical fish scooting around me. I made a mental note of my favorites. There were many species, so I referred to the card often.

It was simple to identify the lionfish's colorful body, with its distinctive red and white stripes, intertwined with other reddish golden-brown and black-brown ones. One lionfish was peeking out from under a coral shelf. I knew a sting from one of its seven poisonous spines could be painful; I hurried away.

I smiled at the clown fish darting from one piece of coral to another, but wondered what sex it was? All clown fish are born male but have both male and female reproductive organs. When the alpha female clown fish dies, a change occurs in their social structure, which causes the dominant male to change to a female and become the new leader.

The brightly colored, yellow-masked butterfly fish always swam in pairs and were easy to spot. An emperor angelfish almost touched me. It was a magnificent eye-catching fish with bold stripes, a vibrant green-blue color, and a flat body. I stared as it maneuvered along, then watched until it nestled in the delicate fan coral.

Swimming always relaxed me and thoughts of competing in the Canadian synchronized swimming championships flooded my mind. Although it was hard to practice while in nursing training, I smiled. It was always about the journey because I cherished it more than the prize, even when I won.

Reaching the shallow water and the seashore for the last time, I sat in the sweltering sun and drizzled the warm sand through my fingers. I felt pure relaxation. I closed my eyes and reflected on my journey. I could feel myself regenerating in these precious moments of solitude and contentment.

Finally, I beckoned the transport boat for a ride back to our anchored vessel. I was ready for dinner. We ate on the dive boat and devoured a meal of either beef or lamb shawarmas, kabobs, samosas, pineapple, dates, and freshly squeezed orange and pineapple juices. I chatted on deck with Bob and his wife, Sally, from California, both experienced advanced divers. Bob was working for one of the oil companies.

"Bob, I love your stories of diving in the Philippines and Australia. But your stories about Turk Lagoon and diving amongst fifty Japanese World War II warships are awesome. You've given me an incentive to get my advanced diver certification and start doing wreck dives."

"Joyce, the marine life is spectacular. Make sure you get to see it. I promise you won't be disappointed," said Sally.

Bob and Sally said goodnight and moved off to another area of the boat to sleep. I rolled out my mattress on deck to slumber under the stars. As I scanned the cloudless sky, looking for familiar constellations like the Big and Little Dipper and Orion, my heart longed to be viewing the stars with my daughter.

Back home, when she was younger, we would scan the night skies above Lake Ontario from our backyard. We would sit on the deck, feeling the breeze and listening to the leaves rustling in our towering red maple tree. Betsy and I had promised when we were apart that we would focus on the Big Dipper and then concentrate on sending a positive message to each other across the miles. We had hugged to seal our plan.

As my gaze fixed on the stars here in Jeddah, I wondered where she was right now. I sensed the sway of the boat while the gentle lapping of the waves against the hull lulled me to sleep.

The sun's intense rays woke me early. It was another perfect day to snorkel. I jumped into the water for my final float over the coral reefs. A coral grouper, with its monstrous mouth and sharp teeth, was crunching the coral. Close by was the dramatic masked puffer, with its white body, a black mouth, and a black mask over its eyes. It was a memorable fish because of its contrasting colors.

I was totally relaxed by the time we were ready to leave but taking the advanced diving Professional Association of Diving Instructors (PADI) training churned in my thoughts. Before I left Saudi, I wanted to be certified and able to handle different water conditions and dives during my travels. The Nike logo filled my thoughts: Just Do It. I signed up to continue my training, and a few weeks later, filled with trepidation and excitement, I returned to Jeddah to take the PADI Advanced Open Water Scuba Diving course.

Our instructor briefly reviewed the course material, including the five required dives: mastering your buoyancy at any water level, a drift dive, a night dive, a navigation dive, and a deep dive. We also practiced lifesaving techniques and listened to lectures focused on protecting the environment, especially not taking any coral as souvenirs. In the evenings, the lights burned late while we completed our homework.

All my fellow students were in their twenties and thirties, male, muscular, tall, and tanned. I was the lone female, nearly fifty-eight years old. We were each paired up with a buddy, and mine was a male Norwegian nurse from Riyadh, who was built like a football linebacker, and about the same age as my sons. My stomach was in knots as I feared I might not be capable of completing the physical part of the course. The lifesaving exercise required me to tow my six-foot male Norwegian buddy through the water to safety.

"Welcome, Grandma," he said with a grin and not unkindly, to which I punched him. He clutched his arm and feigned the impact of my punch as he shot out his hand to shake mine. I grabbed it and gave it a squeeze.

"Hey, buddy, you and I will make an amazing team," I said with a smile and patted him, stretching up to reach his shoulder.

Our instructor stressed the negative effects of nitrogen narcosis on the body during a deep dive. It has also been called "being narked" or depth intoxication, when divers accumulate too much nitrogen in their bodies, resulting in a sense of euphoria, much like being drunk. At depths of more than 100-plus feet (30.5 meters), this was exceedingly dangerous and became life-threatening. Known as the rapture of the deep, nitrogen narcosis–afflicted divers feel a sense of reality and security, hence the absolute need for the buddy system.

The course went exceedingly well until I did the deep dive, 82 feet (25 meters) below the surface. This dive was my test to see if I was susceptible to nitrogen narcosis and succumbing to the rapture. When we reached the depth of the deep dive, we had to spell our name, backward, on a slate. During the dive, I noticed my air consumption increased. In addition, my wetsuit started to compress, making it tough to maintain my buoyancy position.

When I reached the goal and stabilized, I spelled my name on my slate. It seemed simple when underwater, and I was pleased with my effort. But when I examined my slate after surfacing, I could barely read my backward scratches. They made no sense at all, and I stared at it in disbelief. The lifesaving lesson became deeply ingrained: I needed to be careful when doing a deep dive as I could quickly become confused without ever knowing it.

"Well, this was a sobering lesson to learn, especially as the purpose of getting my advanced certificate was to do deep wreck dives," I said to my instructor, feeling disheartened.

He put his arm around my shoulders and said, "Joyce, you will be fine. Just remember to keep in contact with your buddy and watch the time you spend in deep water."

My most unnerving and exciting test was the night dive. I hooked two waterproof flashlights, a compass, and a strobe light to my vest, then descended. The water was blacker than black. My flashlight only lit up an area two feet in front of me. It would be easy to get separated from the group, but I deliberately kept my buddy in sight by focusing on the chemical glow stick attached to his tank.

At night the coral changed color. Some coral appeared much brighter and became fluorescent, while others lost their color. Also, fish that slept during the day were active now.

I could only see the tiny area lit by my flashlight. I found it challenging to get my bearings. A foreboding sensation settled in my belly, and my breathing became rapid. I stopped, stabilized, and concentrated on taking slow, deeper breaths. Finally, I moved forward, with my breathing back in rhythm. I refocused on the glowing coral and the intense colors of the fish in the area, lit by my flashlight, and relaxed. The nighttime coral was so different drenched in a rainbow of green, red, and yellow. I was hypnotized.

Suddenly I panicked; I had lost my buddy. I could not see him anywhere. Where was he? Where was I? I started breathing rapidly. I grabbed my strobe light, about to flash it, when I saw him above me, off to my right. I had drifted down several feet, which was easy to do without realizing. I was beside him again with a few swift kicks, and we gave each other the OK sign.

Soon we all turned off our flashlights and allowed the ocean's bioluminescence to wow us. Chemical reactions inside jellyfish, algae, some fish, and even coral caused them to produce and emit light. Coral angelfish have a light organ dangling from their heads at the end of an appendage. It was like a kaleidoscope all around me. I loved this magical midnight secret garden. I was so happy.

With this dive I had finished all the requirements for my advanced certification.

In the evening we gathered. "Congratulations, Joyce, nothing can stop you now," said our instructor as he passed me my certificate.

"Thank you," I said smiling as I positively glowed. My buddy gave me a bear hug, and the gang gave me a loud, "Yay, go, Joyce!" We all celebrated.

Wreck dives soon became my favorite types of dives. Many ships had foundered and sank in the Red Sea because of frequent course-plotting errors, shallow water, difficult navigation situations, and unexpected severe weather.

On one dive weekend in Jeddah, several months later, I joined a wreck dive group descending to 110 feet (33 meters). The water was calm, the sun was bright in a cloudless sky, as nine of us jumped into the water over the wreck and descended. I examined the sunken ship. The enormous steering wheel looked like it would have been hard to control in a storm. Dishes, with their white and blue floral design, were scattered on the stateroom floors; other settings were still on the table, as if waiting for diners to come for their meal.

We were heading back to our dive boat when I heard the unmistakable sound of someone repeatedly striking their air tank—the universal signal for danger, stop, help. My pulse rate increased. Our guide made the hand sign for a shark. My eyes frantically scanned the deep water for any movement. I held my breath, then remembered I must breathe in a slow, steady rhythm, but it was impossible to relax.

The shark swam into view. Its body was gray, with dark gray vertical bars or spots and a pale white underbelly. This shark was the unpredictable tiger shark. It was exceedingly close and headed directly for our group.

My mind raced. What did I remember about the tiger shark? It was an apex predator, of course, and we were in its environment. As for attacking humans, it was second only to the great white shark. Fishermen had found old tires, other sharks, seals, and even a horse's head in a tiger shark's stomach. Divers knew them as the waste disposal of the sea. And here we were, in the shark's territory.

I was both terrified and awed by this evolutionary marvel before me. I had over a half a tank of air, and we were still 40 feet (12 meters) deep. My mind kept repeating, relax, save your air. I bit down hard on my regulator as I tried, but failed, to control my escalating panic.

We formed a tight circle with our backs to each other, linked arms and kicked, making as big a wave as we could. I chose to be next to the most muscular man I saw. I was frightened and used more physical energy, which increased my air usage. It was hard to produce a surge of water in that kicking position. Within a few minutes, my legs burned, then went limp. My adrenaline-laced energy vanished. Would I even be able to swim back to the dive boat? Protecting ourselves was consuming my reserve energy fast.

Tiger sharks are notoriously unpredictable. This one was at least 10 feet (3 meters) long. Although he stayed 6 feet (2 meters) away, it was much too close for my comfort. His eyes were black and piercing. When he opened his mouth, I knew he could consume me in one bite. After many painfully slow circuits around us, his curiosity seemed to be satisfied, and he disappeared, merging once again into the deep.

Our guide deemed it safe to head to the surface and our dive boat. I pumped my arms and legs like pistons, as fast as I could, forcing my muscles to propel me forward. When I arrived at our dive boat, I was ready to collapse. Luckily, two powerful men grabbed me by my arms and lifted me out of the water.

I lay exhausted on the deck, gratefully heaving in deep breaths of fresh air. We were all safe. As soon as the last person was on board, we spotted a shark's dorsal fin heading toward the boat. When the motor started, the shark disappeared. We bellowed and cheered as the trip ended safely.

Chapter 6

Immersed in an Opulent Arabic Experience and I Was the Only Woman

My daily routine included a morning swim. It was easy to do as the pool was right outside my apartment door. Gliding through the water was a positive way to start my day and worth the scramble to quickly get dressed and catch the bus to the hospital.

To better understand the culture and the world I now found myself in, I signed up for Arabic lessons, offered to the staff to learn reading, writing, and pronunciation. The twenty-eight letters in the Arabic alphabet, all consonants, were differentiated by dots, and written from right to left.

I started to master reading and writing, but I was frustrated as pronunciation was challenging. I tried my best, but practicing in front of a mirror did not bring me up to par. I passed the first level, but since I was not speaking Arabic at work, I stopped. Regretfully, I accepted learning languages did not come easily to me, no matter how often I practiced.

Our quality team—the two Connies, Eppie, and myself—developed many successful hospital programs and held our first citywide Quality Management Week conference in October 1993.

Before the event, I received an elaborate invitation, printed with gold lettering, to attend an evening dinner at the home of Dr. Mohammed H. Mufti, director and chief executive officer of the hospital. I was the only woman and Westerner invited. Senior hospital staff told me it was extremely unusual for Dr. Mufti to invite a woman to his home to dine. I felt exceptionally honored and completely accepted as a team member.

His home was distinctly large with an elaborate pool and a manicured yard. The living and dining rooms contained exquisite furniture and antiques from all over the world, and the Arabic silk rug with gold thread, mounted on the wall, was indeed a museum piece.

The servants announced the meal by bringing an incense burner filled with Oud, the most expensive type of incense in Saudi Arabia, to each guest. Some of the men wore ghutras—long white headdresses, which covered their heads and draped their shoulders. They held up the fabric to enclose the incense burner inside their ghutras to take a deep breath of the fragrance. They looked satisfied after they inhaled.

I waved some fragrance toward my face and took a deep breath. The woody Oud smell varied from earthy to sweet. I detected musk and an aging leather aroma. The perfume reminded me of tales from *One Thousand and One Nights*—mysterious and luxurious.

Our table could easily accommodate thirty people, so the eighteen guests sat nicely spaced. Since my tablemates spoke fluent English, our conversations flowed easily. The meal consisted of a dizzying array of salads, seafood, hot and cold dishes, and Arabic and Western foods. It was hard to choose, but my three favorites quickly became kabsa, considered the national dish of Saudi Arabia, a blend of basmati rice cooked with a variety of meats, vegetables, and spices; dajaj mashwi, a Saudi Arabian barbeque made with boneless chicken breasts pounded thin, then marinated, and grilled. Hot tamees, a Saudi flatbread traditionally baked in a tandoor oven, were also served.

The Saudis loved their sweets, and the servants offered several types of dates. It was like going to an expensive restaurant, with delectable food, superb service, but with the elegance and charm of dining in a home. It was a night I will never forget.

Our conference day arrived. The Security Forces Hospital had extended invitations to the other hospitals in Riyadh, and their representatives all attended. The hospital management was pleased with our success because it raised the hospital's profile and prestige and gave the Quality Management Department and our staff more credibility as internal consultants.

Our Saudi boss rewarded us with praise, and we also received a congratulatory letter from Dr. Mufti. As a result, we had many more requests from hospital departments to help them increase their effectiveness. Our small department celebrated as we felt recognized and appreciated.

A few weeks later, Barbara, an American nurse from another department, invited me to join a group from the hospital to fly to Sanaa, Yemen, for a short holiday. Yemen, a mystical Arab land bordering Saudi Arabia on the southern Arabian Peninsula, had green valleys, bleak cliffs, and white sand beaches. It sounded intriguing and fun, so I arranged for time off and looked forward to adding Yemen to my collection of countries visited on my map.

Yemen is at an altitude of 7,218 feet (2,200 meters). As we walked the streets of this mountain valley city, I was mesmerized by the buildings. The unique rammed earth and mud-brick buildings stand as tall as skyscrapers, giving the city a homogeneous architectural ensemble appearance. The homes had geometric designs and white gypsum windows with red, green, blue, and yellow sparkling windowpanes arranged in semicircles above the doors.

We meandered along the streets for an evening stroll, not wearing our abayas, joyful at feeling free and autonomous. My friends had to return to Saudi, but I stayed and savored the tranquility of being a solo traveler for two extra days.

While solo, I rode a camel in Yemen to see the local sights.
Not the most comfortable way to travel, but unforgettable.

At the end of the two days, I took a taxi to the airport. I checked my bag and noted no other women were waiting to board. I was the first person to board the plane. I found my window seat, inserted my earplugs, and put my nose in my book. Suddenly, there was a commotion on the plane, and the steward walked up and down, yelling in Arabic.

I looked up, as he held my checked suitcase, opened now with underwear spilling out. I was mortified and embarrassed. I did not understand his Arabic, and he probably could not read my English luggage tag. My cheeks blazed with shame, as I claimed my suitcase and stuffed all my belongings back in, closing it so he could put it in the overhead bin.

I didn't know the passengers had to identify their luggage to an attendant on the ground immediately before entering the plane. If there had been a way to remove me from the plane, I think the other passengers would have cheered, but they were gracious. The plane took off, and I pretended to take a nap, arriving safely in Riyadh.

Back at the women's compound, the guard on duty said, "Glad to see you are back from Yemen."

"Thanks," I replied flustered.

How did the guard know where I went? My mind spun. Were they keeping track of me for my safety or for more nefarious reasons?

Chapter 7

Getting Comfortable as I Began to Learn the History and Culture of Saudi Arabian People

To keep a positive attitude, I planned events or activities every weekend. Weeks after my Yemen trip, my friend Sarah and her husband, Barry, both of whom I had met at an American Embassy event, invited me to join a group of expatriates from Canada, the US, Britain, and Germany on an overnight camping trip in the Sahara Desert.

We drove from Riyadh in a caravan of eleven cars, to a spot in the desert and parked in a row on the brown flat shale-like surface. We arrived around 4:00 p.m. as the overwhelming heat of the sun was dissipating.

Everyone spread out, exploring the desert, as if we were on a scavenger hunt, looking for treasures. Mary-Anne and Steven, who were from Canada, had unearthed 3,000- to 5,000-year-old arrowheads on earlier trips. The arrowheads were from the Neolithic Stone Age, used for killing animals. Steven pulled a photo from his wallet and showed me a picture. Together we looked for more arrowheads, but we headed back to the cars empty-handed as dusk fell.

The group enjoyed dinner and drinks around the open fire. The peaceful nighttime atmosphere, in the middle of nowhere, contrasted sharply with Riyadh. I was relaxed, something I had not felt for a long time.

We slept under the stars on air mattresses. Sleeping bags were a necessity as the nights were especially cold. I snuggled into my sleeping bag and stared at the celestial patterns in the clear black sky like velvet sprinkled with diamond dust. The sky was huge, clear, the air arid, and the lack of ambient lighting made the desert one of the world's best places to see the heavens.

Tightly packed stars filled my vision as I used my binoculars—too many to count. Pinpricks flashed like shooting stars, and for a moment, it reminded me of the cold Canadian climate when I was young and had caught snowflakes on my black mittens. Finally, I rolled over to sleep, with thoughts of stars and solitude. Hours later, I awoke with the sun, and after more exploring, the group headed back to Riyadh, before the heat of the day consumed the desert.

Six weeks later, I joined the women's-only excursion with my friend Sally to explore the surrounding area near Riyadh. These excursions gave me a window to expand my knowledge and understanding of Saudi lives and culture. Our movements were restricted because we were single women, not allowed to drive, and we could only travel on the hospital bus to some areas in the country.

On one trip we visited a date farm and processing factory. Dates were a staple in the Saudi diet and a highly profitable business. Endless rows of date palms greeted us, their green fronds swaying in the gentle breeze, set against an almost purple sky. They reminded me of the tropical islands like Tahiti, where coconut palms randomly dotted the beaches. Here the palms were in straight lines, like soldiers marching down the field. They seemed identical in size and shape, making them even more regimental. The Saudi date farm was huge, with palms planted as far as the eye could see, covering many hectares. It felt like a secluded hushed paradise, a relief from the hectic noise and bustle of the busy city.

Mohammed, our guide, was nearly six feet tall. His crooked teeth stood out when he smiled. He wore jeans, which I considered too hot, and a faded red shirt with the top button undone. The shirt's single pocket was stuffed with papers. His eyes pierced through me as he spoke in English.

"When men climb the trees to cut the date pods, they wear heavy material to protect them from the sharp points of the thorns. They look like monkeys moving from branch to branch to get the dates. The points cut many men," he said and showed our group the long and ragged scars on his arm.

He passed a thorn to the group, and I slid my finger along the smooth edge, drawing blood. Ouch, even a tiny cut stung.

"The fronds or branches are strong enough to hold 250 pounds (113.4 kilograms) of weight when men stand on them to pick the ripe dates," he continued.

Looking at the tall trees, I decided the job was not for me; my knees felt like jelly just imagining standing so high in the air.

I recalled my gran making delicious date squares. She mixed the dates with a dash of lemon juice, cooked them until they softened, spread them over the rolled oats crust, and baked them in the oven. I closed my eyes and recalled the taste of the sweet date flavor and the browned oat flakes.

"At harvest time, we taste the different colored dates, from brown to golden yellow, as each date species is unique in sweetness and color," said Mohammed.

A basket filled with various kinds of dates was passed from one person to the next, and I grabbed a handful to taste. The smooth skin melted in my mouth and soon I felt a boost of energy. The sweetness and freshness of those dates was like eating a fresh Canadian McIntosh apple, straight from the tree, compared to one bought in the store. The flavor and the aroma lingered.

Mohammed smiled; his eyes sparkled as he watched us enjoy the dates. He passed the basket around again. I picked out my favorites and stuffed more into my pocket for later.

After the farm, we headed off to climb the famous Red Sand Dunes. It was hard work. I started out walking upright, but that position did not work. So I took off my shoes, tied them to my waistband, then walked on all fours, and made better progress.

"Come on, Sally, walk on your hands and feet like an animal. I find this the easiest and the only way to reach the top," I said.

She was still near the bottom of the dune. Roars of laughter reached me. We both tried to move forward but continually slid back. Mastering this technique gave me confidence, allowing me to climb even faster. I loved the challenge and thrived on my feeling of accomplishment. Reaching the top I stood quietly, scanning the spectacular view of the dunes and the mountains.

It was here on this sand dune, in some strange way, I felt a visceral connection with this desert country. The rugged, rough-faced mountains jutting out of the top of the dunes below were spectacular. A few small green bushes were poking out from the sand at the edge of an oasis. I sensed the immense energy and effort the green plants needed to survive in this desert country, and I was just like them.

I popped the last date into my mouth and breathed in the desert air. What better way to remember Saudi Arabia than enjoying the reenergizing flavor of a succulent date at the top of a sand dune in the Sahara Desert, scanning the 360-degree view, as the sun inched toward the horizon at the end of a day?

When I returned to the compound, sand was everywhere—between my toes, in my pockets, in my shoes, in my hair, ears, and under my fingernails and toenails. Fortunately, my camera remained sand-free.

A couple of months later, our women's-only outing saw us strolling around the famous Al Kharj spring and its oasis, 48 miles (77 kilometers) from Riyadh. The green foliage around the oasis was a welcome break from the brown sand, crushed rock, and bright metallic buildings in Riyadh that pounded my eyes with their never-ceasing glare from the sun's rays.

Leaving the oasis and heading out into the desert, I dropped to my knees beside a stone-like foundation and began scraping at the sand. I let out a scream for joy when I pulled out a petrified camel hoof. I turned it over in my hand slowly, dusted off the sand, and tucked it into my day pack.

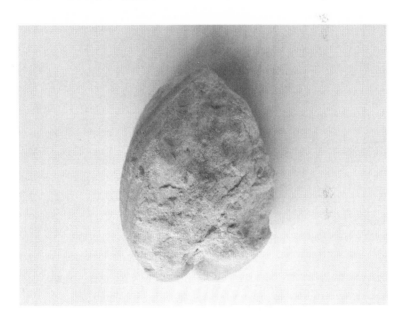

To this day the camel hoof sits on my desk as a paperweight, generating memories of the Sahara Desert.

Not far from where I found the camel hoof, three Saudi men were sitting on their rugs on the hard rocky ground. It was my lucky day. They were hospitable and served me some coffee. It was strong and of course overly sweet.

Sharing strong, sweet coffee with friendly Saudis along the camel trail near Riyadh. We chatted in Arabic for some time about the weather, the camels, their trucks, and shared family stories, especially about children.

Afterward our group walked to the top of a bluff, following the path of an ancient camel trail. The climb was steep, and as I stopped to catch my breath, I called out.

"Hey, Sally, wait for me. Did you know camels put their back hooves into the indentation left by their front hooves when walking in deep sand so they can walk faster. Oh, I would love to be riding a camel right now."

Together we looked at the vistas with the deep ravines, flat areas, and massive dunes. The dunes had been shaped by the wind into smooth curves, and their well-formed ridges reminded me of birthday cakes, with fluffy icing swirled gracefully over the tops and sides. The afternoon sun shone on the sand, spreading a dark amber glow. On outings like this, I missed male company and a firm hand to steady my climb.

But there were consequences to breaking Saudi rules, such as being with an unrelated male. Some actions resulted in security immediately deporting the woman or sending her to a harsh and sparse women's jail. The important thing was for me to know the consequences and then make a conscious decision. Was I willing to take the risk?

Thank goodness I was attending an American Embassy mixed event soon. I loved those events, a chance to dress up and talk to other English-speaking people, and where it was safe to be with unrelated males. The bonus was I could savor a glass of wine or my favorite cocktail, an old-fashioned.

One day I received a fancy invitation with an elegant seal from Abdullah to attend his birthday party at his home. He was one of the two Arab male students who interned for a month in our department. The family's driver drove me to their home where we celebrated with a birthday cake and ice cream. The family sang "Happy Birthday" in Arabic, and I sang in English.

His birthday party began a long friendship with his parents. I spent many evenings with them lounging in their private second-floor quarters. Usually, only family members visited the second floor of a Saudi home. But they welcomed me anytime. Abdullah's father would flip through the TV channels while his mother looked at magazines. Abdullah and his brother would lie on the floor doing homework. I felt their warmth and hospitality, which helped me settle into my new life.

Chapter 8

What Was I Thinking? Traveling with My Young Family Halfway Around the World

At night after work, I would sort through the photos I had brought with me from home. One from our family trip around the Pacific Rim in the summer of 1971 brought back a flood of memories.

Ed and I had met in 1955 at the University of Alberta. He was in engineering, and I was in nursing. After my graduation in 1959, we married and moved to Hamilton, Ontario, Canada. The following August, in 1960, we moved to Boston, Massachusetts, because Harvard Business School offered Ed a spot in the fall class. We were ecstatic. Going to this prestigious school was the opportunity of a lifetime for Ed and our future as a family. Fortunately, I secured a job in nursing administration, close to where we would live.

Going to Harvard was outrageously expensive so we had to spend our money wisely. We bought food at the market on Saturdays at 5:00 p.m. because they would sell some vegetables cheaper at the end of the day. I worked my nursing job during the week and supplemented our income as a special nurse, caring for one or two patients on many weekends. Ed studied and I typed his papers at night. Together we enjoyed as much of Boston as we could during the two years we lived there.

When graduation came, Harvard Business School presented me with a Putting Hubby Through School certificate, and Ed received his master's degree in business administration.

The Boston University offered a master's degree in nursing. I considered applying for the program, but Ed's job was in Michigan, so Michigan it was.

After several years in the States, we returned to Canada, this time to Toronto. Ed worked for a Canadian company as a management consultant. He traveled extensively and left me alone in Toronto with our three young children: Dan, seven; Bruce, six; and Betsy, four. It was a difficult time for our family as we missed him dearly.

One evening, Ed returned from work calling out, "Joyce!" as the screen door slammed behind him. He gave me a big hug and announced, "I am going back to Africa for another assignment in July."

"Oh my gosh, July? That means we will be without you again, just like last summer," I said unhappily, feeling distressed.

Later in the evening we hatched our plan. Since the children would be out of school, we could travel as a family. But with three young children, I felt I needed some help. My mother was healthy and a seasoned traveler, so I twisted her arm to join our adventure. We planned it, did our research, and got all the approvals required to travel to Africa. We all would need multiple vaccinations against tropical diseases. With that job accomplished, we test packed our bags and counted down the days to departure.

"Guess what?" Ed said, returning home one evening close to our departure date. "Our destination has changed." I turned quickly, dried my hands on the towel, and sat at the table waiting for Ed to continue.

"We're going to Papua New Guinea [PNG], an island in the Pacific Ocean near Australia, where I will be working for the Australian government."

Miserably, I saw our plans change in an instant. The reassignment wasted all our planning, research, and money we had spent preparing for our trip.

I was barely listening as Ed continued, "I will monitor the Japanese, fishing in the Australian waters, and live on their fishing boats most of the time while we are in PNG. So, you, your mother, and the children will be on your own."

I suddenly felt completely overwhelmed. How could Mom and I manage with three young children in a remote country halfway across the world? That night we recommitted to doing whatever it took to keep the family together for the summer and adjusted our itinerary.

I completed the monumental task of packing clothes for different climates for the family. To get to PNG we were going to travel through Los Angeles, Tahiti, New Zealand, Australia, and then return home through Thailand, Hong Kong, and Japan. Fortunately, our vaccinations covered these geographic areas, and we packed anti-malaria pills to protect us during our time in PNG. In addition, I packed antibiotics in our extensive first aid kit if we needed to take medication in a hurry and could not get to a doctor.

I prepared identification tags for the children to wear around their necks as a precaution in case they got separated from us. I read *A Bear Called Paddington* by Michael Bond to them, a story about a speckled bear from Darkest Peru. He wore an old hat, a duffle coat, Wellington boots, carried a battered suitcase, and was found alone at Paddington train station in London. He had a luggage tag pinned to his coat that read, "Please look after this polite bear. Thank you." It reminded me of children from England, evacuated from the cities to the countryside for their safety, during World War II. Those children had their names pinned to their clothes, and each carried a gas mask and a small suitcase with their belongings.

I did not want to take any chances. We created identification tags for each of the children listing their names, parents' names, citizenship, passport numbers, flight numbers, next destination, and hotel name and phone number. The boys carried their small Canadian Pacific Air Lines carry-on bags, stuffed with games, books, and snacks. Betsy clutched her little black and white stuffed dog, Mr. No Name, a piece of her blanket, and I carried her games, snacks, and books.

The travel agents made our reservations by telegram and wrote our tickets by hand. It was a detailed, time-consuming job as no one was using computers, faxes, cell phones, and the internet yet. Air travel was new and exhilarating. In the early seventies, the airlines offered children travel books to record their air miles. Sometimes the pilot signed their books, allowed them to visit the cockpit, and gave them airline wing pins for their collection. Airlines offered passengers decks of cards on the plane; there were no movies, and the airlines provided plenty of flavorsome meals.

Our departure day percolated with excitement, yet I was tense as the six of us boarded the plane in Toronto. We made a quick stop in Los Angeles, where we visited a second cousin and her family. We enjoyed a day at Disneyland and later visited the famous San Diego Wild Animal Park, which had just opened. The children marveled at all the animals living at the zoo, as a train whisked us through their habitats. I quietly thanked developers for considering parents and their children and providing a simple way to see the zoo. Remarkably, this set a new standard for building zoos worldwide.

The family is ready to go for our next adventure from Los Angeles to Tahiti: (from left) Bruce, Mom, Betsy, myself, and Dan.

After Los Angeles, our next stop was Tahiti, a South Pacific island in the French Polynesia archipelago. Papeete, the capital, was a paradise with coconut palm trees and the sound of the rhythmic splashing of the blue ocean waves on a black volcanic sand beach. It was a perfect place to catch our breath and relax.

Dan and Bruce met a young boy, probably about ten years old, who climbed a coconut tree in bare feet, then knocked down several coconuts, which the children picked up. Betsy's coconut was one-quarter of her size. She could hardly hold it, so we quickly snapped a photo. After returning to the ground, the boy hacked off the tops of the coconuts with a large machete. I gasped. I wasn't sure I would want my boys at his age handling a knife as large and sharp.

We sipped the clear, refreshing coconut water through a straw and learned the fluid contained sodium, potassium, and other electrolytes to prevent dehydration. In fact, coconut water had been used successfully, as a last resort, for intravenous fluid transfusions in emergency situations.

We toured the island and chuckled at fresh loaves of French bread poking out of the mailboxes as if they were letters. We marveled at the uncorrupted beauty of azure lagoons, waterfalls, and leafy forests while our driver explained how Captain James Cook explored the island in the eighteenth century.

Before our tour ended, we stopped for French crepes, thin pancakes with a sweet orange filling and sprinkled with icing sugar, served at a cozy table along the roadside. My mouth watered as I folded the pancake in half and ate it like a sandwich. Delicious and memorable as only the French could prepare and serve with such class. Words cannot describe its goodness.

On the next leg of our journey, we watched New Zealand's North Island come into view as our plane descended beneath the clouds. New Zealand bragged about the high quality of its air, with fewer smoke-stack industries and more sheep than people. The historical Māori culture thrived there. The landscape included rambling farmlands, coastal waters, beaches, and geothermal wonders.

After we landed, we picked up our car, which we hoped was going to hold the six of us and our luggage. We stuffed belongings everywhere, in the trunk, under the seats, and then Ed secured the rest on the roof of the car. To say it was cozy was an understatement.

Rotorua was our first tourist stop. The Geothermal Mud Pots, or the Boiling Mud Pots, awakened our senses. Betsy's eyes widened, watching the bubbling mud. Then her little hand slipped into mine. I held her tightly as we crept along the wooden platform. Where were the guardrails? The energetic pops from the mud bubbles, boiling below the wooden walkway, and then the smell of rotten eggs overwhelmed us. Betsy held her nose, and I did too.

"Welcome, have you come to see the haka war dance?" asked the Māori tribal leader as we entered the performance hall.

He was close to six feet tall, muscular, older, with tattoos on his chest. His face was soft with kind eyes and his smile disarmed me. I relaxed and knew we were going to have a memorable evening.

"Yes, please, we would love to watch the Māori dancers, we've heard so much about them. We've just arrived from Canada," I said eagerly.

He looked closely at the children as he patted their soft blond hair. "Hello, three towheads."

Bruce cupped his hand around his mouth and whispered, "Mom, what is a towhead?"

"It means people with particularly light blond hair."

The beat of the drums picked up speed, and the male Māori dancers, descendants of Pacific Polynesian tribes, mesmerized us as they moved in unison, pointing their toes out, then pounding their chests while they walked with bent knees in a semi-squat position. The dancers had painted their faces with many lines and circles. They also wore green anklets woven from grasses.

In the past, warriors used the dances to scare other tribes, so these dancers stuck out their tongues, their eyes bulging, shouting, and making a gurgling sound in their throats. Some held poles, which would have typically been spears, as if they were fighting with a neighboring tribe. They made weird sounds and looked scary as they moved, and I felt a strange feeling of excitement as Betsy cuddled in my lap, listening to the loud sounds echoing in the hall.

The women also sang and danced in their knee-length grass skirts and bare feet, moving white pom-poms in unison, moving together rhythmically. I could not understand their words, but the melody, accompanied by a guitar, was energizing.

After the performance, we were invited to join in; the women danced with Ed, and the boys and the men danced with Mom, Betsy, and me. It was a bit of a challenge to follow their footwork. But, in the end, we clapped and gave a deep bow, a brilliant start to exploring New Zealand's North Island.

The next morning, we crammed into our little car to tour the Waitomo Glowworm Caves.

I said, "Hey, gang, listen up, the large sign says, spellbinding, brightest, breathtaking, and incomparable."

Once in the caves our guide said, "It will take about twenty minutes for your eyes to adjust to glowworm light."

"This sounds magical. I think of fairies dancing on dew-filled grass at dawn," I whispered to Betsy.

We had to be careful. If people talked or made a noise, the worms would turn off their lights. We saw the dirty looks we received from other visitors when our three cherubs sat in the boat. We explained the situation to the children, no noise or talking. The boats glided silently through this unusual lava cave, home to the glowworms.

Glowworms travel down a thread attached to the top of the cave, making the thread shine. It was beautiful, like the Milky Way in the sky, with the worms glowing in the dark. The closer we got to the glowworms, the brighter they were, and they lit up the large cave.

After the tour, the guide and several passengers mentioned how well the children behaved, and indeed they had done our family proud.

The three kids were ready to use some of their energy, so we stopped the car to talk to John, a sheep farmer standing by his gate. John's skin was weather-beaten; his deep blue eyes crinkled as he smiled. He welcomed us and encouraged the children to explore the sheep in the fields.

"Come on, Betsy, let's go!" yelled Dan and Bruce.

The children ran as fast as they could, then began mimicking the Māori dancers, pounding their chests, sticking out their tongues, and trying to make low gurgling noises in their throats.

"This farm has been in my family for generations," said John, as he pointed to the landscape and the lush green fields. "I shear the sheep for their Merino wool each year and sell it for a superb price. Later we slaughter the sheep for their meat."

Looking toward the horizon, we saw two riders on horseback and six sheepdogs, guiding hundreds of sheep down a path. If a sheep moved off to the side or stopped, the dog would bark, and the sheep would fall back in line.

"This one is Martha," he said pointing to one sheep around the gate and continued to name others, one by one. He explained the breeds. He clearly loved every one of his sheep and was proud of his farm.

The children came back from the field, jumped into our car, and we took off.

"Joyce, what is that smell?" said Mom.

"What do you mean?" I asked.

"Take a big whiff," she said.

"Oh my gosh, Ed, stop the car. It smells like sheep shit," I said, holding my nose.

"Hey everyone under seven, strip to your underwear and put your clothes in this plastic bag. I know you had fun, but it was a mistake for you to roll down a hill covered in sheep poo. Wipe yourself with this wet towel, and here are clean clothes to wear."

For dinner we devoured a typical New Zealand meal: lamb, potatoes, and carrots. For dessert, we enjoyed kiwi fruit, also called

Chinese gooseberries. The children's favorite was Hokey Pokey—vanilla ice cream sprinkled with caramelized sugar.

A few days later, we flew to Australia. We needed a bit of rest, so we moved at a slower pace. It was also time to start our anti-malaria pills. They were too big for Betsy to swallow, but she chewed them with peanut butter and swallowed them down.

We were introduced to English-style fish and chips, served on wax paper and then wrapped in newspaper. The aroma was enticing, and the fish and chips were flavorful. No ketchup here. Australians splashed malt vinegar on their chips. We loved the tanginess of the vinegar. The family-owned fish and chip restaurant became a favorite.

The children loved crossing the spectacular Sydney Harbour on the passenger boats. The builders had nearly finished building the Sydney Opera House, with its distinctive sails. It was stunningly breathtaking, but not open to the public yet.

We traveled to Canberra, Australia's capital. The Canberra War Memorial housed visual dioramas, displaying PNG's terrain and culture.

PNG sported a wild geography of rivers, impenetrable jungles, and uncharted mountains. Previously the country had had a history of cannibalism, along with numerous violent tribal clashes. But now, instead of fighting, the Indigenous peoples honored their heritage with Sing Sing events, cultural gatherings where they wore traditional shell necklaces with teeth, bones, and seeds strung together with leather and used tapa cloth for clothes. The tapa cloth was made from bark, pounded thin, and then hand-crafted into clothing.

Men and women wore tapa cloth in many South Pacific Islands, including the Māori in New Zealand. The men wore colorful headpieces with expensive and rare feathers from parrots, cocka-toos, the Papua hornbill, and birds of paradise.

The country also had large areas of mangroves, coconut trees, pandanus (a tropical shrub with twisted roots), and bamboo thickets. Plentiful food grew on trees, such as avocados, bananas, and mangoes. I absorbed everything I could about this unknown country and the culture. I was excited. One thing for sure: our lives were about to change.

Chapter 9

The Lessons Learned from Living in Papua New Guinea Shaped My Future

We arrived in Port Moresby, the capital of PNG. The country covers the eastern half of the west Pacific island of New Guinea. It also includes the islands of New Britain, New Ireland, and other smaller islands. Australia administered PNG while we visited, then in 1975 PNG gained its independence.

We rented a small house with a swimming pool, where we relaxed as we recuperated from our travels. The next day Ed left. Mom, the children, and I were on our own.

On our daily walks, we admired the brilliant colors, shapes, and sizes of the many tropical fish in a nearby stream. The only time we had seen similar fish was in a pet store, so we watched them in the shallow water for hours. If we were quiet and listened, we could hear them chewing their food.

Dan and Bruce would fish in the nearby stream and give their catch to Gabriel, our handyman, when they returned. He appreciated their gifts. Gabriel was tall and thin. He was always smiling and moved with a dancer's grace. His wife ironed his pants with a crisp crease, so he always looked neat. Gabriel spoke English, which he learned during World War II, and a grin formed on his face when he talked to us. The children adored him and gave him a welcoming hug each morning.

One day Dan and Bruce came back without any fish. Gabriel stamped his feet and was angry. Later we realized Gabriel had been feeding his family with the fish the boys caught each day. The fish were a staple food for the local people. Knowing someone depended upon them, the boys worked harder and caught more fish.

When the night was clear, we all loved to look at the brilliant star-filled cloudless sky. One night the boys tried to head out on their own. Gabriel was watching.

"Bruce and Dan, where are you going?" said Gabriel in an authoritative tone.

"Oh, to look at the bright stars," said Dan.

"You can't go out," said Gabriel in a somber tone, positioning himself to block their way. "No," he repeated in a firmer voice, "the evil spirits will get you."

Dan ignored him and pushed forward.

"No," Gabriel said, blocking their way.

The boys returned inside. Gabriel stood tall and crossed his arms. His beliefs were unwavering.

Moving from place to place, Mom, the three children, and I took small planes and explored the country for nearly a month. We flew to the Port of Madang, north of Port Moresby. We all loved rambling along the beach, taking in the heady fragrance of the flowering trees, which grew close to the clear blue water. The different species of orchids were a revelation and sheer joy to behold. The colors within the petals masterfully blended, as if an artist had spent hours mixing and applying them, one stroke at a time.

One afternoon I joined an old man who was sitting on a large piece of driftwood on the beach, staring out to sea. We started chatting. His skin looked like leather and his nearly toothless gums showed when he spoke; only a few teeth remained. He was wearing ripped pants, cotton, I guess, and a faded shirt; the second button was missing. Little by little, he began to tell me his story. As he spoke, his shallow breathing became labored at times. His hands, relaxed at first, started to twitch, and he began unconsciously pulling at his fingers. He seemed miles away in thought.

Almost in a whisper he said, "I was young, about ten, and the Japanese soldiers gathered all the people in the village and brought us to this beach, men, women, old and young, all the babies and the children. They put the children in one group and then shot all the men and women, forcing me to watch them kill my father and mother. Some of the older boys dug the graves and lowered the bodies in. Then the Japanese shot them and pushed them in. It was terrible. I remember it as if it was yesterday."

"See the plane over there?" he said pointing to the wreckage of what had been a World War II Japanese warplane. "A kamikaze pilot crashed on the beach. We kept it to remind us of those who died."

I lowered my head as the tears ran down my cheeks. I struggled to squeeze my eyes to stop the flow. The children were playing on another part of the beach. I did not want them to hear this story or see me crying. Palm trees gently swayed in the breeze. The scent of flowers from a nearby bush reached my nose. I listened to the soft lapping of the water against the sand. It was so idyllic and impossible for me to imagine such atrocities and brutality occurring here.

Yet now I quietly sat, next to the old man, my hand in his. I hoped perhaps the beauty and serenity of this place somehow overpowered the evil that had occurred. It offered peace and grace to those who had died. I felt the sweat drip down my back and focused on the sand between my toes. Then the raspy call of a gull broke my reverie, and we said our goodbyes. I went to gather up my children, hugging them more tightly to me, wishing with every fiber of my being I could protect them forever from all the pains of the world.

At night I tossed and turned in my bed. Nothing was right. I didn't sleep much. I thought of the Australian and American soldiers who had protected this country in the Pacific War, the villagers who had perished, and the graves they all now lay in. This plagued me until my eyes grew heavy and finally closed. War has no winners.

While we were in Port of Madang, we discovered mosquitoes loved Betsy. We did all we could, but the mosquitoes continued to track her down. I was worried as her bites were not healing. In the tropical jungle, they could become severely infected. The bites obsessed me. I was like a hawk examining them each day. The locals, my new friends, suggested I take her to the nearby health clinic where the nurse gave her intramuscular antibiotics. This did the trick and the bites healed.

We walked to and from the health clinic because there was no other mode of transportation available, no taxis, and no cart. Walking at noon for an hour was a horrendous mistake. Later in the day, I became especially ill. My mouth was dry, I was continually thirsty, and my body was on fire. My legs gave way as I struggled to walk. Mom had to help me. I became bedridden. She took charge and looked after everything, including me and the children.

I had never been this sick. My fever was exceptionally high. I had stopped sweating, but my extreme thirst went unabated. I would drift in and out of sleep and semiconsciousness. Body quaking chills racked my body. The sledgehammer pounding in my head kept me tossing and turning.

Mom asked our local friends to stop by and see me because I was not getting better. They thought I might have malaria. This diagnosis seemed unusual to me as I was taking my anti-malaria medication consistently. Immediately, I went to the clinic, and they took my blood.

As a registered nurse from Canada, I wondered about their primitive laboratory facilities. But then I recalled my public health professor's lecture. "When you are in a foreign country, remember, the medical staff and laboratory technicians are familiar with the local diseases, and you are not. So follow these simple rules: go to a local doctor, listen carefully to what they say, and follow their advice diligently."

The local doctor informed me, "Malaria was negative, but you have a severe case of sunstroke. Too much heat and sun caused your body to overheat. I am certain your temperature reached at least 104°F (40°C) with the chills you described. Also, being dehydrated, this condition could be fatal. Be careful and do not go out between 11:00 a.m. and 2:00 p.m."

We all followed his advice to the letter, taking lots of time to rest, and soon I recovered.

Mom and I enjoyed our daily trips to the market and continually learned about fresh local foods. The local women were as curious about us as we were about them. Many people spoke English because of the Australians and Americans being stationed there during World War II. The morning walk to the market was always a highlight of my day. Smiles welcomed us. We felt at home.

By talking to the women at the local market, we learned more about the traditional PNG diet. Fish and seafood were the daily proteins; however, most people ate pork on special occasions. Vegetables and fruits included breadfruit, coconut, bananas, mangos, sweet potato, cassava, cassava leaf, edible green leaves, sago, taro, and taro leaf.

It became our regular routine to go to the market early each day to purchase food for our meals. Breakfast would be freshly ground coffee, usually boiled plantains or bananas, taro or sweet potato, and flavorful mangos, if we could get them, or plentiful pineapples.

The women had taught me how to smell the pineapple base, checking for a sweet fragrance, to know when it was ready to cut. The pineapple was ripe when the color of the skin changed from green to yellow and then brown. My skills improved and I always chose ripe, sweet, and firm pineapples. I also learned the most efficient way to remove the skin and cut the fruit to serve.

The noon meal was primarily vegetables, especially yams with fruit. I liked the spinach and aibika. We tried cooked breadfruit mash with coconut milk baked in banana leaves. We didn't like it much. Once was enough.

We loved avocados, and luckily, we had a tall avocado tree in our yard. The women would take a long stick and knock the avocados down. The boys spent a lot of time trying to do the same. Then, when they were successful, they would come running with their bounty for our next meal.

At dinner we ate meat or fish and the same vegetables and fruits we had for lunch. Our family experienced new tastes and textures. It was amazing the children ate all the food. Everyone offered their opinions on each new food, then we gradually settled on the ones we all liked.

We lived with very little and learned to explore new foods, meet new people, learn about new cultures, and enjoy the simple life in our amazing jungle-like environment.

Chapter 10

My Nightmare When I Lost My Son at a Mountain Music Festival

We were lucky. I had purchased the last five plane tickets for Mom, the kids, and me so we could attend the traditional three-day Mount Hagen Sing Sing before we returned to Port Moresby. Mount Hagen was the capital of the Western Highland of PNG, in the mountains, at an elevation of 5,502 feet (1,677 meters). During this famous cultural festival, over one hundred regional or national tribes, many of whom often walked for days on foot or traveled by boat or truck, gathered to compete against each other, singing and dancing.

The five of us could not sit together in the plane. We ended up in different rows, sitting by people who wanted the window seats to observe the jungle-covered mountains below. The weather was cloudy as it had rained, unusual for this time of year. The previous flight had not landed because of poor visibility, and they were forced to return to the city. Now our plane began to descend, but the pilot hastily aborted our landing, and we quickly climbed back to a higher altitude.

"We only have one more chance to land. If not, we must turn back," the pilot announced. Passengers gasped.

A PNG pilot had once told me, "We do not fly through cumulus clouds ever. We call them cumulus granite. We haven't charted all our mountain ranges yet, and we're always at risk of flying straight into the rock face."

I felt secure knowing we were flying in a DC-3, the warhorse of World War II, capable of flying on one engine. But I also knew many airplanes had crashed in this area.

As I looked across the plane my mother and children were here flying in uncharted areas. Were we safe? My hands twisted, my knuckles were white. I took a deep breath and closed my eyes and said a prayer for a safe landing.

Just then, the passengers cheered when the clouds opened and we landed safely. I was jubilant; my family was on the ground.

Our Mount Hagen accommodation was in the school auditoriums, women in one and men in the other. Luckily Dan and Bruce were young enough to sleep with us. Our mattresses were cotton covers filled with sawdust, laid out on the floor. The smell of fresh wood chips was pleasant, but sleeping was bumpy and uncomfortable.

My mom was a star and managed along with the rest of us. The kids slept on their three mattresses, and we slept on ours, at either end, to keep them safe. This was undoubtedly communal sleeping as snores pierced the silence. Fortunately, screens on the windows kept the bugs away, and a cool breeze drifted throughout the room all night.

We were up early the following day and, after breakfast, went directly to a grassy area, larger than a Canadian or American football field, to see the Sing Sing events.

It was mind-boggling to see all the tribespeople in their feathers, with their brightly colored painted faces, pierced noses, and feathered headdresses, wearing decorative shells, beads, and long earrings. There were nearly 2,000 of them, ready to perform and compete for the honors of the best in their class. They made their face and body paint from the reddish earth and local plants, producing vibrant colors. Some colors seemed almost fluorescent. Reds, greens, and yellows were the most popular. They also slathered their bodies with pig grease to make their skin shine.

The performances got underway. The tribespeople competed against each other, dancing and singing and depicting ancient legends passed down in their oral history and daily life. Over in another part of the field, the men would use their bows to shoot arrows at distant targets. We were mesmerized, watching all the movement.

One of the competitors hits the bull's-eye during competition among tribes in PNG.

The competitors would gather before the judges, waiting to be honored with the prizes. This went on throughout the day. We would come and go, get a bite to eat and return. It was challenging for Betsy, but despite all the noise and commotion around her, she caught a snooze now and then wrapped in my arms.

Some tribal leaders caught my eye as we looked around us. One man had white lines painted down the center of his nose with a six-inch piece of wood piercing his nostrils. He had a large white shell, fastened as a collar around his neck, and the end of his short beard rested on the shell. A woven string cloth, rolled up like a rope, was tied around his neck. On his head he wore a conical hat, woven from brown fibers and dyed white at the front. Fresh yellow flowers hung down from the hat, by his ears.

The other men in his group had bright yellow paint on their faces, from their forehead to their noses. The skin between their noses and their chins was painted red and again a line of white was painted down the center of their noses, leading to the thin sticks piercing their nostrils. Some wore fan-like hats of woven feathers, white, orange, and green. I became hypnotized looking at them. Others wore bird of paradise feathers stretching high above their heads. The Sing Sing was like a dreamscape. I was immersed, taking photos.

Suddenly, out of nowhere, I was hit by a sudden feeling of dread. Something was terribly wrong. My stomach roiled as I looked around me. Dan was no longer by my side. I couldn't see him anywhere. I was frantic. My seven-year-old blond-haired, blue-eyed boy had disappeared. To my right was a break in the fence. I saw the blur of thousands of Papua New Guinea tribesmen, moving aimlessly in their finery of feathers, painted faces, and glistening, brightly hued bodies. Nothing was registering except I could not see Dan.

I didn't seem to be able to draw in enough oxygen to breathe as I tried to think of what to do. I was overwhelmed by a terrible wave of guilt and shame. What kind of mother would let her child leave her side at a crowded event like this? A sinking feeling overcame me; I felt light-headed as the blood drained from my head. Would he disappear forever? Maybe the tribesmen would take him back to the Mount Hagen highlands. I would never see or hear from him again.

A woman nearby, whom I had chatted with earlier, saw the terror in my eyes and put her hand on my shaking arm and said quietly, "The police took him to their office at the other end of the field."

I ran in the pointed direction. I am not sure if I bumped into anyone, but I didn't care. Where was Dan? I just had to find him. Arriving at the police office and out of breath, I saw him sitting on a chair and almost burst out crying in happiness and gratitude. My pulse was racing, over 100 beats per minute.

"Dan." I went to hug him. He looked at me as if to say, "Go away. I am having an amazing time."

To my surprise, he was chewing gum. I saw the Juicy Fruit gum wrapper in his hand—a first-time experience. The Australian police were enjoying talking to him. They were having a party. And Dan didn't want the fun to end.

The police looked at him and said, "Dan, are you sure this is your mother?"

He took a moment to consider his answer and then shrugged his shoulders. After a brief conversation, the police released him to me. I felt like I had failed in not keeping my child safe, and I swore it would never happen again.

When the festival was over, I knew this had been a once-in-a-lifetime experience. As we waited for our plane to take us home, the children began playing in a gigantic pile of sawdust, dumped out from the discarded mattresses. They tossed the sawdust high in the air, like fall leaves in a leaf pile, then they dove into the mound. I was glad to see them use their energy before our flight.

All went well until Dan lost his shoe. Soon passersby knew my problem and many helpers were scouring through the sawdust looking for the shoe. I was lamenting as I had only brought one pair of shoes for each child, and I knew it would be hard to replace them. I hugged one of the searchers when he found the missing shoe. We were all like one big family and laughed, as a resounding hooray filled the air. Finally, the plane arrived, and this flight was smooth with no clouds or aborted landings.

When we returned to Port Moresby, Ed finished his assignment. All hell broke loose when he walked through the door. There were yells, kisses, hugs, and all manner of high-spirited joy spilling into the atmosphere. We became a family again.

Mom and I both loved the baskets, bags, and beads we saw during our travels and had bought a variety of each to take back to Canada. Ed bought Kundu drums with their distinctive hourglass shape, carved handles, and lizard skin membrane stretched over the drumhead. The sides of each drum were decorated with etched animals or flowers.

We shipped our purchases and extra clothing back to Canada. We needed space in our suitcases for all the souvenirs we would purchase on the trip home.

These Sepik River Kundu drums from PNG still adorn my home.

Chapter 11

Experiencing Joy and Growth in Traveling, Engraved in My Soul

Our first stop on our return journey to Canada was Bangkok, Thailand. Its crowded streets, crammed with hustling vendors, offered buyers everything they could dream of, especially in the Sunday markets. The nightlife, with its bright flashing lights, welcomed people to restaurants, bars, and brothels.

Tuk-tuks moved through the streets in astonishing smoothness, guided by invisible stop lights. The tuk-tuks were the mechanized version of a rickshaw, small three-wheeled motor vehicles or bicycles. These are common in warmer climates and passengers had comfortable seats.

Mom, Ed, the children, and I adored moving silently through the Taling Chan Floating Market, in a long tail boat. Historically, vendors brought food and vegetables from their farms to sell to people who lived on the canals. Now, it has become more of a tourist attraction. Temples with their majestic spires lined the waterfront along the canals. The flower sellers displayed their wares as they headed their boats to stores in the city. Fresh, colorful orchids, roses, and especially birds of paradise, with their elegant orange crane-like flowers, were stunning and abundantly displayed all around us. We watched as the daily life of the boat residents unfolded.

Later we visited Wat Phra Kaew temple at the Grand Palace with its Emerald Buddha, carved from a block of jade. The Buddha was dressed in one of three royal gowns, depending on the season. Years ago, this had been the official residence of the kings of Siam, but these days it was a place of reflection for monks, who spent their days in meditation.

Back out on the streets we saw monks wearing bright orange robes and holding their begging bowls, waiting for people to give them food.

After our four-day visit we left Bangkok, boarding Royal Thai Airlines, heading to Hong Kong. An attendant, beautifully dressed in an elegant suit and displaying a welcoming smile, offered Mom and me an orchid corsage. The graceful service on the flight was such a pleasure.

Once we landed in Hong Kong, the hot, humid air was stifling as we stepped out of the airport and looked for a taxi. Shopping was on our minds. Mom was hoping to buy made-to-measure evening wear of heavy brocade silk, while I was looking for a pearl necklace and gold charms for my charm bracelet. Ed had his eye on a new camera. The children were on the lookout for new toys.

Neon signs, three stories high, soared above the streets, blinking to catch our attention. Young people crowded the sidewalks, dressed in an elegant formality; men wore suits and women wore jackets and skirts. Their apparel contrasted dramatically with the older generation who looked mundane in their dark pants and loose jackets.

Large, wheeled rickshaws, pulled by men sprouting goatees, moved past us. Available rickshaws were lined up at the curbside, waiting for customers. Restaurant tables were packed so close together we could smell the aroma of the food from the customers beside us. Most diners seemed to be smoking, as the smoke curled around our heads.

On the streets, everyone carried their purchases hanging from sticks balanced on their shoulders. Often two people worked together, each carrying one end. Women used their sticks to carry heavy loads, hanging in string bags. It looked challenging, but the people moved with an easy rhythm. They had mastered their craft.

Many people lived on boats nestled up against each other in the harbor. Wicker baskets were stacked at the back of each houseboat and were used to carry or store fresh fish or fresh vegetables or even transport children.

One evening we dined at a floating restaurant in the harbor. The children loved arriving by water taxi. Well-trained waiters served the food with elegance, and the pomp and ceremony made the evening memorable and delightful—a far cry from our usual day-to-day dining. Plentiful Chinese dishes were spread over the table—an array of delectable aromas wafted in the air. The lighting was restful, a lively three-piece band added to our enjoyment. The atmosphere oozed with elegance.

Leaving Hong Kong, we flew on to Tokyo and, after landing, got on the bullet train to get to our Japanese homestay host family in the suburbs.

The train was crowded. We were jammed tightly together with other passengers. Ed managed the luggage, as the force of the crowd pressed Mom, the children, and me in the opposite direction.

"Dan, Bruce, and Betsy, hang on to my clothes and stay as close as you can," I said. Our children had updated tags tied around their necks, but I was worried my young blond-haired family would disappear. Memories resurfaced of when I lost Dan at the Sing Sing.

It was useless as people pushed and shoved. I was using one hand to hang onto a loop to steady myself, and with the other,

I held onto Betsy. Mom found a strap and was stable as the train raced ahead. The train traveled so fast I lost my balance. When I looked up, Dan had disappeared among a sea of black-haired Japanese passengers. The color drained from my face. Not knowing the language or where we were, I prayed I would not lose him again. My panic increased as I imagined someone grabbing my child and getting off at a stop.

"Can I help you?" a young man said in broken English. I was trying to locate Dan and study the map, to figure out the name of the stations we were passing. The young man was short, thin, and his clothes were crisp, starched, and formal.

"Yes," I said with a sigh of relief. The young man quickly located Dan, looked at the address of our homestay hosts, gathered everyone together, and made sure we got off at the right stop with all our luggage. He was the angel I needed.

Out of respect, three of the Japanese men, who had worked with Ed on the boat in Papua New Guinea, met us at our destination. They had kindly made the host family reservation for us. Relief flooded through me as the husband of our host family also welcomed us as we got off the train.

Soon, we reached their single-story house. My body relaxed as I scanned the yard with its manicured lawn, shrubs, and beautiful white flowers. The Japanese custom was to leave your shoes at the highly polished dark brown front door and then put on slippers before entering. So, a pair of neatly placed slippers was ready for each of us. Next, the hosts kindly showed us our traditional Japanese-style rooms, with futons for sleeping, perched on top of tatami mats.

One of the most memorable parts of the homestay was the authentic food. Our hosts served meals in our rooms—miso soup, curry rice, and all types of fish. I also enjoyed the relaxing custom of wearing a kimono after a bath. Before bed, I would head to the tub room, a separate room inside the house. I would step down into the tub, water coming up to my neck. The warm water would gently swirl around me, my muscles softening as my eyes closed, gentle music lulling me into deep relaxation. Then we put on the soft cotton kimonos and rested. I loved this tradition and my stress vanished.

Each day our host family helped us plan our sightseeing experiences.

One day, while visiting the Tokyo Ginza area, the children spotted a McDonald's sign in the Mitsukoshi Department Store. This newly opened store contained the first of many McDonald's in Japan. The menu included the traditional hamburgers, cheeseburgers, fries, apple pies, and milk shakes. There were no seats or booths, takeout only. Everyone was so proud. Two staff members had gone to America to learn how to make the French fries and cook the hamburgers, US style.

We all felt a wave of familiarity and a high level of anticipation as we ordered our food. Everyone was ready for a taste of home, and it was a delightful change from Japanese fish and rice. We walked along the street munching our first hamburgers in a long time. They tasted fantastic. The fries were salty and crisp.

We had an extraordinary experience when the Japanese Tourist Association arranged a home visit with a Japanese family who spoke English. The hostess was the wife of the physician caring for Emperor Hirohito. We arrived at the appointed time at their home. The physician's wife was a petite Japanese woman who wore a tailored beige suit. Her eyes were kind and dark, but there was sadness in them as she mentioned the terrible sorrow of World War II.

The living room was tidy and clean, everything had its place. The furniture was delicate and intricately carved, polished to a high sheen and placed strategically around the living room. The windows looked out onto a manicured garden filled with shrubs and flowers. Our hostess had placed several floral bouquets in what looked like Ming vases, adding to the elegance of the living room. The vases were the typical blue and white design complete with the bristling dragon. In addition, tall room dividers, crafted by accomplished artisans, decorated with inlaid mother-of-pearl designs of dragons and flowers, gave the room a sophisticated backdrop.

We were offered green tea made with loose tea leaves, always lukewarm, and store-bought Western-style cookies. My white and blue bone china teacup was translucent. The cookies were plain, but the flavor and smell were familiar. I was disappointed as I was hoping for traditional Japanese sweets.

During our conversation our hostess asked where we were staying. She was surprised when we told her we were staying with a local family. We told her we wanted to enjoy the Japanese culture and were so grateful for the opportunity. Immediately, there was a brief conversation with the server; then the Western-style cookies disappeared, and the server replaced them with traditional Japanese sweets. She was happy to share her Japanese foods with us and knew we wanted to learn more.

"Joyce, I served Western cookies because I wanted to show my respect for your kind of food," our hostess said.

"Oh, thanks for thinking of us, but I love the new flavors of your traditional foods."

The children sat quietly as we chatted. Once again, I was proud of their behavior.

We forged a friendship that lasted long after our return to Canada. Each Christmas, the physician's wife would send my mother a small gift—an exquisite silk scarf, a silk handkerchief, a small statue, or another souvenir from Japan. Mom sent a Canadian gift to her. She treasured their bond, which lasted until the lady's passing.

One day we visited two new residents of the Tokyo Ueno Zoo—a two-year-old male giant panda, Kang Kang, and his constant companion, a three-year-old female named Lan Lan. Here we watched the black and white pandas play and move around their enclosure. Communist China had given the pandas to Japan in recognition of the establishment of diplomatic relations between the countries. The pandas had black ears, eyes, and noses, noticeable on their white fur heads. Black fur encircled their torsos and legs, and the back of their bodies were white. I wanted to hug them.

While we visited the zoo, several Japanese people came up to us, hesitated slightly and then quickly touched the children's arms, then mine. I was curious. What was going on? They turned to their friends, nodding their heads as if to say yes. Other families stopped and through a series of hand gestures, asked if they could also touch my arms. We learned later because we were so blond, from being in the tropics all summer, the Japanese could not see our fine blond arm hair. They were astonished when they felt the hairs. So, I guess that day, my family and I became a kind of impromptu zoo exhibit ourselves.

Canada beckoned as our departure day arrived. We were ready to go home and snuggle into our own beds. We flew Japanese Airlines to Vancouver. Unfortunately, the airline staff refused to give us anything for the children to eat for the initial four hours into the ten-hour flight. I pleaded with the flight attendant to provide the children with something, but without success—what a terrible time to forget to bring food with me.

When Mom boarded her plane to travel from Vancouver to her home in Edmonton, tears welled in my eyes. She had been a fantastic support, companion, and source of strength. I was incredibly grateful and treasured the time we had spent together, furthering our bond as mother and daughter.

By the time we arrived in Toronto, all we could do was crash in our beds. We rested and slept on and off for a couple of days, until our bodies became somewhat adjusted to Eastern Daylight Time. Our day-to-day Canadian life returned quickly as the children headed back to school and Ed returned to work.

My mind returned to the present and I smiled as I put the photos away, thankful for the opportunity to revisit long-ago travels with my family. I was grateful my new senior management job here in Saudi Arabia offered me the luxury of privacy—living alone in the compound. It gave me time to think. My work was gratifying, but I wanted my life to be more than just work. I pondered my future.

I wanted my life to be an adventure, to continue to learn from others, to share my professional expertise and discover more about myself. I wanted to embrace a sense of freedom, make my own decisions and explore, as much as possible, the amazing planet I called home.

Right there I made a pledge to myself. This new job was just the beginning. I would keep on traveling and explore at least one hundred countries, including the Antarctic. I would contribute, paying it forward as it were, whether by teaching or consulting in healthcare and do whatever it took to explore, to touch, to taste, to smell, and to live as best I could for as long as my health and finances allowed. I would find a way to give back. Lady Baden-Powell's quote, "Happiness comes not from what we have, but from what we give and what we share," has been my guiding light.

Chapter 12

The Balancing Act That Was My Daily Life in Saudi Arabia

Before I could hit the road again, I slowly adjusted to living in Saudi. Months passed and I crammed my days with eight-hour workdays, fitness programs, and women's outings. I managed limited contact with mixed company at Western embassies.

My expat friends warned me feelings of loneliness would come in waves, triggered by a small memory or those joyous letters from home. I knew these feelings were normal and I found ways to cope. The monthly get-togethers at the American Embassy, with their country-western dancing and line dancing groups, provided exercise and socialization. Often 150 people attended, which allowed me to share experiences with others and cement lasting friendships.

One evening I hosted a potluck dinner at my apartment. Twelve women from several countries attended: Canada, India, Ireland, the Philippines, the United Kingdom, and the US. Most of the women wore their national dress. I admired the distinctive styles, brilliant colors, and extraordinary fabrics.

Each guest brought their traditional favorite foods to share and provided a recipe card for each person to take home. We displayed scrumptious dishes, each with their own unique flavor and aroma, on my dining table: Canadian butter tarts, Indian butter chicken or

Makhan Murg in Hindi, Irish stew, a Philippine sour soup named Sinigang, British fish and chips, and American apple pie.

Everyone shared interesting facts about our homelands, including the culture, the geography, and the history. It was an entertaining and memorable evening. I believe it also helped us alleviate any homesickness and bonded us deeply as expats. We also realized we shared many more similarities than differences in our hopes and dreams.

In August, five of my new best friends left Riyadh. I had worked hard connecting with them and felt devastated and a profound loss when they returned to their home countries. I was lonely. For a while I pulled myself into a protective cocoon and concentrated on becoming my own best friend. Luckily, my isolation did not last long, and soon I was reconnecting with others.

I accepted an invitation to attend a traditional Saudi wedding. The ceremonies started late in the evening. The driver picked me up at 10:30 p.m. To my amazement, I was the only non-Saudi there. I took my cues from those around me and stuck close to the ladies, helping them practice their English.

Saudi weddings are a big event. Unlike Western weddings, there was no religious ceremony. Instead, women assemble in a separate room wearing the latest expensive designer clothes, as if they were in a fashion show. I felt I was at a bachelorette party. Men hang out in another room.

We were all happily chatting when suddenly the room became silent. The women scrambled to find their evening bags and secure their veils because a male, the groom, had entered the room. He and his bride sat at the front of the room on raised, decorated chairs. The bride wore a beautiful white gown and the groom a thobe, a white ankle-length robe and ghutra. Both appeared nervous. Finally, the bride and groom spoke and welcomed the group. The women cheered and clapped. Then, turning abruptly, the groom left.

I wondered how many times the couple had been together before the wedding. Sometimes, the bride and groom meet on several occasions, in secret, before the wedding, but often, a marriage broker arranges the union, and they would not meet until the big day.

After the groom left, the women removed their veils, and once again, the atmosphere filled with conversation. The servers rolled out plastic tablecloths on the carpeted floor, placing plates of food and paper towels down beside each of us. I followed the women to the sink to wash my hands, then we sat on the floor. There were no knives and forks. I realized I would have to pick up the greasy chicken and other food with my hands. My appetite vanished.

The woman sitting across from me stared at me far too long. I pulled off a leg from a roasted chicken, and someone handed me a chunk of white meat from the breastbone. I placed the food on the plate and glared at it. Another lady passed the samosas, and I grabbed two and dumped them on my plate. I hesitated. I felt self-conscious and uncomfortable. Using my fingers, I finally picked up the food and stuffed it into my mouth and chewed and chewed. But my throat tightened. It was hard to swallow.

A woman nearby sensed my resistance and seemed to feel my agonizing discomfort. She leaned toward me and softly whispered, "You may leave the food." Her comment and moment of thoughtful understanding and empathy broke my tension. Soon I joined their conversations and laughter.

I eventually made it to my bed at 3:10 a.m.—happy, full, and too tired to think about anything.

Activities such as dining out at the local restaurants brought me joy and happiness. I put on a few extra pounds but maintained my weekly fitness program of swimming and aerobics to keep my weight in check.

Abdul's small friendly Arabic restaurant usually had a line of waiting customers.

Abdul was portly, with a belly that fought rebelliously against his white thobe. He would greet me, show me to my table in the restaurant's women's-only area, and hand me the menu. His eyes constantly darted everywhere, making sure his customers were content.

"Welcome, Joyce, what would you like today, perhaps your favorite?" said Abdul with a wink.

"You know me too well, Abdul," I said with a laugh. "How is your family doing, especially the little one, Ali?"

"My family is well; thanks be to God. Ali is sprouting, did I tell you he's walking now?" Abdul, a proud and doting father, showed me a picture of Ali. Abdul knew my favorite meal. The shawarmas were a quick and tasty meal; the lamb was my choice, although it was more expensive than chicken or beef. His perpetual smile set the tone for the restaurant as he wielded a long narrow knife and skillfully carved slices from meat, stacked in a cone-like shape, rotating on the spit. This method of cooking continually browned the meat on the outside.

Immediately, he wrapped the meat in freshly baked, still warm, flatbread. Carefully he added the correct quantity of tomatoes, cucumbers, onions, pickled vegetables, and extra tahini sauce. Each restaurant used its own unique mixture of cardamom, cinnamon, cumin, turmeric, and paprika. Abdul's resulted in a delicate flavor only he could produce. The restaurant became my home away from home, my safe place to relax and enjoy the local happenings.

Over the months, I developed a small group of female friends and we often talked, late into the evening, sitting on the sofa in my apartment. We sipped freshly squeezed mango juice and enjoyed samosas and each other's company as we chatted and unwound from the day's work. One evening Karen, an intensive care unit nurse at the hospital, who came to Saudi from Texas after seeing an ad in a nursing journal, asked me a question.

"I've always been curious, Joyce, how on earth did you end up coming to Saudi Arabia?"

"Well, let's see," I said, sinking back into the comfort of the sofa and closing my eyes. I told her I was a divorcée in my fifties and the life I had expected to be living in Canada with my husband was long over.

"When all my children were married, I had the opportunity to travel, which had always been a lifelong dream of mine. So here I am in Saudi. Unbelievable, isn't it?" I smiled suddenly, shaking with laughter.

"Absolutely," declared Karen. "I think you're amazing, and incredibly brave."

Then she dissolved into fits of laughter too. "Unbelievable? Well sure! But honestly, I ask you, Joyce, who among us expats haven't pushed their limits over here?"

After we had recovered from our fit of giggles, Karen looked at me thoughtfully for a moment and said, "You know I never married, it's always been just me. I think that's why I'm so grateful we met and for the fun and friendship we share, especially in a country so foreign and restrictive at times."

"I couldn't agree with you more, Karen," I said as I reached over to hug my dear friend close.

Two weeks later, Karen and I met for dinner at a nearby Indian restaurant. We entered, passed the men-only area, then sat in the women's section, as unescorted ladies. The owners had placed six-foot-tall black screens to seclude our space. Two Filipino servers were friendly and chatted as we decided on our choices from the menu.

We settled in for a quiet, relaxing meal. Our server brought samosas, fresh naan bread, and tandoori chicken. Then the restaurant turned off the lights in respect of evening prayer. As a regular customer, I knew the routine. We sat in candlelight, eating our food, and spoke in hushed tones.

I loved enfolding the chicken within the warm naan bread, savoring the delicate flavors. The smoky scent and bouquet filled my senses, which came from slow cooking with Indian tandoori spice. The rich orange and yellow from turmeric and saffron made the dishes a visual delight. The desserts, my favorite, were heady, syrupy, sweet, and satisfying.

"Someday, I am going to India to explore the various cultures and taste the specific traditional dishes of each region," I declared to Karen while licking my fingertips. "Would you come with me?"

Before she could answer, there was an uproar in another part of the restaurant. Yells, screams, and the sounds of people desperately pushing and shoving to exit the premises as quickly as possible reached us. We stared at each other, frozen. I whispered, "Mutaween?"

We sat unmoving and waited. Two mutaween wielding their canes rushed into our area, knocking over the screens. They came crashing down into a pool of darkness on the floor. Bright overhead lights suddenly flickered on, causing me to blink several times to clear my vision. I found my purse and clutched it tight.

"Go, go," a mutawa yelled, his cane held threateningly high above us. I could imagine his rod striking my back in one brutally swift action. His jaw was tense, and his eyes glared at us menacingly. Sweat dripped from my forehead.

Panicked, I hurriedly put on my abaya and headscarf, then rushed toward the door—Karen beside me. The cane hit a piece of furniture, the sound deafening. I froze, waiting for the next crack, and felt a rush of air pass close to my face. He yelled at us again, and, keeping our heads bowed submissively, Karen and I rushed through the door onto the sidewalk.

The mutaween brutally shoved the two Filipino staff members, who just moments earlier had been serving us dinner. My stomach tightened. I got a sick feeling inside. The mutaween forced the men into a waiting car, its engine running. They drove off, tires screeching, obliterating the evening's stillness.

I stood on the pavement, my fists clenched, and stared as the car disappeared into the distance. I glanced at Karen. Without a word, we began our walk back to the compound. Our appetites had vanished. We knew they would likely send the servers to prison and then after their release they would have to return home. The Filipinos worked hard in Saudi to support their families who depended on their paychecks.

The following week, I walked back to the restaurant to pay for our meal, but the authorities had boarded it up. Again, the power of the mutaween hit home.

Living and working in Saudi, for me, was a way to add money to my bank account, to try to understand a new culture, and to travel and see the world. But often it was hard to feel at home in a country where I was constantly looking over my shoulder to see if the mutaween were nearby. My headscarf covering my hair and my abaya were my constant companions.

Chapter 13

I Invited My Son and Daughter-in-Law to Join My Explorations When Cambodia Opened Up

"I realize you can't tell me if my son and daughter-in-law Bruce and Cindy Perrin are on the flight from Toronto," I was on the phone with someone from the Bangkok airport. "All I'm asking you is should I go to the airport or not?"

There was a moment's silence, "Yes," said a male voice, the phone disconnected.

It was June 1994, and I was standing at the arrivals gate, understandably impatient. It had been forever since I had seen Bruce and Cindy. It had been quite an accomplishment to get our holiday schedules to line up. I had traveled from Riyadh to Bangkok, and they were coming from Canada. I kept glancing at my watch, while pacing back and forth. What was keeping them? Finally, I spotted their smiling faces. We hugged, grabbed their suitcases, and headed to our hotel.

They were exhausted after the fourteen-hour flight. Cindy had never been far from Ontario. Bruce couldn't remember anything from his visit here when he was five. Like most travelers, their eyes opened wide at the sight of Bangkok City—the noise, colors, neon lights, and crowded streets.

The next morning, we checked out of our hotel to meet up with Thomas, a coworker from Saudi Arabia, and his friend Steve. Both were Americans, traveling with us to Cambodia, Vietnam, and Laos.

Cambodia is in Southeast Asia. Thailand borders to the west and northwest, Laos to the north, Vietnam to the east and southeast, and the Gulf of Thailand to the southwest.

Cambodia was slowly emerging from its two decades of warfare and violence. The Khmer Rouge, Communist Party members who had ruled the country from 1975 to 1979, were responsible for the genocide of at least one million of Cambodia's seven million people.

We taxied down the runway for our one-hour flight to Cambodia, the five musketeers, heading off to a somewhat unknown country, still in the throes of recovery from this violent and savage government.

On arrival in the capital, Phnom Penh, we checked into the Hotel Sofitel Cambodiana, with its pagoda-style temple roof. We were ready to explore, so we hired an English-speaking guide, Boran, whose smile was welcoming.

Boran explained, "Pol Pot, the leader of the Khmer Rouge, wanted Cambodia to be an agrarian socialist one-party state, eventually becoming communist. The population was forcibly moved from the cities to the country to work in collective farms."

We headed to the Tuol Sleng Genocide Museum, formerly a high school, which had been a prison. I was not sure what to expect. Walking through the museum, I saw the tools that had been used to torture people. At some of the displays, I had to turn away quickly. Waves of disgust and disbelief welled up inside me. The exhibits showed how the guards tortured the prisoners, with electric shocks to their ears causing deafness, or how many others died of suffocation when a plastic bag was tied around their heads.

Sometimes the guards pulled off a prisoner's toenails, increasing their punishment if they yelled out or screamed in pain.

After this intense cruelty, prisoners would sign anything their tormentors wanted them to sign, real or imagined. Their forced confessions formed the basis for future government propaganda purposes. My rage increased as I paused at each of the displays.

One of the museum guides expanded on what we were seeing when he told us, "The guards treated the prisoners harshly and kept detailed records to report to their bosses. They took multiple black and white mug shots when prisoners were admitted, and especially during their torture, to confirm to the generals the guards had completed their orders. The guards delivered unrelenting beatings, numerous electric shocks, along with other creative torture methods. They usually got the confessions they wanted, or the prisoners died in the process."

Boran looked at me, then quickly grabbed my hand to steady me. The story of the Khmer Rouge genocide rolled on as if it were a movie, playing in one room after the other.

Outside, the hot, humid air smacked me in the face, sweat ran down my neck, yet I felt totally chilled to my core. Across the street, I saw a man with one leg and another missing his right arm and shoulder. I assumed they were victims of the torture I had just learned about. Even though I was a nurse, I looked away, trying hard to process all I'd just seen. I felt a deep sorrow for what human beings as a species do to harm each other.

Next, we made a brief stop at a former execution site, now a memorial, the Choeung Ek Genocidal Center. Hundreds upon hundreds of skulls of the victims of the Khmer Rouge were randomly piled on top of one another, in glass cases. I tried to imagine each of these skulls as a living, breathing person with a family, hopes, and dreams for their future, all gone. It was horrifying. It was overwhelming and raw.

"An estimated 1.5 to 2 million Cambodians were killed during the reign of the Khmer Rouge, and unfortunately, the technical and professional classes were eliminated, leaving a void in those skills," said Boran.

We drove from the Genocide Museum to the Killing Fields. When we arrived only a few people were there. I felt an eerie silence, just the rustle of the leaves in the stifling hot breeze. The air was heavy with despair and sorrow.

"Come in the shade and listen," Boran said. "The history of the Khmer Rouge's barbarian actions during its genocidal four-year reign is one of mass torture and starvation. They brutally murdered men, women, and children in one of their 196 torture and execution centers. They preferred to kill people by slitting their throats, delivering a blow to their heads, or bludgeoning and mutilating them with a pickax. This way, they saved their scarce supply of bullets, which they used in other devastating ways.

"Soldiers hung babies from trees and forced young boys to batter them to death," he said in a tone so hushed it was hard to hear. "Young boys also dug the mass graves and pushed all the dead people into the pits. They killed every member of my entire family."

As I listened to him, all the air left my lungs. It seemed as though all the oxygen had left the atmosphere. I felt myself struggling to breathe. I wanted to hug Boran, but somehow, I knew it was not the right thing to do. Instead, I stared at the trees and visualized babies, hanging from branches and boys hitting them. Unspeakable memories must stalk those young boys' minds, if any had survived.

As we continued our tour, I asked Boran a question that had been nagging at me: "How did the Khmer Rouge get their funding?"

"Well, some say the North Korean and the Vietnamese governments were helping the Khmer Rouge. Others say the drug lords, who sold opium in the occupied area, used the money to continue the war, or money came from the sale of gems such as emeralds, sapphires, and rubies found in the mines. So, it was probably a bit of all of the above.

"The Vietnamese troops eventually toppled Pol Pot and his Khmer Rouge regime in January of 1979 when they seized Phnom Penh, the Cambodian capital. But then the Khmer Rouge retreated into the jungle," Boran said.

I did not want to hear any more tales of the country's devastation and horror, as it was emotionally draining. Yet, these thoughts now played in an unending, uncomfortable loop in my head. We said goodbye to Boran and returned to our hotel.

All five of us felt empty and were glad to find ourselves in a more relaxing setting. It was a relief to squeeze into a booth at Phnom Penh's Hard Rock Café, with its welcome air conditioning, as we downed a local beer. We discussed our feelings, thoughts of horror, and the devastating history of the country. Again, the cold Angkor Premium beer helped us unwind. Later we snapped photos of ourselves at the café. When we shared the photos with our friends, our smiling faces would mask the gut-wrenching experience we had just gone through.

Back in my hotel room, in the shower, I thought of the day's events and how blessed I was to be from Canada. I suddenly felt overwhelmed with emotion and sobbed uncontrollably as the warm water washed away my tears. I felt both anger and horror, but also enormous gratitude. My loved ones and I were safe.

I was here with my family; we would meet again within the hour for a delicious evening meal together. We would never have to experience what so many Cambodians had had to face. Life indeed was tenuous, haphazard, and a random toss of the dice for so many people. Yes, I was blessed. I was grateful.

In the evening, the five of us headed to a typical Cambodian restaurant and were greeted with wonderful aromas swirling in the air. We chatted with our server, and he explained a typical Cambodian family would eat fresh fish, rice, and vegetables as their evening meal. We ordered a banquet-style hot pot called "Yao hon for dipping," which included beef, shrimp, spinach, rice noodles, dill, napa cabbage, and mushrooms, with an unusual tangy coconut broth that enhanced the beef and shrimp combination.

In the early morning my anger and sorrow had subsided somewhat, and the five of us headed to the Silver Pagoda, a Buddhist temple, for a glimpse of the richness of the Cambodian civilization. The pungent smell of burning incense greeted us before we had reached the pagoda's threshold. I closed my eyes and my hands moved the bouquet toward me. I inhaled. It was pleasant, complex, and relaxing.

Sadly, the Khmer Rouge had removed half of the pagoda's original treasures in order to obliterate Cambodia's former culture. The Silver Pagoda had over 5,000 silver floor tiles, weighing up to one kilogram each, and were strategically placed, resulting in stunning silver reflections. The early artisans were known for their meticulous beautiful designs and artifacts.

The most impressive was a bejeweled mask, worn while performing a Cambodian classical dance. Years ago, the artisans originally embedded 1,516 diamonds onto dozens of solid and hollow gold buddhas, which adorned the mask. However, the current government had removed most of the diamonds, and only the gold buddhas remained.

There was a serenity and peacefulness to the temple and the royal palace grounds. I felt the hope and appreciation when a government works to protect and promote its history through the breathtaking work of its artisans.

In the afternoon we flew to Siem Reap, in northwestern Cambodia. From my window seat, I looked down and saw the extraordinary monuments in the Angkor Wat complex. It had been built as the headquarters of the Khmer Empire, which had ruled Cambodia for more than 600 years, from the ninth to the fifteenth century. Smaller temples dotted the grounds some distance away. I was excited about the opportunity to climb in and around the buildings, and I was anxious to explore this historical site as soon as we landed. After settling in our rooms, we headed over to the complex to see the unique temples.

I was sweating within minutes from the blazing sun and humidity. I grabbed my water bottle and took a gulp. The water was already warm. I looked at the thermometer on my bag, which read 100°F (37.8°C). I felt wiped. I thought about how this humidity contrasted with the dry heat in Saudi and decided I would take the dry heat, even if I had to wear my black abaya.

It took Suryavarman II, king of the Khmer Empire, forty years to build Angkor Wat, between 1110 and 1150. The Purification Pool, dedicated to the Hindu God Shiva, surrounded the buildings. Rising above the temple were five corn-cob–shaped towers, a typical Khmer design, which represented the homes of the gods. As I walked over the bridge that spanned the Purification Pool, I felt a strange sense of peacefulness and awe. I was embarking on a sacred journey. I felt small and insignificant, starting on a pilgrimage to the gods, in this massive complex.

Kneeling next to the Purification Pool at the Temples of Angkor Wat.

Once over the bridge, we hired a guide, Arun, who immediately said, "The Khmer Rouge killed all of my family." I was shocked by his bluntness. I gulped and looked away. So many questions ran through my mind.

Dark hair curled over his forehead, a well-manicured mustache covered his upper lip, and his piercing eyes moved over each of us. He started telling us about the temple's intricate details; however, when he spoke about the people's hardships, I saw his eyes glass over. I wondered what he was thinking. I wanted to hear more about his family. How did he survive? My mind began to drift. I wanted to get away and not hear anything more. How could humans be so savage to each other?

Stopping to pose at one of the entrances to the temples.

We wandered among the temples, learning about the statues positioned on each side of the doorways. We noticed several soldiers patrolling the area. Cindy and I made our way through the smaller temples. Unfortunately, due to lack of maintenance, trees had twisted and turned and grew in and over many of them.

It reminded me of the story of "Jack and the Beanstalk" with one main tree reaching to the sky, held down by roots pushing through the ground. How I would have loved to climb these trees as a child. There were so many places to put your feet and hang onto the branches. Hours passed as we wandered, feeling safe in our peaceful exploration.

We stopped to rest. Two young girls playing homemade bamboo flutes serenaded us with Cambodian music. We tried to engage in conversation with a few of the children, then one young boy, Charya, braver than the rest and obviously smart, asked us short questions in broken English. Soon I learned he could not go to school and therefore would not get an education.

"His family is too poor," one of the girls said.

The lack of opportunity for an education was heartbreaking. I stared at his face. His eyes burned with curiosity and abundant energy as if to say I want to learn, teach me. He seemed like a natural leader, so I encouraged him to join us as we meandered through the rest of the temples. He learned new English words quickly. He challenged me to think of questions to keep his interest. His smile was so engaging, it felt like a big hug to me.

We kept exploring until we couldn't take another step in the heat and humidity. We left Angkor Wat and headed back to the hotel in search of much-needed air conditioning and some relaxation. The men enjoyed a few games of pool as Cindy and I watched, and then we all downed more of the famous Angkor Premium beer with its red label showing pictures of the Angkor Wat temples. The flavor was strong, refreshing, and cool as it slipped down my throat—a pleasant relief from the oppressive heat and humidity.

At night before bed, I thought of little Charya, who could not go to school. My great-grandfather, Matt McCauley, a member of the Alberta Legislature, was instrumental in passing legislation in the Alberta government in the early 1900s to make schools free and accessible for everyone. As a result, all children were able to go to school and have more opportunities and choices available to them when they grew up.

The next morning before sunrise, Bruce brought baguettes from our favorite French-style bakery. They were still warm, light, and crispy, with a rich buttery flavor. Complemented by our robust coffee, it was a special start to our day. We were heading out to explore the more unusual and elaborately carved temples, in the remote areas of the Angkor Wat complex, rarely visited by tourists. As the sun rose, we piled into a car with Arun.

Our driver slowed down at what appeared to be a checkpoint. He knew the Khmer Rouge might be in the nearby jungle, but nobody was staffing it, so he shrugged his shoulders and drove on.

We wandered among these extraordinary, more obscure temples, feeling the serenity of the environment. Only bird songs broke the stillness. The sun's heat was just beginning to build for the day. It was like a fairy-tale land from a children's book. I was happy and felt like I was in another world.

"Artisans built these structures in the twelfth century. Each male and female figurine, facing toward the open door of each temple, represents the purpose of the temple. The position and direction of their feet indicate a significant religious meaning," said Arun.

"Arun, how many hours do you think it would take to carve one of the figures?" I said.

Before he could answer, the sound of gunshots pierced the air. They sounded extraordinarily close.

"Get in the car right now and put your heads down. We must leave immediately!"

More gunshots rang out as our driver gunned the engine. The five of us scrunched down in our seats. I looked at Cindy and Bruce. The color had drained from their faces; my chest was tight. I was taking rapid shallow breaths, bent over, trying to make myself as small as possible. The return trip seemed to take far too long. We made it back to our hotel, but I felt like a limp dishrag and was emotionally exhausted.

We were shocked to see soldiers, positioned with guns, standing outside our hotel and in the lobby. A soldier turned to us and said, "All tourists must leave tomorrow morning on the last plane from here as the Khmer Rouge has advanced to this area. You are unsafe to remain here."

I grabbed Cindy's hand and squeezed it. I needed her for support. I wanted to leave right now, but the plane would not come until morning.

That night we ate another typical Cambodian meal, but the atmosphere was heavy and somber. The joy we had experienced in Siem Reap had vanished. Even a few Angkor beers did not help.

Finally, morning arrived, and we were the first to board the twin-engine plane, followed by two Asians, then United Nations members, and the staff from other international organizations. We taxied and rose into the air, the pilot making a sharp banking maneuver to the right to avoid possible ground fire from the Khmer Rouge.

With a sigh of relief, we touched back down in Phnom Penh. After settling into our hotel, we spent the rest of the day wandering through the market and picking up some souvenirs. The smell of food being cooked at various stalls, the abundance of color, and the noise of sellers on the street helped quash my thoughts and fears of having narrowly escaped any danger the day before.

People moved swiftly among the shops, and store owners welcomed us with smiles and slight bows. My favorite store was the one selling silk fabric. The smell of incense hung in the air, giving the store a touch of elegance. The owner showed me beautiful silk for a blouse, which I would have made in Saudi Arabia when I returned.

The five of us were restless and anxious to leave Cambodia, so we hired a taxi to take us to the Vietnam border. When the cab arrived the next day at dawn, for the four-hour trip, we were so crowded Cindy had to sit on Bruce's lap. We felt like sardines crushed in a can. Nevertheless, the drive was uneventful. As the miles clicked away, I tried to focus on the flat countryside, dotted with gently moving palm trees.

I liked the Cambodian people and was happy we could visit. But I was more than a little relieved to be leaving the civil unrest behind us. I could put myself in danger, but to invite my son and daughter-in-law on a trip, putting their lives at risk, had been a terrible thing. I felt an extraordinary responsibility. The heavy burden I had been carrying lightened when we crossed the border into Vietnam. I said a silent prayer of thanks because we arrived safely.

We were lucky. Some months later, I learned tourists who were traveling on the same road to Vietnam a few days after us were kidnapped and killed by the Khmer Rouge.

Chapter 14

I Was Overwhelmed—Learning about the Sorrows of the Vietnam War

After the usual immigration and customs procedures, the five of us hired a comfortable taxi at the Vietnam border to take us on to Ho Chi Minh City, formerly Saigon. Vietnam had just opened the country to visitors, and they welcomed us with open arms. The Vietnamese government encouraged travelers to speak English to school children. The children wore T-shirts with questions to ask English-speaking tourists: What is your name? How old are you? Where are you from?

The government knew speaking English promoted tourism, which would be essential to grow the country's economy. The children we encountered were timid when they approached us, but their natural curiosity and excitement to practice their English overcame their shyness. After I helped them with certain pronunciations, one child would correct another; without a doubt, these children learned fast.

Bicycles and motorized scooters bunched up at intersections, waiting for the traffic lights to change. It reminded me of horses champing at the bit behind the starting gate before a race. We always ensured we were standing safely on the curb when the light turned green. It was every person for themselves as the road became a sea of battling bikes.

Stalls at the central market drew our attention; it was the place to shop. Hand-embroidered linens and clothes, such as tablecloths and blouses, were incredibly sophisticated, with intricately detailed needlework. I was thrilled to find blouses for my granddaughters, the work of each one unique to a particular artisan.

On our second day in Vietnam, after a typical breakfast of sticky rice called xoi, served with fried onions and beans, the five muske- teers, as we still called ourselves, went to visit the Cu Chi tunnels, built by the Viet Cong to house troops and move supplies dur- ing the Vietnam War. I had no idea how alarming the experience would turn out to be.

The five of us maneuvered into one of the dark tunnels, cramped and damp; spiders were everywhere. My son turned his cap around to prevent cockroaches from crawling down his back. Our only light was one flashlight, and people at the back had no light at all and just followed the leader.

I twisted my body, as I squatted down and crawled through one of the shorter tunnels, which the soldiers had enlarged to allow a Westerner's body frame to make it through. My leg muscles began to cramp, but it was impossible to straighten them in such close quarters. I was glad to see daylight and to work myself free from the tunnels' dark, suffocating, claustrophobic environment. Everything about the experience was disorienting, disturbing, and unreal.

Next, we viewed a video showing how the Viet Cong had won the war and how the underground tunnels played an essential part in the fall of Saigon and the South Vietnamese government. The Viet Cong were tenacious, despite facing a formidable foe as well as the relentless bombings. They could live underground for weeks or months at a time while waging modern-day guerrilla warfare. The countless deaths of their comrades and families, along with the thousands of deaths of American soldiers, were a stark testimony to the heartbreak and ultimately the human cost of war.

During the war the Viet Cong had laid cunning booby traps and mines in the jungle. Our tour included entering a part of the jungle, laced with harmless hidden traps, where we tried not to trigger a firecracker. The firecrackers were meant to simulate the lethal mines and grenades that maimed and killed so many American soldiers during the Vietnam War.

I turned to mention something to Bruce, and suddenly a firecracker exploded; in my carelessness my pant leg had snagged on a clear plastic fishing line. I searched about me but saw nothing. Was there another one close by? I kept on looking and I finally saw the shimmering clear plastic line catching the light. I was momentarily shocked. It was almost impossible to fathom if it had been a real mine or grenade, I would have caused my death and possibly the deaths of those around me. By the end of our jungle ordeal, the five of us had set off every one of the booby traps, effectively killing ourselves and alerting the Viet Cong. It was both sobering and jarring to realize this had been the fate of so many young men.

A little farther along, I saw a demonstration of how the Viet Cong created a trap, digging a small indentation in the ground, filling it with poisoned bamboo spikes and covering it with brush. When an American stepped on the brush, the force of his weight pierced the sole of his boot with the bamboo spikes, causing injury or death. The Viet Cong knew the US forces would never leave an injured soldier behind, and carrying the wounded would slow their progress.

I was thinking about the mines and the traps when we came to a clearing, and our guide told us to watch. He lifted up some sod, the size of a piece of typing paper, which covered a hole cut into the ground. He disappeared into a tunnel, dropping the sod back down behind him to cover the hole.

The guide shows us how small the entrance is to the hidden tunnels at Cu Chi.

I looked carefully and did not see the cut in the ground. The Viet Cong are tiny, and with their slight bone structure and body build, they were masters at disappearing. It took our guide a split second to vanish into the underground tunnel.

Although I saw it, it was hard to believe. I imagined how infuriating it would have been, tracking a Viet Cong, only to find the soldier had evaporated before your eyes. It must have been like trying to catch mist.

During the tour I remembered conversations I had had with Sam, a US soldier in Riyadh, who had fought in Vietnam.

"It was impossible to tell who the enemy was," Sam had told me. "The people, mostly women, went from planting rice in the fields one minute to planting mines in the path of our troops the next. Then they went back to planting in the fields again. So how could I know who our enemy was? Who or what intelligence could I trust? The answer was I couldn't tell. We couldn't tell. At best, it seemed it was only a guess. It was an impossible situation."

I remembered Rob, an American pilot who served during the Vietnam War and now flew for Saudi Arabian Airlines. Rob had said, "It was impossible to fix your bearings in the jungle. So, the night of a raid, helicopters landed first and gave the aircraft a tracking point for the bombers to know their target location. The Viet Cong were safe in their tunnels. Only a spiral bomb could reach and destroy their underground network. I still suffer from flashbacks thinking of the effects of those bombs. You know, Joyce, post-traumatic stress disorder is a real thing."

I had wanted to give him a hug to show him I understood, although how could I? So instead, I had simply whispered, "I am so sorry, Rob."

No more tunnels or Vietnam War museums; I had had my fill. I knew after the war, the North Vietnamese immediately displaced the South Vietnamese teachers, university professors, medical doctors, and lawyers. These South Vietnamese professionals had to eke out an existence as cycle drivers or manual laborers. They were similar to the technical and professional classes in Cambodia who were on the losing side at the end of the war, and they had felt the same effects.

In the evening under the shower, no amount of hot water could unknot the muscles in my neck and back. The anxiety I had felt walking through the jungle was real. I thought of the sheer terror those American soldiers must have experienced. I understood on some minuscule level how those young men, those who were lucky enough to get home, had changed so much when they returned. The trauma they must have experienced was so significant and profound, nothing could ever be the same for them again.

At dawn the following day, as the sun started to break gently over the horizon, we headed northeast of Ho Chi Minh City to the small town of Dalat. Lakes and waterfalls filled the landscape, while vast evergreen forests made the panorama complete.

Once in Dalat, we happily devoured tasty food from the market, which was overflowing with fresh vegetables. Rosy red tomatoes, deep green bundles of leafy spinach, and large perfect avocados spilled forth from the baskets trying to contain them. Buckets of flowers exploded with colors and fragrance, covering every walkway. People carried their flowers carefully, almost like cradling a baby.

The women wore conical hats, cotton shirts, and baggy pants— typical Vietnamese clothing—and all had welcoming smiles. I bought some handwoven fabric coasters from a smiling, dark-haired lady who proudly showed me a photo of her working in her home. A bit further along, Cindy, Bruce, and I bought three original paintings from a young man selling his work. The picture I chose was a street scene, with one man riding a bike and another man carrying packages hanging from a wooden stick over his shoulder and wearing a conical hat; palm trees and houses filled in the background. The colors were muted greens and browns and projected a gentle yet characteristic scene.

A funeral procession suddenly filled the street around us. The mourners wore ornately designed, brightly colored cloth-ing. One man carried an umbrella, shading who I assumed was a noteworthy man walking in the procession. Others followed, carrying a tall canopy hung with multicolored streamers. More men, dressed in white shirts and dark pants and wearing the conical-type hats, led a large crowd that filled the road. It was orderly, somber, and respectful.

After Dalat we visited Hoi An, a quaint, friendly place. We strolled around, visiting the old homes, now unique museums filled with priceless antiques. I loved exploring Hoi An. Exploring old buildings was one of my hobbies, and I noticed some similarities to buildings I had visited in Japan.

After a brief overnight stop in Da Nang, just north of Hoi An, we continued up along the coastal strip. We saw rice paddy fields built on the sides of hills. The hills sparkled with all hues of green, from dark forest through bright emerald. Women were still wearing the familiar conical hats to protect them from sun and rain, tending the rice paddy fields from dawn to dusk.

Vietnam has over 1,800 miles (3,000 kilometers) of coastline, considerably longer than the West Coast of the United States. Once we arrived at our hotel at the Gulf of Tonkin in North Vietnam, we set out to investigate. The five of us sunbathed on the pristine beaches in Ha Long Bay and admired the spectacular scenery of lagoons, shaded by coconut palms. It was marvelous having the beach to ourselves in this undeveloped area. We wandered over the endless expanse of dunes, with their finely ground sand, and viewed the rugged mountains where many hill tribes lived. I fell in love with the sublime beauty of Vietnam's natural terrain.

It was a sad day when we returned to Da Nang and said goodbye to Cindy and Bruce as they headed back to Canada. When they boarded the plane, I felt a deep emptiness. Yet, despite inevitable loneliness that night, I felt happy about the adventures we had shared. We had built some unique life experiences together and formed a closer bond in doing so.

Steve, Thomas, and I carried on, visiting the magnificent nineteenth-century Dai Noi Citadel in the town of Hue in central Vietnam, then headed to Hanoi via an overnight train. I slept little at night even though I bought a soft seat for the trip. The chair looked comfortable enough when we researched the train trip and made the reservation, but it turned out to be a big mistake. The "soft seat" was actually rigid wooden slats. No cushion. It was devilishly uncomfortable, so I walked up and down the carriage, buying snacks at each stop. I thought the eighteen-hour train ride would never end. Nevertheless, we survived an awkward night. The following day, we found a place to stay in Hanoi, showered, and were ready to explore the city.

The summer monsoon or rainy season occurs from May to October. One day, after shopping, I was sitting comfortably alone in a rickshaw when the afternoon cloudburst started. The heavens opened, quite literally. Torrents of water swirled and surged through the streets. The driver jumped off the bike and pushed the rickshaw, with me in it, through the rising water. I was soaked. Water came up to my waist, and I struggled to keep my parcels and backpack dry. Fortunately, my sandals were waterproof. The rain did not last more than ten minutes before the sun came out, high in the sky. The water drained from the roads. My cotton clothing dried quickly, but the extreme heat and humidity sucked my energy. I learned that floods were common during this time of year and what to expect next time.

One evening in Hanoi, we enjoyed a water puppetry performance, a uniquely Vietnamese art form, depicting legends and folklore. The puppeteers stood in waist-high water, behind a backdrop. They skillfully moved elaborately dressed puppets to the rhythm of traditional music, played by a live orchestra. I was impressed by how well the puppeteers controlled the puppets' movements; they appeared to glide over the water. It was a magical night, and right then, I became enthralled by Vietnamese culture and was glad they treasured and shared their history.

We explored a quaint French-influenced city quarter in Hanoi. The many family-owned gift shops beckoned me to examine their items for sale. I took advantage of the beautiful silk available and had several blouses made before I left Hanoi for Laos. The city pulled on my heartstrings. The time to head on was approaching. I wished I could stay longer, to enjoy the rich culture, which continually was summoning me to poke into the winding streets, stores, and ornate temples. I felt the rush and excitement of a country changing, developing, and growing.

Chapter 15

Resting and Relaxing When I Stayed in Vientiane

Laos, a landlocked country, shares its border with Thailand, Cambodia, Vietnam, China, and Myanmar. The country is slightly larger than Great Britain. The rugged Annamite Mountain chain and the Mekong River dominate the topography. Laos embraces the Hmong-Mien, Khmer, and Thai cultures, which have significantly influenced the country. However, to the Western traveler, Laos may appear underdeveloped and relatively undiscovered.

It would have been expensive and time consuming to obtain a visa permitting travel outside Vientiane, Laos's capital city. Instead, I had purchased a tourist pass, which allowed me to explore just the city. I only had four days in Laos before returning to work in Saudi Arabia, so this was perfect.

The day was magnificently clear when Thomas, Steve, and I flew to Vientiane. I liked visiting with the pilots whenever I flew. My conversations with them were fascinating. As well, the view from the cockpit was spectacular. As we headed to Vientiane, the land below was a kaleidoscope of sights and colors. The Mekong River wound through the deep forests, and the trees and grasses ranged from silvery sage green to the deepest green blue. The rich fertile soil along the riverbanks supported abundant vegetation.

The weather was hot, humid, and sunny as we disembarked from the plane. Short, sporadic showers provided some relief.

Thomas, Steve, and I had arrived midmorning, and we got a taxi to take us to a hotel, recommended by some expatriates we met at the airport. It turned out to be comfortable, with air conditioning, centrally located, and quiet.

As the city was small, we decided to start exploring on foot. Our first stop was a local pastry shop near our hotel. The Vinh Loi Bakery House, or Sweet Home Bakery, took its name seriously and the food was delicious. The bakery instantly became our breakfast and snack hangout. The aroma in the bakery was always heavenly as we entered to place our order.

Sitting outside in the café chairs, we enjoyed split French baguettes stuffed with Lao-style pâté called Khao ji ji. Then we sampled numerous sweet tarts, French pastries, and other baked delicacies, all made in the wee hours of the morning. All types of people stopped by to grab a morning coffee or pick up fresh pastries for lunch. It was easy to lose an hour or more as we happily watched life in Laos unfold on the street around us.

Dinner was always an adventure. I tried to follow the local customs and enjoy the unfamiliar aromas and flavors, even if I did not know what I was eating. Only occasionally, the tastes were an unpleasant surprise, but that was the chance I took when I explored different foods.

Sticky glutinous rice called Khao niao was a staple at each meal. I would grab a small handful of the rice, form it into a ball, then dip it into one of the condiments before popping it into my mouth. In Laos, workers carried their midday meal of rice in woven baskets, which they hung over their shoulders. I purchased a memorable souvenir in Laos: three smooth brown woven wicker baskets, used for holding sticky rice. When empty, they fit inside each other like Russian nesting dolls.

At dinner one evening, I devoured sticky rice between sips of fiery rice whiskey. Larb was another Laos staple: seasoned pork, cooked and then served with vegetables and rice. I tried it along with a highly aromatic fermented fish sauce called padaek, to spice up the dish. The whiskey enhanced the meal wonderfully.

After dinner, we watched men and women perform traditional dances, which originated from the Khmer Empire. Our table was right in front of the stage, our view unobstructed. The dancers told a story through unique and graceful hand movements. Their feet, often bare, moved simply, as their dance was accompanied by traditional Laos musicians. They danced slowly, in a circle formation, the men and women never touching each other. Their clothing was elaborate; the women wore heavy-looking gold headpieces, which never seemed to move during the dances.

Shopping was a delightful adventure. I spent hours wandering the many stalls and viewing the wares in the central market. Stall after stall displayed beautiful materials and exquisite woven hangings. I bought two different fabrics, intending to have them made into custom-made evening jackets for my mother and me. I knew an excellent seamstress back in Saudi Arabia.

Fellow expatriates who joined us at the bakery filled me in on changes happening in Laos. Matthew, a businessman from Australia, told me the government was in the process of restoring the glorious old buildings in the city, through the Vientiane Integrated Urban Development Program. Many old homes, instead of being torn down, were now being given a fresh coat of paint, woodwork repairs, and some reroofing. Once repaired they were ready to coexist among the new steel and concrete buildings. Their rich history and legacy were being preserved.

Chris, an Australian whom I met at the bakery as I ordered a cup of Robusta coffee sweetened with condensed milk, was convinced

Laos was just ten years behind Vietnam and its economy would soon take off. He had started a fruit farm and said he'd seen positive changes with the introduction of limited free enterprise.

During our visit we all rented bikes and cycled around the city's flat terrain. Our 12-mile (20-kilometer) tour was planned by another local expatriate. It was hot and humid when we headed out, just after sunrise. I took plenty of water, wore my Tilley hat, and applied lots of sunscreen. We stopped when we wanted, and, fortunately, we didn't puncture a tire, as there were no bike repair shops to be seen.

We biked past elaborate embassy buildings and large, extravagant private homes with their lush, manicured gardens. They seemed out of place, towering over the smaller, poorly constructed buildings, which most city dwellers called home.

We stopped to visit the Buddhist monasteries, clustered together along the embankment of the Mekong River. Most Laotian people were devout Buddhists. In their language the word for monastery was *Wat*. The oldest and most exciting Wat was named The Heavy Buddha because of a massive sixteenth-century bronze Buddha inside the main hall.

The monks, wearing their brilliant orange robes, were happy to greet us even though we couldn't speak their language. We removed our shoes before we entered the sanctuary of the Wat. The Buddhas were sacred objects, and people were requested not to pose beside them for photos.

I learned there were protocols to follow when speaking to a monk. Males kept their heads lower than the monks. Women were not permitted to touch the monk directly or hand them any object. I practiced the Laotian greeting, placing my palms together in a prayer pose and learned to return the greeting if someone welcomed me this way.

The people of Laos showed me warmth and friendliness with genuine smiles. My experience was rich and deep, as I felt the quiet, relaxed culture.

But all too soon, it was time to say goodbye to Thomas and Steve and head back to work in Saudi.

Chapter 16

The Challenge of Changing Jobs in Saudi but the Joy of Mother's Visit in Riyadh

I needed to make serious decisions. The Ministry of Health in Saudi Arabia had cut funding to the Security Forces Hospital. My department was closing in the spring and now my team and I were without jobs. I knew I needed to find work immediately and wanted to continue working internationally.

I considered my options and planned to head to England and enroll in an English as a Second Language (ESL) teaching certificate program. I thought this would be a straightforward way to continue working abroad. Although I felt sad, I was ready to say goodbye to Saudi Arabia. I certainly wouldn't miss abayas and the mutaween. I had already packed my belongings when, to my surprise, another well-recognized healthcare facility in Riyadh, the National Guard Hospital, contacted me and offered me the job of director of their quality improvement program. I was ambivalent because travel was on my agenda, but they were persistent.

The opportunity was appealing. They were willing to wait for me while I took the ESL program and would give me two months off to travel to Canada to attend a family reunion and my mother's ninetieth birthday celebration. After several sleepless nights, I decided to take the position. Later, it became clear I might have made the wrong decision.

The new job was a challenge as I tried to understand the hospital's total quality management systems and get to know the staff. I quickly learned not all staff were welcoming. During my interview I had understood I wasn't replacing or displacing anyone. However, that was not the case; the department's former head became my assistant and was unhappy with my arrival. The tension in the department was high and meetings were stressful.

I asked myself why I took this job, especially when new funding became available at my former job and the executive director of Security Forces Hospital asked me to return. I was afraid funding would be withdrawn again. So I decided to stick it out at the National Guard Hospital, determined I could improve the office situation.

My brother Peter secured a fantastic spot for our family reunion to celebrate Mom's ninetieth birthday back home in Canada. My mother, brother, sister, my children, grandchildren, an aunt, and cousins all spent a week at a cottage resort. We reminisced about the many summers we had spent as an extended family at our home at Kapasiwin Beach near Edmonton. We all had fond memories of swimming during the day, bonfires at night, and board games on rainy days. We celebrated Mom's zest for living by acting out skits and viewing a slide show of exciting events in her life.

Mom loved to travel. After my father and grandmother died, she explored the world with family and friends. She had the time, the energy, and, most of all, the motivation. She visited seventy countries. Her life was rich with adventure. I felt in awe of this tiny, feisty woman, as we applauded her accomplishments and endless vitality. As she shared her stories, I realized she was my role model and my loudest cheerleader. My goal was to follow in her footsteps.

In a quiet moment, with just my mother, I shared more with her about my life in Saudi: "Mom, Saudi Arabia has many differences from other cultures you have seen. I wish I could show the country to you. I think you'd love the experience. Saudi Arabia is a closed country, meaning you need a sponsor to be permitted to enter and stay there."

"Well, if you can find a way to make that happen, I'll come and visit. I know you can do this, Joyce. You'll find a way, you always do," she said knowingly.

When I returned to Saudi Arabia, my assistant, the former director, had resigned, and the staff began working as a team. As a result, our department's work started moving ahead, but progress was slow.

Soon, I asked my boss if I could sponsor my ninety-year-old mother for a month's visit. I knew the Saudis respected their elders, so I was hopeful. I felt elated when he approved my request. The wheels began to turn.

Mom would arrive in time for Christmas when the weather was more agreeable and Ramadan was around the corner. Her visit inspired me to organize my work, to allow time to be with her. Mom would learn about a new culture and meet my Saudi friends. I wanted her stay to be as memorable as possible.

I bought new high-thread-count cotton sheets and placed red roses on her bedside table for her arrival. I hoped she would not be lonely during the day and the air conditioning would not be too cold. Her health was excellent, as she did not take any medications, and if she had medical issues, we were in the right place. I arranged for a wheelchair so Mom could join our women-only trips.

Mom flew alone, from Calgary, Alberta, to Saudi Arabia, a long-haul flight of over fourteen hours. She set the bar sky-high for me, to be like her at ninety. Our arms outstretched, we hugged, and she smiled from ear to ear.

She rested during the day, while I was at work. We were together during evening hours and weekends.

With her quiet charm and sincere interest in people, Mom was soon flooded with invitations for tea and dinner. She was an inspiration to all who met her. The way people interacted with her was a delight to watch. Even my boss spent time with us over a cup of coffee, ceremonially served in the Arabic style. The server held the small cup in one hand and raised the brass pot, with its long spout, two feet into the air. He poured the coffee into the cup without making a splash.

One day when I was off work, we took the hospital bus to the Camel Souk (camel market). Mom used her cane to walk around and was enthralled as they auctioned off the animals. Saudi camels are typically dromedaries, with long legs and one hump. The camel stores fat inside the hump and metabolizes it when food and water are scarce. Mom was fascinated by how the camels adapted their bodies to live in the harsh desert climate, protecting themselves from frequent sandstorms.

Camels have three sets of eyelids. The middle eyelid is a transparent membrane, which drops down to protect against sand. Camels can also close their nostrils in a sandstorm. They are the beasts of burden in the desert and have been used this way for thousands of years.

Young boys showed off the camels to prospective buyers, leading the animals with a single rein. Some camels refused to budge. We laughed as it became a fight between the camel and the boy. At first the camel won, but once they got moving, the boy directed the camel to follow him with gentle movements.

Mom and I are wearing our required abayas as she gingerly pets a camel. We were warned that the camel would turn and spit at us.

Another night, at the gold market, we shopped until 2:00 a.m. Mom was an adventurous customer and bought an eighteen-karat tricolored gold bracelet and earrings. We visited many shops. The sellers treated her with the utmost respect and attention.

Saudi friends invited us for meals. Mom's eyes widened at the luxury of some of their homes decorated with Iranian handwoven rugs, marble floors, elaborate silk window treatments, antique furniture, and outstanding world-famous artwork. Mom enjoyed the different flavors of typical Saudi foods and charmed our hosts with stories of growing up as a young girl, from a pioneer family, in the early 1900s in Edmonton. She shared highlights about her trips around the world, especially visiting India, Russia, and China.

I marveled at how fortunate I was to have a mother who, at age ninety, was alert and physically able to have traveled the distance to be with me. We cherished our extraordinary time together in this unique Arabian country.

What a role model. I loved her fiercely. When I waved goodbye, tears welled in my eyes. I could not help wondering when I would see her again. There was a huge loss and void in my life when she left. My apartment felt empty and far too quiet.

Chapter 17

I Said Goodbye to Saudi and Moved on to Explore Africa

The silence left by Mom's departure quickly disappeared as I refocused on improving hospital programs and enjoyed the final months of my year-long contract. Work became more manageable as our team gelled. I began to focus more on social activities and attending Canadian Embassy events and other functions.

A friend told me how to make wine. Intrigued, I started to brew wine in my apartment, which of course was highly illegal. I rigged up large empty bottles, with plastic tubing, in the closet of my extra room, mixed all the ingredients and waited. The aroma almost knocked me over when I walked into my apartment, especially as the wine began to ferment. The compound's housekeeper, who cleaned my apartment weekly, knew what was going on, and of course the hospital had access to my apartment at any time. But my expatriate friend Robert, who also made wine, warned me, "Just don't get caught."

It wasn't long before the wine was ready and I enjoyed a glass, made more delicious for its pure subterfuge. And hence I named my homemade wine The Subterfuge. It accompanied many wonderful and memorable evenings with my female friends in Saudi.

At a British Embassy event, I met an engineer, Tom, from Ireland. He was always fun to be with, so we would go out to dinner with my New Zealand nurse friend Lois and her date John.

Lois and I took risks every time, as it was against Saudi law to be with an unrelated male. Tom lived in another compound, and we often went to his place for a barbeque with his workmates. It was fun and we were safe while we were there.

The four of us pushed the boundaries by going out to dinner at international hotels. We knew it was unlikely the mutaween would be there, bothering guests from other countries. It was getting to and from the restaurant or between our compounds that was risky.

As my contract continued to wind down, Tom and I got more serious. Tom showered me with exquisite jewelry and a sapphire ring. He happened to mention in passing it had a matching wedding band. I visited his family in Ireland. They were extremely welcoming, and we had a lot of fun, especially at the pub.

Tom and I enjoyed our final months together, but our relationship ended when I left and we parted as friends.

My contract with the National Guard Hospital was up, and it was time to leave. I'd accomplished my goals and objectives after three and a half years in the Kingdom. I was ready to travel to more new places and expand my horizons.

One night, after shopping, just three weeks before I was due to leave, I was in a car accident. The driver of my taxi ran into another car. There were no seat belts in the backseat. I flew forward and my left wrist hit against the console dividing the front seats. I heard a crack and pain shot along my wrist, up to my elbow. Ouch! I had never been in an accident in Saudi.

People on the sidewalk yelled, "Leave! Leave! Go! Get another taxi now."

They were right. As crazy as it might seem, I needed to leave the accident scene immediately. I had heard the police and the taxi driver customarily blamed the passenger, if she was an expatriate, as the cause of the crash. Dazed, I grabbed another taxi. The crowd cheered. This driver dropped me off at the National Guard Hospital's emergency department. An X-ray confirmed a fracture in my left wrist. I left with a cast, which I had to keep on for six weeks.

I only had three weeks left on my contract, and I was grateful my boss gave me special permission to live in the compound for the full six weeks, so my wrist could heal.

While I was healing, Dr. Mufti, my former boss at the Security Forces Hospital, again invited me to return. I thanked him immensely but declined his offer. Then he asked if he might send my name to the World Health Organization (WHO) in Egypt to be a consultant. He thought the WHO would welcome his recommendation because I had worked in this region and knew a lot about healthcare here. I felt honored. It would be another way to help others and share my knowledge.

The six weeks seemed to drag as I waited for my wrist to heal. I planned to do some exploring so I packed my belongings and shipped all but my backpack and day pack home. When the cast came off, I left Saudi Arabia with mixed feelings.

I would miss my friends, but I felt deep joy leaving the restrictions behind. My time in Saudi gave me the satisfaction of having made small differences within the Saudi healthcare delivery system, even if those changes might only last a few years. It allowed me to learn about other cultures, live and work in a foreign country, and travel with family and friends. The money I earned was significant and added to my bank account. I was content with my time in Saudi Arabia, but definitely now wanted to see more of the world. I was restless.

Leaving Saudi and heading out to traverse the African continent from north to south, east to west. Everything I took with me fit in the backpack pictured.

Chapter 18

I Was Ecstatic Starting to Work with the World Health Organization

After leaving Saudi in October 1996, I traveled throughout the African continent and the Middle East, as I waited to hear back from the WHO. I explored as many countries as I could, often consulting or teaching English in schools, and mostly traveling on my own, bumping along the roads in local buses.

One memorable stop was in Beirut, Lebanon, where I gave several lectures on quality improvement at the Sahel General Hospital. Part of the lecture included dividing staff into smaller groups to work on problems and solutions.

I enjoyed seeing the sights, with my friends as guides. I stayed with a family who served delicious food. I especially enjoyed the grape leaves, stuffed with lamb and rice and flavored with cinnamon, mint, marjoram, cumin, and allspice. The aroma and flavors make it one of my favorite recipes.

After a short stop in Eritrea, a country in the Horn of Africa on the eastern side, I traveled on and stayed with my mother's friend in Cape Town, South Africa. She suggested I use her apartment as my home base as I explored South Africa, Mauritius, Rodrigues (an island off Mauritius), Madagascar, Reunion (another island), and Lesotho. Each country had its own charms. Most of the time I traveled solo, but for difficult trips I traveled with a group for safety and to reach remote places.

*An audience of doctors, nurses, and administrators paid close
attention to my presentation in Beirut at the hospital.*

People welcomed me, opening their hearts and often their
homes wherever I went. If I wasn't staying with a family, the hos-
tels were always the best places to learn the local information and
make new friends.

I loved the energy of young people, and they treated me with
respect. One of my most exciting experiences was being invited to
join them and learning how to abseil. We vertically descended the
rock face of a waterfall, safely attached to a rope, and then dropped
into the river below. I loved the challenge.

As you know I love handwoven baskets, and South Africa offered amazing integrated designs and high-quality containers. Of
course, I added more to my collection.

These baskets are from South Africa, and their detailed designs make them exceptional art pieces.

In late April 1997 the WHO invited me to be a consultant throughout the Mediterranean region, and I headed to their Egyptian office. A WHO driver met me at the Cairo airport, and we drove for three hours to Alexandria, where I would be based. It was a Thursday, the beginning of the weekend, and the sky was clear; the traffic was light. I was nervous about having accepted an assignment from such a prestigious organization. I'd dreamed of working with the WHO for as long as I could remember. When I thought of international health, the WHO was the pinnacle, the gold standard. I was thrilled to be joining them.

The warm welcome by the WHO office staff was relaxed and friendly. I was extremely grateful, especially as I seemed to have picked up a cold on my flight. I spent Friday and Saturday in bed trying to kick my cold before work started the next day.

On Sunday, back at the WHO office, I learned my first assignment in Kuwait had been postponed. Instead, because of my background, I was asked to plan and write a continuous quality development manual to be used by staff in the WHO Member States of the Eastern Mediterranean Region.

I was given a short time to write the manual and then develop the plan to deliver an accompanying workshop and leadership program. It was a challenge. My workbooks from Saudi Arabia hadn't arrived, and I had to rely on my memory to write the content. Unfortunately, the internet was not available as a resource at this time. I also had to learn how to format the manual on a computer to print it out like a book—a new skill I quickly learned. The secretaries became valued friends and full members of my team.

I took pleasure unwinding from the time pressures at work by visiting the small shops in the area. Discovering Ahmed's tailor shop was a bonus. He made me a travel outfit: slacks with an inside zipper pocket to keep my cash safe when shopping and a matching blouse with pockets and a zipper, fashioned in exquisite finely woven Egyptian cotton. It was light and kept me comfortable in the sweltering and humid climate on the Mediterranean coast.

Mohammed, Ahmed's brother, spoke English and invited me to join him and his friends at the shop for an evening of Egyptian guitar music. The evening was magical. I swayed back and forth to the beat of the music, clapping my hands. I wanted to get up and dance, but there was limited space.

Across the street from the shop was a pizza restaurant. It soon became my treasured haunt. Students attending the nearby university were there and always friendly. Their passion, drive, sense of adventure, and zest for life regenerated my soul.

"Can we help you with the menu?" asked a young student seated in the restaurant. Her eyes were the color of pale amber and stood out against her deep Egyptian complexion. She smiled expectantly at me. A handsome young man sat close beside her.

"Oh, thanks," I said. "Your pizza looks delicious; I'll have one just like yours."

"Well, I always get double cheese, does that work for you?" she asked. "Oh, and by the way, I'm Fatima, and this is Mohammed. Come join us at our table; there's plenty of room."

Fatima ordered my pizza with tomato sauce, oregano, goat cheese, sun-dried tomatoes, black and green olives, and double mozzarella cheese. The waiter placed it in front of me. The aroma alone created a sense of anticipation. I knew I was about to enjoy a delicious meal.

I stuffed part of the large wedge into my mouth and closed my eyes. I wiped tomato sauce from my lips. The flavors were sublime. Salt met sweet, met tangy, met perfection. I was not disappointed. The pizza melted in my mouth, with just the right amount of everything, including extra cheese. Fatima and Mohammed laughed at my obvious delight.

On my days off, I hired Osiris, a knowledgeable guide who had studied Egyptian history, to show me the sights. She arranged for a car and driver who took us 50 miles (80 kilometers) to El Alamein. The town had been the site of two critical battles during World War II, helping the Allies to win the African offensive.

The first of these battles prevented the Axis from moving further into Egypt and protected the Suez Canal. The second was the battle for El Alamein itself, led by General Montgomery's forces. It resulted in the end of the Western Desert Campaign. I wandered about the Allied cemetery. The inscriptions on the headstones touched me deeply. I remembered the stories of my two uncles who died in France during World War II. We returned to Alexandria.

The next morning, I woke up tired and unsettled. Touring the cemetery had left me restless and agitated. I felt the lingering effects of our somber visit to the cemetery for several days. But Osiris had other artifacts for me to see.

We headed to the Alexandria Museum, and she told me everything I wanted to know and more about the artifacts. I was fascinated learning about the Egyptian mummies, which were housed in a temperature-controlled room.

Moving on we stopped at Rashid, a port city along the Nile. This was the site where the original Rosetta stone had been found in 1799 by a soldier in Napoleon Bonaparte's Egyptian campaign. After Napoleon's defeat, the British placed the Rosetta Stone in the British Museum, where I saw it while visiting London. We stared at a replica, showing detailed carvings, which historians had deciphered. It had allowed them to gain an understanding of Egyptian hieroglyphics and establish a complete list of symbols and Greek equivalents.

We stopped for dinner at a hotel in Alexandria, on the water's edge. As we entered, music from a string trio drifted into the dining room. The tables were elegantly set with linen tablecloths, crisply folded napkins, and sparkling crystal glassware. The sun's setting rays bounced off the immense cut-glass chandeliers, making light dance over the walls.

The waiters served our meal flawlessly. I watched in anticipation as they lifted off the silver covers to reveal the aromatic dishes of chicken and rice, encircled with asparagus almondine. Then, as I broke open a warm fresh roll and smothered it with butter, I felt myself physically melt and unwind. The meal and ambiance offered a wonderful and relaxing environment to close out the day.

Back at work I met my WHO supervisor Dr. Sayad Fatimie. He was the former Minister of Public Health of the Islamic Republic of Afghanistan, and he welcomed me with a smile, clasping both my hands in his. He had a warm spot in his heart for Canada, having visited when he spoke at the "Health as a Bridge to Peace" WHO conference sometime in the early to mid-1990s. He told me he'd shared a story at the conference of successfully negotiating a cease-fire in the war-torn country in order to undertake a massive country-wide immunization program. His goal had been to have the cease-fire last for two weeks, but he arranged for it to last two months. I was amazed he was able to accomplish this in a country engaged in civil war.

Dr. Fatimie was exceptionally pleased with my manual and the plan for the accompanying workshops and leadership program and gave me an exciting opportunity. He scheduled me to travel to Yemen in May and to Sudan in early December to deliver the continuous quality management program workshops and leadership program and evaluate how it could be implemented in all countries in the WHO Mediterranean region. I was ecstatic and felt so proud I could make a difference in people's lives.

I tidied up a few loose ends and said a heartfelt goodbye to Dr. Fatimie, who once again praised my work and wished me well. I also gave a big thank-you to the staff who had worked tirelessly with me to develop the manual and program. I was proud of our work and excited to test it and tweak the necessary changes to ensure it was the best it could be.

Chapter 19

I Reached Out to Lend a Helping Hand on World Health Organization Assignments

In May 1997, I was excited to return to Yemen with the WHO. Previously, I had visited Sanaa with colleagues while working at the hospital in Saudi Arabia.

Yemen is a mystical land set in the southern Arabian Peninsula. It's full of green valleys, bleak cliffs, and white sand beaches. Hidden gardens in time-tested villages overlook gardens with old buildings. Zigzagging paths led up the cliffs, many reaching thousands of meters above the sea.

On arrival, Abdulla, the WHO driver, and Samir, my translator, both middle-aged men, met me at the airport and took care of my bags. They made sure I was comfortable en route to Aden, one of the biggest cities in Yemen. Samir helped with the logistics of my trip and arranged the meetings.

The building architecture was as diverse and complex as the country itself. Yemeni men built structures made from local materials, like mud, brick, reeds from the plains, and stone from the mountains. Simple thatched huts lined the coastal regions, and spectacular mud-brick houses perched like eagles' nests, towering on the top of the mountains.

Every time I looked in another direction, the view seemed more spectacular than before, with some homes several stories high. They were the most impressive buildings I had ever seen. Were skyscrapers invented here and are all Yemenis architects? Their homes were four- to six-story towers, imposing and remarkably stable. Despite not having any steel incorporated into the structure, they had stood for centuries.

During the week, I delivered my quality improvement workshops where the participants, selected from various parts of the country, learned research methods to address healthcare quality issues by changing processes and creating improved ones. We worked in teams and learned how to use problem-solving strategies to come to a consensus. Coming to an agreement and then supporting the decision was one of the significant difficulties facing the teams. However, the participants were attentive and creative and demonstrated a desire to learn and came to class early to chat. They told me about some of their challenges: new computers still sitting in boxes and not being used because of dust and sand in the air and government-rationed access to electricity.

The staff worked around these challenges by using manual systems for daily work, running a generator one day a week to compile their financial accounting summaries. It was hard for the Yemeni Ministry of Public Health to move forward when they were hampered by the environment and a lack of resources.

One evening I joined Samir, Orysia, his Ukrainian wife, and their nine-year-old son, Khalid, in their home for dinner. Their marriage was indicative of Yemen's close relationship with the former Soviet Union. I thoroughly enjoyed our conversations and the home-cooked Ukrainian meal, which brought back memories of the Ukrainian food I had experienced in Edmonton as a child.

Late one morning, I stopped to visit a khat dealer who welcomed me graciously and gestured for me to come into his store. He had dark curly hair, deep brown eyes, and wore an expensive-looking watch on his left wrist. His left cheek was bulging; it looked like a Ping Pong ball pushing out his cheek, but I knew it was khat.

The dealer said, "Early in the morning, men pick the khat leaves from the tall *Catha edulis* plant, which grows in the highlands. The plants consume much of our scarce water supply, causing concern in this desert area. Then men deliver the khat to me in packages covered with cloth or plastic to ensure the leaves maintain their freshness. If the leaves are dry, unfortunately, they lose their potency."

"It takes a lot of work to have khat to sell here," I said.

He nodded and continued, "After someone chews the khat, they push the wad into their cheek, where the leaves produce a recreational type of drug-producing stimulant and euphoric effects, then the person sleeps and rests until evening. But unfortunately, it often causes insomnia, so the person's sleep cycle is challenging to manage."

I looked at the many packages of fresh-looking khat ready for purchase. By noon, customers would have purchased their supply for the next three to four hours. The bags would be gone. The dealer smiled and proudly showed me the different fresh leaves. He offered me khat to try. I shook my head and said, "Thank you for your hospitality," and walked out onto the street.

At one of the healthcare meetings, we had discussed the terrible toll that chewing khat was having on the population. The current khat epidemic was negatively impacting the country's progress. Chewing khat caused anxiety, increased blood pressure, paranoia, talkativeness, aggressiveness, and energy loss—all common symptoms. Officials had tried for years to stop the fallout from the addiction, but the culture was firmly ingrained. The researchers determined approximately 90 percent of all Yemeni men and 25 percent of women were addicted to khat. I felt a pit in my stomach.

One afternoon after a workshop, the senior male staff from the Ministry of Health invited me to join them and their secretary, Araya, on a boat tour of the Aden harbor. It would not be appropriate for me to be without another female companion on the boat. Araya wore her abaya. I did not have an abaya, and thank goodness no one asked me to wear one. I loved boating on the water, so this was a special treat.

The Aden harbor is one of the oldest ports in history and played a significant role for the Allies in World War II.

One evening in Aden, at the Beach Club, I enjoyed my first cold beer in a long time. I was celebrating the success of the Aden workshops. The beer slid down my throat, cold and flavorful. After spending a few relaxing hours, chatting with other expatriates, the lady at the reception desk called for a taxi to take me back to my hotel. As we headed to the car, the driver said, "Come and sit in the front."

"No thanks," I said and climbed into the backseat.

I didn't think anything of it as I often sit in the front seat, but I wasn't in the mood to chat. I was deep in thought, going over my next day's presentation. Soon I didn't recognize the road and realized the driver was on a different route to the hotel, along what seemed to be a desolate desert road. My primal instincts kicked in. My fight-or-flight sense went into overdrive. I was on my own, no WHO driver here.

I had told the clerk at my hotel I would be going to the Beach Club and back by 10:00 p.m., but would he even remember? It was now 9:30 p.m. The driver began to slow down as if he was looking for something. I only saw the sand, road, and the stars, nothing else and no one else. I was scared. I kept forcing myself to breathe calmly and pretend to be asleep. But my mind was racing, and I was sweating. How would I escape? Eventually, the driver sped up and we arrived at my hotel. I got out of the taxi. My nails had pierced my palms, and blood was on my blouse.

As I turned away and headed up the hotel steps, he taunted me, "I always wanted to do it with a white woman." My body went cold, and a wave of nausea hit me. I was shaking involuntarily.

"Glad you are back, Joyce, you look pale, are you okay?" said the hotel clerk.

"I will be okay after a rest," I said, trying to smile.

I had forgotten how Western women were viewed in the Arab countries. I silently offered up profound thanks for being safe and vowed never to forget.

The next day Samir and I drove to Sanaa to deliver more workshops. Sanaa had a medieval charm, friendly streets, and unique architecture. I loved it just as much as I did on my last visit. People had lived there for over 25,000 years, and in the seventh and eighth centuries, Sanaa became a center for the expansion of Islam. Sanaa was tucked in a mountain valley at an altitude of 72,178 feet (22,000 meters).

The higher altitude caused me to breathe deeply and gasp for more oxygen. Our hotel was six stories high. It was difficult to climb the narrow stairway, with its fourteen-inch-high steps. I was huffing and puffing by the time I reached the top floor. The increase in altitude was making me tired, and I took it easy my first day, allowing my body to adapt.

The hotel's main entranceway was decorated with an elaborate semi-circle of blue, green, and yellow glass windows above the door. The original builders had constructed the windowpanes from different colored alabaster, but now they were replaced by glass. While I walked along Sanaa's streets in the evening, light shone through the decorative windows with appreciable beauty. I felt tranquil.

Changes had appeared everywhere since my last visit three years ago. More colorful metal doors had replaced the traditionally carved wooden ones along the commercial and residential streets. The metal doors were bright blue, with red and white leaves and geometric designs, which seemed uncomfortably out of place. The contrast between the old and the newly built metal buildings jarred me.

Standing by old Yemeni doors—the slats open to promote air circulation.

Women's clothing varied from area to area in Yemen, but now more women were wearing the black abaya, which was new since my last visit. Others wore more colorful cloths over their heads and kept their faces covered, leaving two slits for their eyes.

Men's dress customs had continued to evolve over the centuries, and an experienced eye could tell the value of the jambiya, especially ones made of gold or embedded with precious stones.

The jambiya was a sharp and lethal dagger with a curved blade, used to settle arguments, worn at the waist by Yemeni men over fourteen years of age. The value of the jambiya established the status of the man. The jambiya I purchased for my son on this trip had a metal handle and silver twisted thread in floral designs with turquoise stones in the center of the flower.

Shopping was a bargain, and it was hard to keep money in my purse. I bought lots of containers, used to hold kohl or charcoal eyeliner, while in Yemen because the oval-shaped containers were small, easy to pack, and affordable. They were about three to four inches high, some simple silver, and others elaborately decorated with semi-precious stones. Each one had a silver stick attached to the container by a chain. It would be used to apply the kohl.

Arabic men, women, and sometimes children applied the kohl to their eyelids. There were concerns about the lead found in the kohl, and health studies discouraged its use but to no avail. It was a well-ingrained custom in this culture.

The more expensive kohl holders had a large amber, sapphire, or ruby stone affixed to the center of the container and were exquisite. However, I preferred the antique silver filigree designed containers and was thrilled to add four to my collection as I browsed the shops.

After touring and shopping it was back to work. The Sanaa workshop was a replica of the program in Aden, with three modifications: the group spent an additional hour on techniques managing change, and we completed more listening exercises and added several new activities for members to practice reaching a group consensus among difficult choices.

For example, we practiced selecting a lead. Then I coached the leader on achieving a decision within the group. To my surprise, the group stayed for an extra three hours to practice. Again, the results were positive. The participants grew more confident working in groups, especially as they increased their cooperation and listening skills.

Their appreciation for the workshops and their thanks made the work worthwhile. The success of any program depended on how upper management introduced it to the staff. When senior staff were cheerful and supportive, my success rate was higher.

Chapter 20

Ants in My Pants

After leaving the WHO in July 1997, I headed to Zimbabwe in Africa. Zimbabwe, now officially called the Republic of Zimbabwe, has had a history of name changes. It was formerly called Southern Rhodesia, Rhodesia, and then Zimbabwe-Rhodesia. Zimbabwe is a landlocked country surrounded by the Republic of South Africa to the south, Botswana to the west, Zambia to the north, and Mozambique to the east. The current capital is Harare, though it was formerly known as Salisbury.

A brightly colored sign, posted in the Zimbabwe Tourist Board in Chimanimani, the easternmost part of Zimbabwe, offered an authentic homestay with Banga, a member of the Shona tribe and his family. This opportunity was important to me as I wanted to experience how local women lived and went about their daily activities, so I signed up for the educational, experiential adventure.

While I was waiting for the bus, sweat was dripping into my eyes, I rubbed them, only making them sting more. I needed to save paper tissues for emergencies, like using the toilet—a lesson I had learned the hard way. Body aromas floated around me from the other people waiting, so I moved farther away.

"Excuse me, sir, do you know when the bus will arrive?" I asked an older man wearing torn blue jeans and a faded lemon-colored shirt. The veins on the backs of his hands were raised and scarred. He appeared weary; his skin looked rough from years of hard labor, making it impossible to guess his age. I wanted to learn about his life. He looked me up and down as if trying to determine whether he would answer my question. Finally, he sagely whispered, "It will come when it comes," and then he turned away.

I repeated it as a mantra, "It will come, when it comes" over and over in my mind. Others looked tired too. My eyes scanned the road, and I saw a woman trudging along carrying a child on her back and a pot filled with fruit and vegetables on her head. The man walking beside her carried nothing.

A heavy load as a woman carries produce on her head and a child on her back in Zimbabwe.

An hour had passed. I was fed up standing in the brutal heat, shifting my weight from one foot to the other, and getting more impatient by the minute. I had checked out of my hotel with the goal of heading to the homestay. The hotel might not have a room for me if I returned. I felt stuck and so I waited.

Frustrated, I threw my scarf on the ground and then sat on it to wait. Other people kept looking at me, almost as if they wanted to say something but didn't. Soon I realized why. I jumped up quickly, yelling and swatting madly. I had ants in my pants. They were taking chunks out of my legs. I threw my arms everywhere, trying to dislodge the invaders. I did the Highland Fling. I did the Irish River dance, with several freestyle moves thrown in.

My exhibition caused quite the stir among those waiting. I finally stopped and looked at them. They had smirks on their faces. The women politely hid their laughter behind their hands, but the men just howled at my expense. Some of them were practically holding each other up. Then I burst out laughing, the whole spectacle just too hysterical despite my somewhat bruised ego.

That broke the ice. The women beckoned me over and spread their skirts out around me so I could drop my pants to get the rest of the ants off my body. I hugged each one in gratitude, we bonded. From that second on, I took my clues from them, standing in the shade, waiting, shifting my weight from one foot to the other.

I checked my watch. Two hours had now passed. It was getting late and soon it would be dark. My mind raced ahead. Would I be safe walking to Banga's house by myself? I had a flashlight, but I felt unsettled. I didn't know where his home would be once I got off the bus.

One man kept staring at me. His body language seemed welcoming, so I approached him slowly.

"Hi, I am Joyce, and I am supposed to be staying with the Banga family. Do you happen to know them?" I offered my hand. He shook it. His skin was hard and rough, but he broke out into a big smile.

"Oh, yes, everyone knows Banga; he is the big boss of the community and lives with his four sisters. We are hugely proud of him for building the proper toilets for the Tourist Board to allow him to have visitors. My name is Garal. I live nearby." Finally, the bus came.

The bus bumped along the paved road, filled with potholes.

I realized it had been a mistake to have a light lunch. I sipped my water, not wanting to drink too much for fear of having to go to the bathroom. I chewed some chickpeas to tide me over and looked forward to joining my new family for dinner. Soon the dark shades of night descended. Being close to the equator, there was little twilight in Zimbabwe. I dozed after being in the sun all day.

The bus pulled up at the side of the road. Some people had gathered, waiting to greet passengers.

A tall, imposing man with piercing eyes and dark skin said, "Welcome to my community. I am Banga." I had to look up; I was five feet two inches tall, and he was well over six feet. One look at him and you knew he was in charge. His skin was soft, but his handshake was strong and firm.

Garal waved and ambled in the opposite direction.

"Thanks, Garal. Thanks for your help, it was nice to meet you. I hope to see you again," I called out, waving back.

"Come, come, we have dinner waiting for you. You must be tired," said Banga.

He put his hand out again. I gave him my backpack, then followed, taking two steps to his one.

The house was small, made of wood, and extremely tidy. He immediately showed me to my bedroom, just large enough for a single bed pushed up against the wall. It was dark except for the light from the open door. One of the sisters had left a small blue towel on the bed. It was rough against my face yet had the delicious smell of fresh air and sunshine. Immediately it triggered memories of fresh sheets after they dried on the clothesline in Edmonton.

My thoughts were disturbed by Banga. "Dinner is on the table."

I sat on a straight-back wooden chair, painted lime green, which wobbled and creaked. In front of me was my meal. Cornmeal called sadza, cut tomato, and some spinach-like greens filled the cracked, lime green plate. One of the sisters had placed a cup of lukewarm tea beside it.

"Thank you, Banga," I said, trying not to show my disappointment. I was so hungry. Thankfully I still had more dried chickpeas, my staple emergency food.

Banga said, "The national dish of Zimbabwe is sadza, which is also our primary dietary staple. It tastes like an extraordinarily thick porridge of maize made from ground corn. Sadza masikati, lunch or sadza of the afternoon, and sadza manheru, dinner or sadza of the evening. You will eat this for lunch and dinner."

I sat alone, the flickering candle on the table casting shadows on my plate. Other family members sat across the room, sitting and chatting while a young girl did her homework, aided by another candle.

As I ate my simple meal, Banga explained the primary purpose of my visit was to learn what the women do. He explained I was to experience their lives and work with them, but he made it clear I would eat with him.

The young girl, Mudiwa, his niece, was slim with long jet-black hair. I noticed she kept looking over toward the table while I was eating, trying to listen to our conversation.

Banga continued, "Mudiwa is studying hard at high school, and she is determined to get into law school at the college. Tomorrow, I would like you to spend time with her." He said it more like a command rather than offering a suggestion.

"Certainly, I will be happy to help her," I said. "What time should I get up tomorrow, Banga?" I asked, hoping he'd say about 8:00 a.m.

"The ladies are always up at six with the sun."

"What time do you get up?" I inquired.

"Oh, any time, about eight-thirty when my sisters bring me breakfast. In the afternoon we will visit my uncle. He is one hundred years old."

"Oh, I would like to visit him. Can I meet your sisters now?"

"No, they have settled in for the night."

I felt uncomfortable. His eyes seemed cold, and something did not feel quite right. I felt inferior. I finished my dinner and went to my room. I found my flashlight, got undressed, and was ready to climb into bed.

As I lifted the light blue tattered bedspread and the soft blue sheet, something scurried out from the bed. I dropped my flash-light and let out a yell.

Banga came running and knocked on the door.

"Is something wrong?" he yelled in a powerful voice.

"Oh, a large lizard just ran as fast as he could out of the bed as I was about to crawl inside."

"Oh, all right, I thought you were in trouble," he said dryly.

I grabbed a handful of chickpeas, munched on them, gulped water from my water bottle to wash them down, and fell into bed.

Before coming to Zimbabwe, I had researched the culture and learned about male domination, deeply woven into the Shona culture through solid patriarchal practices. Young boys were often given more opportunities to go to school than girls. Mothers trained their girls to rely on their husbands for support. Banga demonstrated the Shona culture clearly in his authoritative tone. I thought of life as a Shona woman and wanted to experience their day-to-day activities.

It wasn't until I heard scratching outside the window the next morning that I stirred. What was that sound? I rubbed my eyes and listened again. Was it branches rubbing along the side of the wall, pushed by a gentle wind? No, it was too steady and consistent. One of the sisters was sweeping with a broom made of branches, clearing the dust from the house and the yard of leaves.

I dressed, clutched my toilet paper, then headed to the newly constructed toilet with its cement floor and holding tank. It was spacious, clean, and impressive. The government had loaned Banga the money to build a "long drop" with metal walls and a cone metal roof for his paying guests. It looked like the grain storage bins on the Canadian prairies.

As part of the women's seemingly never-ending chores, they put a scoop of lime down the hole, which took away any smell, just the way my family did when we had our summer house at the lake. I felt right at home.

After washing my face and hands in a bowl of water, I went for breakfast. As I came inside, the four sisters, Japer, Malba, Rufaro, and Jacolin, greeted me warmly with smiles.

They had been up since dawn and had prepared breakfast, swept the house clean, and Malba was getting ready to head to the river to do the laundry.

"Do you want to come with me after your breakfast?" Malba asked.

"Sure," I replied with a smile, then sat at the table. The sisters had set up two places, and I wondered where Banga was. It was apparent he was not up yet.

My breakfast was a free-range egg with a dark yellow yolk and a bit of dry toast, no jam or butter. The tasty egg will give me energy to do my chores. My beverage was a cup of lukewarm instant coffee with a few drops of canned milk.

"Thank you," I said. Then I realized I was alone.

I studied the simple wooden interior of the house, painted wooden chairs lined up like soldiers against the walls. A well-used sofa took up most of the space and a few china dishes were on display, along with a green vase, empty of flowers.

I finished eating and headed out to find Malba, who stood ready, a large basket of laundry on her head. Her feet were bare as we walked along the gravel road to the river. She didn't flinch or appear to feel pain. My feet were protected from the sharp stones on the road by water shoes.

We walked along, then worked our way down the steep decline to the river's edge. Much easier than bringing water to the house. Quickly, Malba stood knee-deep in rushing cool water, washing the clothes.

First, she slapped clothes, including several pairs of jeans, on the rocks to loosen the dirt. Then she rubbed the material together and scrubbed each piece of clothing again and again. I remembered my gran doing the washing in a tub with a washboard. She warmed some water as it removed the dirt more easily.

I joined Malba. Soon my muscles ached as the cold water rushed by and froze my feet. I almost lost my balance and dropped Banga's shirt I was washing. The current stripped it out of my hand, but luckily I was able to catch the edge of the sleeve before it disappeared.

"Where does the river flow?" I asked Malba.

"Oh, over the falls below," she said with a smile. She must have sensed what I was asking. "We can never get anything back if it slips from our hands."

"Really?" I nodded and looked at my white knuckles as I tightened my grip on Banga's white shirt.

We did laundry until midday. It was hard physical work.

Malba brought me back to reality. She said, "That is the washing for the day. Now let's take the washing up to the house, hang it on the line, and put the rest on top of the bushes to dry."

My heart was heavy as I looked at Malba, a dark-haired woman perhaps in her thirties, but who looked older. Her hands were strong and capable, her skin rough. She had many calluses on her palms from daily labor in the fields and the never-ending daily routine of washing, cleaning, gardening, gathering fuel and water, and cooking. I was exhausted after my short time washing clothes.

As we headed up the riverbank, I slipped back, grabbing a plant on the bank to stop my slide.

"Ouch," I cried out as thorns pierced the skin of my left hand. I let go and proceeded to slip back even further, sinking deep into the mud.

I looked up. Malba was laughing so hard she had to remove her basket from her head and put it on the ground. I was sure she was about to start rolling on the grass, she thought it was so funny.

After composing herself, she came down to get me out of the mud. Gripping her strong hand, I started to take a step. My foot came out, but my water shoe decided it liked the soft gooey mud and stayed behind. I reached down, the mud squishing through my fingers, found the shoe, rinsed it in the water, and then put it back on my foot.

I tried to balance myself precariously, lifting one foot at a time, and finally got to the top. My hand was burning with the embedded thorns, so when we reached the house, I grabbed my tweezers from my first aid kit and pulled the thorns out. I swabbed my hand with an alcohol swab and sat down for lunch.

The sadza and greens were the same as last night. While sadza masikati filled my stomach, I smiled. I might lose weight on this trip.

Chapter 21

Living with Women in Zimbabwe and Experiencing Their Life Under the Burden

After lunch Banga appeared. "Time to visit my uncle Rudo, who is one hundred years old and lives alone in a small house made from mud bricks."

As we walked along the road to Rudo's house, Banga said, "The trees around his house have been cut down and not replanted."

Immediately, I grabbed a fallen tree limb I saw on the side of the road and dragged it along behind me. Soon Banga looked back, not offering to help me as I struggled. This branch was too bulky for me to manage. I was determined not to give up.

I clenched my jaw and yelled, "Hey, Banga, how about taking some wood to your uncle?"

He turned, his eyes drawn together, bored into me, then said in a humiliating tone, "That is not my job. It's yours."

"Oh, really?" I replied defiantly, leaving no doubt about my thoughts on the matter.

"That's women's work," he said decidedly.

I began to walk slower and with tiny steps. Finally, after continual prodding, Banga grabbed a smaller tree limb and pulled it behind him.

The trees disappeared; the landscape was bare; only scrub bushes were visible.

When we arrived at Rudo's house, the cooking area was outside at the back of the house, tucked under a canvas awning, safe from rain. I victoriously dropped my tree limb beside the fire pit.

I studied Rudo as he hugged Banga. His bones shaped his skin. He was exceedingly thin. The deep grooves in his ebony skin looked like the bark seen on ancient trees, full of character and beauty. His eyes were cloudy, definitely cataracts, but reflected a shining light and his smile was welcoming. I was riveted on his face. I couldn't turn away.

He turned to me, and I held out my hand. I felt an overwhelming urge to hug him and did. We both were a bit surprised, then his arms squeezed around my back. His body odor was different, not unpleasant, just unusual. I am sure he smelled my body odor but didn't indicate it was bothering him. He smiled.

Banga was taken aback by my actions but just looked at me with his piercing eyes.

We sat down on the mud floor. As I held Rudo's left hand, I could sense an incredible energy flowing through his hand to mine. My hand was tingling. I wished I knew his language so we could communicate. I could ask Banga to do the translation, but I didn't want to ask him. I learned Banga was unprepared to give me anything, even a helping hand with my large tree branch. So instead, we sat still together, and I settled into Rudo's shallow breathing.

I wondered what Rudo's actual age was. Under a hundred, over a hundred, maybe 110? He had survived many years without antibiotics, other drugs, surgeries, and our generation's medical miracles. In any case, he seemed happy without modern conveniences and his life seemed serene.

Banga interrupted my inner thoughts. "Joyce, get up; let's leave now."

Rudo quickly got up from the dirt floor without any help. I was beyond impressed. I had a long way to go before I reached his age, and I had to give myself a little push off the floor to stand up. I would need to do at least seventy-five squats a day to build up my thigh muscles to match his.

I squeezed Rudo's hand, gave him another hug, then waved goodbye.

Banga and I walked back in silence as I tried to keep up with Banga's longer stride. I pondered how different Rudo's life was from mine. The monotony of the walk gave me a chance to think of the differences between life in Zimbabwe and life in Canada.

Would I stay in my Canadian home if I were ninety or one hundred years old and in robust health like Rudo? I pondered that thought. We returned to the house, and I was ready to rest, but Banga had other ideas.

"Joyce, go to the rondavel, the round thatched mud-brick cookhouse at the back of the house, to help cook dinner with the rest of the women," Banga demanded in his authoritative voice. "We need enough food for ten people."

Tired, I got up and moved toward the rondavel, but stopped along the way to help one of the sisters pound the corn into meal used to make the sadza. She was using a heavy log, 3 feet (1 meter) long and 4 inches (10 centimeters) in diameter, to pound the corn. I picked up a second log and joined her, working together in a rhythm to crush the kernels against the bottom and sides of a hollowed-out log container. When I finished, I gave my arms a shake, stretched them and took a few deep breaths. I was glad the sisters were there to share the workload.

I pounded the grain with wooden poles in a rhythm with one of the sisters. It was heavy work.

After washing my hands in the creek's running water and shaking them dry, I stepped into the rondavel. Within seconds, I was furiously blinking my eyes, and tears streamed down my cheeks. Smoke filled the rondavel blocking my vision. A hole in the thatched roof was supposed to allow the smoke to go out like a chimney, but, instead, the smoke settled around me, filling my lungs and causing me to cough.

My job was to stir the sadza, which was cooking in an eight-inch pot, resting on stones, surrounded by a wood fire. It brought back childhood memories of learning to cook on an open fire as a Girl Guide.

Rufaro handed me a sturdy wooden spoon, and I bent down to stir the sadza. The pot sat on five-inch-high stones. Rufaro squatted on her heels to stir the sadza, and when I tried my knees creaked loudly. The sisters all turned, stared, and shook their heads. I needed both hands clenched around the spoon to stir the sadza. A young boy, about fourteen years old, held the pot to keep it in one place. Bless him, I couldn't have done it myself. Rufaro and her sisters had developed strong arm muscles, so they held the pot with one hand and stirred the sadza quickly with the other.

I tried hard to do the same, but my knees gave way and I fell to one side. Rufaro brought me a small piece of wood to sit on, but it was too low and unstable. Thank goodness this was not my permanent job. My arms ached, my eyes teared, I was embarrassed, frustrated, and tired.

I couldn't stay in the rondavel any longer. I burst out of the hut and inhaled a huge breath of fresh air. My eyes needed a rest.

Rufaro continued my job so the sadza did not burn. I was grateful to her.

My next task was to prepare and cook the staple green vegetable. The greens, like spinach, were grown in their kitchen garden beside the house, just a few steps away. This staple was nutritious and formed a significant part of the daily diet in rural Zimbabwe.

"Come pick the greens; it's easy," said Japer.

I followed her and we picked and washed the greens, breaking them into five-inch lengths.

We headed back into the rondavel to melt chicken fat in a six-inch frying pan, then added a handful of chopped onions. The aroma of the onions, together with the smoke, drifted in the air. Next, I began filling the pan with enough washed greens for ten people, but it was impossible to fit them all in. I was exasperated.

My eyes watered from the smoke and my vision was blurred. The smoke was bothering me again.

"May I have a bigger pan, Rufaro?"

"This is the only pan we have; we cook in small batches and eventually have enough for everyone," said Rufaro.

I felt indignant and angry. The rondavel was confining and un-comfortable. I couldn't imagine doing this day in and day out. The greens quickly cooked down to a small, shriveled pile. We put them aside and filled the pan again, starting the process all over until we had enough. Every second I spent in the cooking hut was one too long. My eyes were so sore, and my tears didn't stop. Finally, we had enough greens, and then we added cooked tomatoes to make a sauce.

"Dinner's ready. Joyce, come to the table," called Banga. The ladies had set two places, and I looked surprised.

"My sisters don't eat with you and me; they eat in the rondavel," said Banga.

The frustration and sadness inside me was like an inferno ready to explode. I could hardly contain myself. "Oh, why do they eat in the smoky cookhouse?" I asked, trying to control the anger in my voice.

"That is the Shona custom," he said. "In fact, all the men eat first and then the oldest woman to the youngest."

Conversations like this made me realize the Shona culture was difficult for women. My body was tense; my muscles were quiver-ing. In reality, of course, I knew this was the experience of many women in cultures around the world. It was a long quiet dinner.

My mood improved when Banga's niece, Mudiwa, came over to me.

"Would you help me with my algebra?" she pleaded. "I have to do it tonight because it's my turn to take the textbook home. We share this one textbook with all the students in the class."

I looked surprised. "I can't remember the last time I did algebra, but okay, let's give it a try," I said, trying to disguise my shock at this lovely young girl and her classmates' total lack of resources available to them.

"Please bring me the book, a piece of paper to practice on, and let's go," I said with a smile as I clapped my hands.

Mudiwa brought me a newspaper.

"We don't have extra paper," she said, looking down at her feet, not making eye contact.

"I'll practice on the border." I smiled at Mudiwa.

Why did I throw away the scrap paper I had a few days ago, I thought. There was barely enough space to write the algebra formula on the edge of the newspaper.

My other challenge was having enough light to see the questions. The constant flickering from a solitary candle flame provided the only light to work out the answer. By the time we finished the questions, my eyes felt strained. As we answered the last question, I said, "Mudiwa, enjoy your day at school tomorrow, and I'll be happy to help you again with your homework."

"Thanks, Joyce," she said with a bit of a curtsy and a luminous smile.

"Sleep well, everyone," I called out and went to my room.

That night I pulled back the covers to check for a lizard. None.

Chapter 22

My Life with the Family and Living Under the Burden

Breakfast the next day was sadza, and a few slices of tomato. Banga came over to the table.

"Today is a special day at the health clinic, called World Health Day," Banga said. "The director would like you to be the guest of honor because you work for the World Health Organization."

"Oh, I would love to go and am grateful for the invitation."

"They would like you to say a few words about the World Health Organization. We need to be there at ten. It will take us thirty minutes to walk to the health unit, so wear your walking shoes," he instructed.

"Thank you, I am interested in participating and learning from the nurse and doctor how they deliver care."

Soon Banga and I walked down the road toward the local health unit to celebrate World Health Day. I had a bounce in my step. The road was a deep red color, and fine dust coated everywhere I looked. The local farmers had planted corn, but the crops looked marginal at best, with only a few plants producing more than one cob of corn. Without irrigation, they waited for rain.

"Sadly, droughts are common, and food is scarce," said Banga.

The celebration was about to start. I was seated in the front row and given one of the few wooden chairs. The students sat in an orderly fashion on the ground, and parents and guests either joined them or stood at the back.

After the introductions and speeches by the local doctor, the nurse, a government official, and myself, we watched students from the local school, in each of the grades, perform skits depicting current health issues.

The high school students performed a fantastic skit about the dilemmas of dating, sex, and using condoms to protect against HIV/AIDS. It was a topic close to their young hearts. Although I couldn't understand the local dialect, their message was clear. Everyone was proud to perform their school skit.

The audience, students, and parents howled with laughter, and I almost fell off my chair. HIV/AIDS was a major problem here among those ages twenty to fifty. Providing education and open discussions were the best deterrents. The message was vividly direct and understood.

The worst part of being the special guest was being part of the judging team. I found it hard to choose winners because everyone had worked diligently on their presentation, sharing clear messages with the audience. First prize was a new mop and pail; second prize was a broom and a dustpan. Useful for the school, but nothing for the students to take home and pin on a bulletin board.

Frankly, if I had known there were only two prizes, I would have brought an award for the third team and a notebook and pencil for each student.

After the prizes were handed out, the organizers invited Banga and me to the reception where they served sandwiches, cake, and sodas.

As the crowd drifted away, the doctor and nurse asked me to stay to suggest ways to tackle some of their challenges. We chatted for several hours. I spent most of the time listening, trying to understand their overwhelming problems with lack of equipment, supplies, and basic health tools such as vaccinations, hospital avail-ability, and money to meet the needs of patients. My heart ached for the dedicated health professionals trying to spread their limited resources among far too many people.

As I was leaving, the nurse and doctor gave me a warm em-brace, thanking me for my comments. Somehow, I felt a connec-tion with them through a deep understanding of their struggles. I hoped I helped in some way and was grateful that they shared their struggles with me. I wished time were on my side, but I had to leave the next day.

Banga had headed back earlier, so I returned by myself, walking slowly, pondering the meaning of the day. I could see the celebra-tion was the culmination of hard work, composing and practicing the skits. Each team developed relationships, new skills, teamwork, and ways to support their school.

I thought of my grandchildren. But I could not imagine a prize for the best skit to be a mop and a pail or a broom and a dustpan, given to the school. The participants received nothing but knowing they performed well and the community supported their activi-ties. Here no students received a medal for participation. Life was exceptionally different here, compared to Canada.

Dinner was the usual, sadza and greens, and Banga again as-signed me to the rondavel to help the sisters. The result was the same—more smoke and tears, but this time I finished all my jobs. I felt as if I had passed the test, and I smiled from ear to ear when a sister gave me a hug realizing how hard this was for me.

After dinner, we watched TV. The sisters had set out several chairs and people from the community joined us, paying money for the privilege. The electricity to power the TV came from a car battery.

"What are we going to watch, Banga?" I raised my eyebrows and looked at the TV.

"Oh, we watch two programs, a religious service from Harare, and can you imagine the other program?"

"I have no idea," I mused. I could not think what program Banga would consider watching that would be worth the expensive battery power.

"Oh, the wrestling programs," he said, puffing up his chest. "Are these fights real?"

"I have no idea," I said.

I was surprised and chuckled inside.

I watched for a while, laughing at the antics of the wrestlers, then went to bed. Before drifting off to sleep I thought of my experience being welcomed into the family with warmth and respect. I was grateful.

The following day was my last day, and the bus would arrive just after lunch.

After a breakfast of sadza, Banga and I trekked around, climbing the steep stone slab hills. We had a chance to chat, and he talked about my visit. I was one of the few women who came. We both had mellowed a bit. It was getting hot by 9:30, so we walked back to the house. I stopped to watch the corn being ground.

Soon I marched to the only store in the area. I looked for two large twelve-inch frying pans and lids, but they only had one. I picked up a large saucepan and lid—wanting two, again they only had one. No broom or mop for the sisters either. I looked for something for the third prize at the presentation yesterday, but the store was empty. I purchased all the notebooks, pencils, and erasers for Mudiwa to have and share with other students, but unfortunately there were not enough supplies for the teachers and the school.

Swinging my purchases at my side, I wandered over to where the sisters were making mud bricks. They were working hard, their feet bare; they were dirty from the wet red clay. The clay squished between their toes, as they worked straw into the mud with their hands, packing the mixture into wooden molds, and then dumping them out on the flat ground to dry in the sun.

As they saw me approach, the sisters stopped working and whispered to each other, expectantly pointing to the pot and the pan. When I gave them the pot and pan, the smiles and hugs were my thanks. They warmed my heart. I felt blessed to have this experience, my vision blurred.

My bus arrived, and to my surprise, Banga gave me a goodbye hug. We both respected each other and our cultures.

My visit was incredibly worthwhile.

I experienced firsthand the sisters' full and hard labor-intensive days. They swept the house with a stick broom; they walked barefoot to the river to wash the clothes. They planted the seeds, then cultivated the plants. They ground the corn by hand, picked the vegetables, prepared meals, walked about a half-mile several times a day to gather drinking water, carrying it back on their heads and also looked after the children.

I thought of Banga and his sisters while I lived as part of the Shona culture for a few days. Each culture is different in its history and customs.

It was not easy being a woman in rural Zimbabwe, living under the burden of their everyday lives.

When I visit a country, I am their guest. I am open to learning and try to understand. Sometimes I do well, but other times I cope with the challenge.

Several months later, I received a letter from Banga. He thanked me, on behalf of his sisters, for the pot and frying pan they were using each day. He wrote Mudiwa had passed algebra and completed high school and was now studying law at the University in Harare.

I was ecstatic and so proud of her and supported Banga for giving her the opportunity.

I was happy to learn life was changing with more opportunities for younger women in Zimbabwe.

Chapter 23

Giving My Time and Energy to the International Executive Service Corps

In September 1997, after Zimbabwe I traveled to Botswana. I saw how this country was suffering from drought affecting people and all domestic and wild animals especially the elephants. The lack of water left dead animals everywhere. The sight was gut-wrenching.

After my trip to Botswana, I returned to northern South Africa to join a safari group heading in two 4x4 vehicles to explore the remote Richtersveld area. One day we drove on a dry riverbed and set up our vehicles and tents on the bank for the night. We were hot and dusty and to our surprise the guide told us we could take a dip as water slowly started to seep along the previously dry riverbed. It was refreshing.

Suddenly we heard crashing sounds, and the river began rising at an alarming rate. The rains from the mountains flowed quickly and created strong currents as the water started to rise and began lapping at the wheels of our vehicles.

Now it was unsafe to swim, and we got out of the water immediately. We all scrambled up the bank and helped to move the tents and the vehicles to higher ground. It was an experience I will never forget. The force of the water was so strong, shrubs were floating in the river. After two days the river water disappeared and it was now safe to drive on the riverbed to continue our trip into other parts of this remote area. Now I understand what a flash flood means.

One happy experience was offering a ride on top of our 4x4 to an elderly man who had been walking along the road. His smile enlightened his face. He was the only person we had seen for several days.

Returning to Tanzania, I took a canoe trip on the Zambezi River where we maneuvered around submerged hippopotamuses. Our guide slapped the water with his paddle and the hippos would poke their heads out of the water to see what caused the noise. Hippos have been known to bite a canoe in half.

One day our guide in my canoe slapped the water so hard, his paddle broke. Lucky me, I was a queen for the rest of the trip because I had to give him my paddle.

On our last night we camped on the road in tents waiting for our pick up the following day.

"Come and see these lion paw prints around our tents," yelled our guide the next morning. There were several of them.

I gasped! We were lucky the lions were not hungry. Everyone was safe.

After these electrifying adventures, I returned to Egypt and volunteered with the American-based International Executive Service Corps (IESC). This nonprofit organization focused on improving conditions in economically developing countries. They had recruited me to share my expertise as a quality improvement consultant, and for the next three years I accepted a series of unique assignments in between exploring new countries.

I was excited and nervous in equal measure as I greeted the staff and management on my first IESC assignment at a hospital in Alexandria, Egypt. During my seven-week placement, my job was to introduce and implement quality improvement systems, helping the staff to assess and streamline procedures and set up new operational practices. I would be developing programs to train staff from a quality improvement perspective. I worked long days during a six-day workweek.

I worked with the medical director who was also the hospital owner, and we agreed on the teaching schedule and implementation plan for each department. Everything went smoothly during this phase. However, encouraging the staff to take responsibility and make changes in their operations became a significant challenge. By the end of the first week, I was mentally exhausted.

On Friday, my day off, I rested and hung out with other IESC volunteers who were my support system, offering social activities and the freedom to speak without a translator.

One evening in the market, an artist hand painted a bookmark for me on papyrus paper. It was decorated with a picture of Nefertiti at the top and JOYCE spelled out in Egyptian hieroglyphics in gold.

This Egyptian bookmark with Nefertiti and JOYCE spelled in gold hieroglyphics is another one of my treasures from my travels.

My hotel room became my private cocoon as its large balcony offered an expansive view of the Mediterranean shoreline. I loved sitting there listening to the soft hiss as the waves gently rushed onto the sand before slowly retreating as dissolving foam. The pleasant rhythm soothed my nerves and allowed me to relax.

As night fell, stars in their millions began to bloom across the heavens to sparkle and wink over the water. I was secluded from the activity below, yet able to watch lovers holding hands as they walked along the shore or others running to maintain their fitness.

My days were full and demanding as I tried to meet the medical director's high expectations through teaching, training, and effecting changes throughout the hospital. The staff were busy doing their daily work, but many of their systems duplicated others and were unproductive.

This was my first IESC assignment. I was on a steep learning curve to adapt to Egyptian culture and replace current hospital systems with more effective ones. The attitudes were different from those in my previous assignments in Saudi Arabia, and I quickly lowered my expectations so I didn't get frustrated.

Soon the staff and I were forming teams to work on replacing any inefficiency and helping people to accept change. I felt I was making inroads as the staff continued to be more secure, asking for permission to take specific actions; however, maintaining sustained progress was painfully slow. The culture tended to promote a "do as you're told and follow my directions" attitude, which was deeply embedded into the working mentality.

One successful change was to the admission process, where we managed to eliminate half of the steps. They were pleased with their progress. I was happy to see them begin to ask more questions about the hospital systems. They revised the method of delivering medications to the inpatients and thus streamlined the process. I cheered them on as the medication errors stopped. We also evaluated the process for filing medical records and reordered all the active and closed charts. These changes saved hours of medical record employee time in retrieving information for clinical staff.

At the end of the seven weeks, as we planned for my departure, the owner asked if I would stay on. He was grateful for the staff's progress and wanted me to continue.

"Thank you, I appreciate your support, but I have made plans to travel," I said.

"I am disappointed. Could you perhaps come back later?"

I shook my head, then gave him a slight smile as I clasped both my hands over his, and said, "Thank you for your kind words. They mean a lot to me."

The next day the staff honored me with a festive birthday dinner, complete with a delicious chocolate cake glowing with lit candles, and they serenaded me with "Happy Birthday" in Arabic. I managed to blow out all the candles, and with delight we devoured the cake.

The head nurse said, "Joyce, you remind us of Nefertiti and the qualities she represented in our culture. We immediately thought this was a gift for you."

She presented me with an eighteen-karat gold necklace and pendant of Nefertiti's head and a gold circular charm with the hospital logo engraved on it.

A flush crept across my cheeks as I held up the necklace and carefully studied the engraving and design. I was thrilled to be regarded as a modern-day Nefertiti.

"Sukran (thank you)," I nodded and smiled. I was overwhelmed with their thoughtfulness; it was unexpected.

As we departed, the female staff hugged me, the men shook my hand. I felt the gratitude of their kindness and we sensed our collective successes.

I knew I would take on other IESC volunteer assignments, but, first, especially after the busy and somewhat stressful last seven weeks, I decided to immediately head out to explore the remote and relatively unknown and unusual Egyptian White Desert near the town of Farafra near the Libyan border.

Chapter 24

Wow, Overnight in the Egyptian White Desert and Exploring Unique Chalk Rock Formations

The White Desert gets its name from the color of the white and cream sand and from the large chalk rock formations, created by sandstorms that blew across its landscape. These unique formations had caught my attention in a travel magazine, and my plan was to camp in the White Desert with a guide in November 1997.

Mohammed, my driver, picked me up at my Cairo hotel precisely on the dot of 6:30 in the morning. He was a large man with a dark complexion, whose body betrayed his love of food. He had a smile coming straight from his heart. We immediately connected, and I was excited and impatient to get on the road.

We were on our way to meet Saad Ali Mohammed, my guide, a thirty-five-year-old Egyptian entrepreneur who lived in the west Egyptian town of Farafra. His business interests were varied and included farming and also running a tourist service. Saad had graduated from the University of Bavaria in Austria with a degree in agriculture. With support from his mother and brothers, he had built a forty-hectare date plantation that produced superior quality dates.

Mohammed and I arrived at Saad's large estate. I saw a boy and a girl, about seven or eight years of age, pass us riding donkeys. It was harvest time and the children had large wicker barrels, overflowing with dates, strapped to the donkeys. They were heading to the market. They sat up straight and seemed proud of their responsibility to sell the dates. They smiled at me, giggled, and covered their faces, then waved as I snapped their photo.

When we arrived in Farafra, we had dinner at Saad's home. His mother, wife, daughters, sons, spouses, children, and extended family gathered around to greet us. Saad was married with two children, who were both extremely polite. His son did the honors of pouring water over my hands to wash them before the meal and handed me a clean, pressed cloth to dry them. Next, the men and I went into one room and sat on the floor while the women served a tasty soup made from rice, fresh garden vegetables, and lamb, along with warm freshly baked bread. We finished our meal with dates from the plantation, so soft and sweet they seemed to melt in your mouth. I tucked dates into my pockets to have later.

Saad built and managed the Farafra Bedouin Village-Hotel, where I stayed in a comfortable, clean room the first night. I took a dip in the local hot spring. The water was forced through pipes producing strong water jets, which massaged my muscles. It was a form of sleeping pill. The orange red colors smeared across the sky, as the sun dipped below the horizon, restoring a sense of peace.

The following day Saad and I headed out in a 4x4 on our camping trip. First, we paid a visit to Mr. Sox, a tall thin man, with deep creases in his face caused by the relentless harsh desert climate. He was friendly and wore a light blue thobe. Despite the sweltering heat, he also wore a long beige camel-wool scarf wrapped around his neck. I thought it was strange because of the sweltering day, but this was the way he marketed his handmade camel-wool socks, scarves, and sweaters. I bought a pair of socks for my son.

Abda Badr, a local sculptor and artist, invited us into his studio. His 1.5 feet (0.46 meters) high sculptures of the local people depicted them in their daily activities such as drinking coffee, playing backgammon, and smoking waterpipes. His watercolors were skillful and used vivid colors and bold strokes to portray triads of birds, camels, and the desert.

As we arrived at the sand dunes, we met one of Saad's other tours, a group of Egyptian school children from Cairo. Their exuberance was contagious as they rolled down one of the dunes with the energy of a runaway snowball, rolling faster and faster until they reached the bottom. I tried to climb to the top, but my feet just kept sinking into the soft cool sand. I removed my shoes, tied them to my belt, hunched over, and climbed using my hands to assist me.

At the top, my eyes widened. I suddenly became still as I absorbed the expansive view of dunes as far as I could see. Staring at the sand was mesmerizing, and I fell into a trance, soaking in the vista until I heard Saad call my name, bringing me back to the present. I ran down the dune with the joy of my childhood in my heart. More fun than the climb up.

Just before the sun went down, I was exhilarated as we went dune climbing in our 4x4. Saad ran our vehicle up the dune, turning quickly at the top and heading back down. We repeated this several times. I was excited; the thrill of turning on the sand caused me to let out a squeal. It was breathtaking. As we made our last turn, we got stuck—not a smart thing to do as no one else was around. My heart raced. We didn't have any way to communicate with others. I wondered if we would spend our last days here; I said a prayer for our safety.

Immediately, Saad assessed the situation. The sand covered two-thirds of the front wheels. But he had all the tools ready as it was not the first time this had happened. We each grabbed a shovel, and after much digging, we were able to lift the wheels using the jack, then placed a wire mesh under the front wheels. Gradually we worked our way out of the sand. We let out a loud cheer as we were on our way again just as the sun was beginning to set. All was well.

A little farther along we found an ideal spot to set up camp and settled in for the night. The next morning Saad made a fire, and when the wood had burned down to coals, he removed them, placing a flattened circle of dough carefully on the hot sand, then covering it up again with more hot sand.

I thought the sand would grind against my teeth, so I decided to pass on breakfast, but curiosity got the better of me, and I forced myself to taste the cooked bread. To my surprise, I couldn't find a single grain of sand in my mouth when I ate the delicious, warm bread.

Later in the day, Saad and I headed out for a walk. He showed me the flora and the fauna of the desert. I was wide-eyed to see small flowers poking their heads out of the sand when we found water holes. I wore my sunglasses and squinting through my partially closed eyes, I realized the sun was as bright as if it were reflecting off the snow in a Canadian winter.

This unique desert had taken millennia to create, and when I looked out into its vastness, the result before me was stunning. The rock formations, with their stark white appearance, stood out against the desert golds and browns, not seeming to fit, giving the landscape a strange otherworldly vibe. They were like icebergs, but set in the sand, not water. Some took on the magical shapes of trees with stems and bushy tops. Others looked like mounds or immense hills. One massive silhouette was shaped like an hourglass, broad at the top and bottom and pinched in the center. I was struck by its size, I guessed the height of an eight-story building.

Astonishingly these structures were cool to the touch, even in the midday sun, when everything around them burned with heat. The whole scene was breathtaking, strange, and awesome—a striking art exhibition by an original and skilled master sculptor.

That night we joined another one of Saad's tour groups for dinner. The group consisted of six Germans and one person from Holland, all with various backgrounds including a marathon runner, a doctor, and several business professionals. A photographer had spent six months in the desert and six months in Amsterdam and was holding a one-person photography exhibition in Cairo later that month.

This group was on an eight-day camel trek; the camels carried the luggage, bedrolls, food, and other supplies while they walked. Although most of them couldn't speak much English and I couldn't speak German or Dutch, we managed with sign language. We laughed and enjoyed sitting around the campfire after a nourishing meal of chicken shawarmas. The chicken was rolled in flatbread, stuffed with hummus, pickles, and a few French fries, and we devoured freshly sliced mangoes for dessert.

It was early to bed and early to rise in the desert. Sunset was about six in the evening and sunlight woke me up just after five in the morning. One evening we rolled out our sleeping bags on a rug, and I moved around to make the suitable hollows in the sand for my body. The sand was as soft and comfortable as my mattress back home. The dead silence of the desert was heavy and still. The desert air drugged me to sleep in a flash, but I awoke about four in the morning, just after the moon had set. I reached for my binoculars. The sky was like a fireworks show. Stars were everywhere. They burst forth with their brilliance in the Milky Way, sparkling like diamonds.

The next day, after continuing our drive through the desert, we found a bit of relief from the sun in the shade of one of the rock formations. It looked like a house balanced on top of a column.

*I crouched below a rock sculpture carved by the wind
in the White Desert.*

Soon the wind would sculpt more of the column away, causing it to collapse. Saad lit a fire and prepared our lunch, a vegetable stew. The onions, okra, cloves, tomatoes, turmeric, cinnamon, paprika, and cumin simmered in the pot. The aroma soon had me ready to devour a delicious meal. Satiated, I pulled out my stash of fresh dates as a sweet treat for dessert.

At the end of our trip, we found a secluded oasis, which relieved my eyes from the brilliant white of the desert. I talked to a German hiker who had been camping at the oasis for six days. He was enjoying the solitude and isolation, so different from his demanding life back in Germany. I had to agree with him.

The White Desert was a rare experience, with its thrilling vistas. It was another of Egypt's treasures. The rock formations were unique and with the constant wind would change over time and probably disappear. I felt blessed to see this natural wonder.

The solitude of the desert had been welcoming, but now it was time to say goodbye and head back to Cairo.

Chapter 25

Viewing Where the White and Blue Nile Rivers Join, but Then

In early December 1997 I flew to Khartoum, Sudan, to deliver another quality improvement workshop for the WHO. My United Nations passport whisked me through the customs and immigration procedures. A representative grabbed my luggage and quickly we moved through the crowds to the waiting automobile.

Sudan is south of Egypt and its borders include Ethiopia, Eritrea, the Red Sea, the Central African Republic, Uganda, Chad, and Libya. This water-scarce country is part of the geographical Sahel region between the Sahara and coastal West Africa.

Women wore white robes, a nice change from Saudi Arabia's and Yemen's black abayas. In addition to the white robes, some women displayed their individuality by wrapping a brightly colored scarf—usually pinks, reds, and yellows—around their shoulders and heads, covering their hair and securing the scarf with a small pin. Younger girls wore white dresses and a white headscarf, contrasting with their dark brown skin and dark brown eyes.

I considered the challenges of keeping everything clean when there was a water shortage, but I knew the communal laundry area was the community gossip station and meeting place, no men allowed. Women didn't miss this opportunity to learn the latest news.

The next day, I met with the Sudanese Ministry of Health senior staff, and we began to plan the quality improvement program and my teaching and presentation schedules. The discussions lasted well into the evening.

The staff seemed interested in the program and committed to making some changes in their healthcare delivery systems, which was the first step to success. I headed back to the hotel with a spring in my step. It was a productive day, even if it was a long one. It was at times like this that I felt happy with my job.

Before the workshops got underway, I headed to the market with my driver, Ameen. I was struck by the image of all the women wearing white robes as we were about to drive across the White Nile Bridge, so I asked Ameen to stop, intent on capturing it all on film. Below me, the fast, narrow, dark, muddy Blue Nile River and the wider, slower, light gray, White Nile River merged into one and became the Nile River, known to millions around the world throughout history. I'd seen the beginnings of the Blue Nile in Ethiopia, and the White Nile in Lake Victoria, along with the Nile's final journey into the Mediterranean Sea. I had promised myself that taking a photo of where they met would be one of the first items on my to-do list in Khartoum.

I was so intent on my picture taking and transfixed by how the colors of the two Niles were mixing I didn't notice the plainclothes security guard and Ameen approaching.

The security guard spoke Arabic. Ameen translated, "No photos. A high-security military building is in your photographs."

"Ameen, tell him I will give him the film."

"She will give you the film," Ameen said.

He shook his head, no, and pointed to stairs leading down to the ground at the end of the bridge. We followed him below.

"Sit on this bench outside the office and wait."

No one spoke to us for almost twenty minutes. We were both getting agitated.

The White and Blue Nile merge. It is not apparent in the photo, but the Blue Nile is a pale greenish blue color and the White Nile River is a light grey color. The waters remain separated due to sediment, but mix as they flow together making the Nile River.

Finally Ameen spoke to the guard. "She is a visitor on a United Nations passport and should be released immediately." Then, he whispered to me, "They want money."

With my hand over my mouth, I mumbled, "I can't pay them because I'm on a United Nations passport. By bribing them, we could be in significant trouble. I was instructed not to get involved with the police and under no circumstances to bribe them. Often, people set you up, and it causes the United Nations a lot of trouble. The local WHO staff will protect me and take care of our current situation unless I make it difficult for them."

Time continued to pass. I desperately wanted to get to the market before noon to buy some famous Sudanese pottery beads to have as a souvenir of my trip.

I mulled over my options and whispered to Ameen, "Stand up, look the guard in the eye, point to me and tell him in a demanding voice I want to see their boss immediately."

My demand offered the guards a solution to save face. Ameen returned with one rather pale-faced security guard, who would not look me in the eye. We all got in the car and drove to his superior's office.

We were met by a gray-haired man in a crisp uniform, his widely set dark brown eyes drilled through me. His face was stern, his hands clasped together on his desk, like a school principal waiting to mete out punishment to a pupil who has done something wrong. I felt slightly unnerved. The silence seemed to stretch too long.

The guard finally spoke and said, "The lady took a picture of the military building from the White Nile Bridge."

I smiled and slowly spoke with my best apologetic voice. "I'm extremely sorry for causing this situation. I wasn't taking a photo of a military building. I wanted to take a photo of the two Nile rivers becoming one. I wanted to show this famous spot to my family in North America because, well, because the view is incredible."

The boss's hands relaxed, his eyes softened, and he smiled. "I'm sorry for your delay. Unfortunately, there has been a misunderstanding."

"Thank you for your assistance in resolving this situation so nicely. Would you like me to give you the film?"

"No, keep it. It's okay to show your family. And you are right, of course, yes, the view is incredible."

"Thank you again for your kindness and consideration," I said and turned quickly to leave.

We rushed to the market, arriving just in time for me to purchase enough beads to later string a necklace. I was glad for my colorful handmade beads, but I was especially happy for my photograph, which had been the source of all the trouble. Thank goodness for the United Nations passport. Who knew what might have happened without it? I had my photo and had achieved one of my personal objectives on this trip.

Ameen and I stopped for lunch in a small restaurant where we ordered some kisra, flatbread made from sorghum flour, along with moukhbaza, a paste made from mashed bananas. Next, we added jibna salata, a crumbly, white cheese salad with cucumber, tomatoes, spring onions, a pinch of salt, and rocket greens called young mustard greens. The servings were large, tasty, and filling. I added karkade, a tea made from hibiscus flowers. The pleasant floral aroma filled the air, and the sweet clear tea calmed my senses and relaxed my muscles after our adventures.

We continued our drive after lunch. I visited an open-air market that had all types of consumer items for sale. The carved gourds, attractively etched with flowers and unusual geometric shapes, were unique and one of my children has one now. Another stall displayed beautiful handmade necklaces and bracelets. A lady at one of the stalls handed me a bottle of perfume she had distilled from the petals of a mix of flowers. I loved the scent. She refused my money and seemed rather indignant when I offered to pay. She was giving me a gift, which I accepted with a smile and a hug.

"Sukran," I said, bowing slightly to her while clutching the small bottle tightly to my chest. She watched approvingly as I placed it carefully in the safety of my purse. I showed her a Canadian flag pin and she nodded. I pinned it to her blouse, and she smiled shyly. Her generosity and the unexpectedness of the gift made my heart sing with pure delight.

The next week our workshops got underway. One afternoon, when I finished work early, I slipped over to the National Museum of Sudan to study the many displays. Just outside the main entrance stood beautifully carved wooden figures of a man, woman, and child, surrounded by a shallow reflective pool, a serene, picturesque sight.

Inside were a number of interesting displays about camel travel in the desert. The museum highlighted the many pyramids found in Sudan and the Sudanese claimed they had more pyramids than Egypt.

While in class some of the Sudanese trainers who were helping with the workshops arranged a cruise for me one evening on the Nile River. Glorious deep rose-pink colors spread across the sky as the sun went down, lending the evening a magical and informal atmosphere. We laughed and enjoyed our social time together. Their thoughtfulness touched my soul.

One day we traveled outside the city to meet with local healthcare providers. Two young boys were riding donkeys along the side of the road, bundles of branches tied to the animals' flanks. A white truck sped down the highway, loaded with people sitting everywhere, on the roof of the cab, in the back, and even on the bumpers. I estimated there were at least fifteen to seventeen people. They waved, smiling as we passed.

Hand-carved statues outside the National Museum of Sudan.

Being in Khartoum also allowed me to see the whirling dervishes again. I had seen these swirling, twirling performances in Egypt and was anxious to view them here. Tourists and locals flocked to the whirling dervishes' location to see men from the Sunni and Shia Islam branches practice Sufism. The men who whirl were called Sufis or dervishes. I stood at the edge of the grassy dance area, the size of a basketball court, as the sun began to set. The dervishes discarded their green robes and began dancing in their long white gowns and caps.

The women didn't dance. Instead, they were enthusiastic spectators, clapping their hands and singing, keeping the rhythm. As the men swirled and twirled, a trance overtook them. Their robes flared out, blurring at the speed of their turns. They seemed to levitate off the ground as they twirled faster and faster. The women's voices were chanting, the clapping of their hands marking the rhythm, and the dancers' arms flailing like windmills. I felt dizzy watching them perform and, at one point, needed to look away, but my eyes pulled me back to their circular movement, almost becoming hypnotized.

The performance lasted for hours. I felt transported to another world, but I could not say exactly where.

The two weeks of workshops passed quickly; I finished my assignment and read the evaluations. A big smile broke out as I read their positive kudos. One lady wrote: "I will never forget you. You have made me more self-confident, and I hope to be more like you. Good luck." Another person wrote: "We certainly hadn't enough of you, Joyce. Come back soon." Another person wrote: "Your beautiful smile, I will miss you so much, I'd like to thank you for your great effort you have done." Another person said, "To the most loved teacher."

I hoped the staff would put what they learned into practice, thus using it in their work and personal lives.

I returned to Egypt for a final debriefing on the Sudan workshops. I felt pleased that my quality improvement program would help people. With minor adjustments, it would be ready for the WHO to use in other countries. I was happy to have touched a few lives along the way, and my hope was the workshops could prove valuable in other countries as well.

After Sudan my goal was to continue traveling. However, my boss in Alexandria persuaded me to accept one last project presenting two papers on quality improvement at a conference in Casablanca, Morocco. I was incredibly happy to be invited because many of the conference participants had attended my previous workshops in different countries. This was my opportunity to find out if what I taught was, in fact, beneficial. It was vital to know if I made a difference in their lives—personal, workwise, or both. The driving force throughout my career had been to teach and help others. I believed I had accomplished my goal wherever I traveled over the world. But here in Morocco was the proof. Would the answer be what I wanted to hear?

The day arrived, and I was understandably apprehensive about asking the attendees my questions, seeing their reactions, and hearing their replies.

Before I could say hello, I was surrounded by former students from various countries. Everyone wanted to talk at the same time, giving me hugs, and shaking my hands. They blurted out their successes using the techniques they learned. I couldn't follow all their answers. I felt overwhelmed and blinked my eyes as tears welled up. Later in the day I got the chance to ask Huda from Yemen about the specific workshop learnings she had been able to apply to her daily practice. I asked her for feedback, which could improve future programs.

"I used the voting method to solve family disputes, and that's a big help to me. I was happy, and my family was happy," Huda said, smiling at me. "Thank you for that skill; it's been invaluable." Then almost as an afterthought, she tapped me on the arm and said, "We also use it at work, you know."

Kamal from Sudan said, "I liked how you divided the groups into two sections. First, two people got together and decided on something, then four people decided together, then eight decided until the group came to a consensus. It works for anything, even where to go for a picnic." He laughed at some recent memory. "Since we all learned it together, we have become a solid team at work."

My heart was singing and I felt fulfilled. The hours I had spent planning and preparing to meet the participants' needs and deliver specific programs, geared to their level of concerns, seemed to have proven worthwhile and were paying dividends for my diligent effort and worry. If only one person benefited from these programs, that was a gift enough for me. But the fact they had been emboldened and saw a value in my programs, then chose to share and pass them on to someone else, well, that was a bonus and a true gift. It was, in fact, the living embodiment of my motto and belief—touching one person and one life at a time.

Chapter 26

The Gorilla Family Touched My Heart in the Middle of the Ugandan Jungle

I took a break from my travels after my trip to Sudan and then spent most of 1998 in Canada and the United States, visiting loved ones. Of course, the grandchildren had grown, and I shared new travel experiences with them and their classmates in their schools. I loved the way we took treasures from my travels to their classrooms and shared my stories with their friends.

Even after six years of traveling, I was still deeply committed to continuing to explore the world. I was sixty-three years old, my investments had done well, and I felt free and focused.

I also accepted a few more IESC assignments, including opening a private eye hospital in Cairo, which was a rewarding and successful experience.

So in September 1998 I started to travel again and visited Germany, then headed back to Africa, visiting the Canary Islands and Egypt, then worked my way down the west coast through Morocco, Senegal, Gabon, Gambia, Guinea, Guinea Bissau, Ivory Coast, Ghana, Togo, Benin, and Burkina Faso.

In January 1999, after I traveled to Uganda, a landlocked country in central East Africa, I had the chance to check out a natural phenomenon that attracted a lot of tourists. In the northern hemisphere water drains clockwise. In the southern hemisphere water drains counterclockwise. Uganda straddles the hemispheres because the equator runs through it. I stood at the tourist attraction, one foot in the northern hemisphere, one foot in the southern hemisphere, the equator cutting me in half and watched water go straight down a drain.

I am standing over the equator where I am half in the northern hemisphere and half in the southern hemisphere.

Uganda is home to a significant gorilla population, and I joined a tour group visiting the lush green slopes of the Buhoma Mountains in the Bwindi Impenetrable National Park (BINP) in southwest Uganda, hoping to find the M or Mubare gorilla group, with a huge silverback (some weigh up to 430 pounds or 195 kilograms) and his family, one of the country's fourteen endangered mountain gorilla groups.

It was 6:45 in the early morning and the air was cool as I crawled out from my sleeping bag. Our group had slept in tents, pitched on the Abercrombie and Kent hotel site. During the night we were protected by guards, armed with bows and arrows. We had been assured the locals welcomed the tourists and the contribution we made to the local economy. It seemed safe; I slept deeply.

The other early risers and I were sipping coffee before the day's rugged climb to search for the shy mountain gorillas began. Others were still snuggled in their sleeping bags, catching the last of the shut-eye. The sun hadn't pierced the dense forest canopy, but it would, and we would feel the heat before our trek began. After a substantial breakfast of eggs and toast, I was ready to tackle the lush green slopes of the Buhoma Mountains.

Our guide, Bret, told us how the World Wildlife Federation had worked with local leaders in this part of Uganda, convincing them to stop hunting the gorillas for meat. With the gorillas now protected, tourists could see them living in their natural habitat, and the community shared in the fees paid by the tourists, which supported the community. I was anxious to start as I put my supplies of food and water into my day pack.

By 8:30 a.m. we arrived at the base of the mountain, and Bret said, "We're going to walk in a single file. I'm the lead and the slowest person will walk behind me; the rest will follow. We will only have one hour to watch the gorillas once we find them, so take your pictures, but no flashes, please, as the light may bother the gorillas. And do not get too close."

I stepped up, thinking I would be the slowest person, but to my disbelief Bret placed me behind two others. Not too bad for a grandmother, I thought. The first part of the trek was easy, a slow rise, and my breathing was regular. We took a five-minute rest, and I guzzled my water.

The second part of our walk was through the dense jungle. Earlier, before we had left the hotel, other guides had found where the gorilla family had slept the night before and slashed a path to their location. As we arrived, I heard them slashing more of the bush. The other guides were tracking the gorillas' movements and guiding us forward by talking to Bret over a walkie-talkie. My walking stick helped me to balance as I stepped on spongy ground, my foot sometimes breaking through branches that covered the path. I wore heavy hiking leather boots and tucked my pants into the tops of my socks to keep bugs out.

I trekked through dense vegetation to find the M gorilla family in the jungle in Uganda.

The jungle was alive with sounds and fragrant with the smell of the bushes, the soil, and the leaves. A beautiful blue butterfly hovered around me for seconds. Its blue wings were iridescent. I wanted to follow it, but I had to stay in line and march on. Everywhere I looked there were birds—brown, blue, red, and yellow—and noisy monkeys, chattering high in the trees, swooping from branch to branch.

It was 11:00 a.m. when we spied the M group or the troop. I counted one silverback male, fourteen females, and several younger males and females moving through the thick bush.

The silverback male was massive, regal, and had a demeanor of intelligence. This silverback's head was the size of a lawnmower engine, and his muscular hairy arms stretched long and limp. My pulse raced, and my eyes widened, peering through the bushes, as he stood up.

He was tall, heavy, and his hands were so large they could easily crush me. It's honestly hard to put into words the sheer awesomeness I felt seeing these magnificent elusive creatures in their natural habitat. Bowing came to mind. I'm not sure anything could have prepared me for how emotional I felt. I moved as close as I could and was mesmerized watching the troop through the bushes. The gorillas looked so docile and friendly, I had the urge to join them.

I watched the silverback swing his arms at his sides as he walked about, and I could see his eyes blink through my binoculars. As the leader he was responsible for the safety of his group. He sauntered over to a tree, defecated, wiped the stool from his fur, then moved to a shaded area and stretched on his back. Soon a loud snore filled the air. With his eyes still closed, he scratched his face, then his right ear. I was not sure if he was sleeping or just dozing.

Two younger gorillas started playing in a flat grassy area nearby. They somersaulted, playing what seemed to be a game of tag and then picked up some fallen branches and threw them back into the bush. I smiled. They acted like my two sons when they were young.

Two older females were keeping an eye on the youngsters, just like mothers do. Another female came closer to where I was standing with a young baby hanging onto her fur on her chest.

It was hard to get clear photos because of the darkness and dense green foliage of the jungle. I concentrated, watching their every move, so I could remember this experience. The gorillas looked happy and content, and I was glad we were not disturbing their day.

The air was hot, humid, and still, and we stood in the shade, mesmerized by the gorillas as we ate our lunch. Our hour disappeared and time was up, so we headed back to our camp. We walked silently, each one thinking about what we saw and how we felt. I smiled as I treasured the memories of seeing the gorillas and their family life.

To my horror, I stepped on a sharp thorn, hidden by the branches that littered the path that had been slashed by the guides. I fell to the ground. The thorn had cut my leg and blood flowed quickly, soaking my sock. Lucky for me, Ian, another tourist, and an emergency room nurse, was behind me and had an excellent first aid kit handy. He secured two tight bandages with wide tape, stopping the flow of blood. I was embarrassed to delay the group, but they were more concerned about my well-being than rushing back. My leg was fine during the remaining trek.

In the evening we all thanked our guides as we recounted our memories and prepared to leave for Kampala, Uganda's capital city, the next day.

Chapter 27

My Black Eye and the Horror of Uganda's Lord's Resistance Army

In February 1999, our group returned to Kampala. Three members from the gorilla trip and I, along with two young men, had signed up for a white-water rafting adventure. Our guide Chris was dressed in navy blue shorts and a red long-sleeved T-shirt, his bulging biceps straining the fabric. He wore a baseball cap and sunglasses and welcomed everyone with his smile.

"You will get tossed out of the raft, so be prepared. It will be a wild ride," he bellowed. "I've been a guide for three years and know the river. Are you ready?"

His voice reassured me he knew the river and how the Nile flowed at this water level. My breathing relaxed; besides, he was gorgeous.

"Gather round and listen up," Chris continued, black hair poking out from under his hat. "Nothing on your feet; no flip-flops, no water shoes, no necklaces, no rings, they will disappear. Do not wear anything you are not prepared to lose; only bathing suits, life jackets, and helmets are okay. When we flip, hang on to the raft if you can," he said with a wink. "Let's go, gang. We are the lead raft."

"We are lucky," he continued. "The authorities have opened the five gates that control the water flowing to Egypt. As a result, the river will be swift, and we'll have grade four and five rapids. The Rafting Association rates the rapids, one through six."

"Hey, Chris, break down the difference for me," I said.

"One is smooth, two and three can be bouncy, four and five are extremely tough, and six? Well, let's hope not to try that one today."

We grabbed our paddles. Chris taught us how to use them, how to climb back in the raft if we got tossed out, and what to do if we came up under the raft. We practiced hand signals and safety procedures.

Chris yelled, "Remember this cardinal rule: never hold on to someone else, because you will both go under and may never come up. All hands up if you can swim?"

Everyone raised their hands.

The river was as smooth as glass. The idyllic and tranquil flow of the river removed any thoughts of fear to come. I felt calm before the expected adrenaline rush.

The rapids' names were descriptive: the Bad Place, the Nile Special (also the name of a Uganda beer) and the Fifty-Fifty rapid, with its steep elevator-like plummeting drop.

As we approached the first rapid, the thunderous sound of flowing water broke the silence. Now I was nervous. Anxiety pushed away any thoughts of relaxation, and I paddled hard as we were thrown into the grade five rapid.

Suddenly I was out of the raft and sinking in the water. Someone else who had been thrown was grabbing manically at my arms, as if they were drowning and in the throes of intense panic. Instinctively I held my breath—both of us were going down fast. I heard Chris's voice in my head, never hold on to anyone, ever. In an instant, I knew exactly what I had to do. With all the remaining energy I could summon, I broke free from his iron-clad grasp on me. My lungs were bursting. I kicked hard to get to the surface, gasping for air. One of the other guides, who was paddling the safety kayak, towed me back to the raft. I was furious.

People should not be on these trips if they were not accomplished swimmers, for their safety and for others. Chris talked to the young man who had been holding on to me. He was visibly shaken and apologized profusely. Chris put him on the other side of the raft from me for the duration of the trip.

I had just enough time to get resettled and relaxed before we hit our next grade four rapid. We were paddling better. A few quick twists forced our raft backward, but we stayed upright and made it through without dumping. "Yay," we yelled, lifting our paddles into the air.

We floated on the river, eyeing the local thatched huts, with their circular roofs, perched on the riverbank, and watched children playing near a house. We took turns floating alongside the raft as we made our way downstream. The guides in the kayaks kept watch for crocodiles that liked to hang out in well-known spots along the riverbank. When they spotted them, we stayed in the raft.

We stopped for lunch and relaxed for some time before heading off again. We managed to stay upright throughout the next few rapids. But now we were heading to the final and most treacherous one.

Chris gave us specific commands for the last rapid, saying, "We will almost certainly flip. Follow these instructions. When I say duck, put your head down. That will prevent any paddles from hitting your face. Do not wait to see if I fly off the back. If you see me fly off the back of the raft, you missed your chance, and we are toast; we are already in the water."

Not exactly the most comforting speech I've ever heard.

I was ready, squatting in the raft, prepared to duck, but I waited too long. Then, I saw Chris fly through the air. It was too late for me to get safely tucked down. A paddle smashed into my nose just beneath my eye; the pain was immediate and intense. I submerged into the water.

I came up for air on the other side of the rapid. I touched my nose. It was sore. I wondered if I had broken a bone. We all hauled ourselves back onto the raft and headed toward the shore.

When we landed, I scrounged some ice and a cloth to make an ice pack. Then I grabbed a window seat near the middle of the bus as others climbed on to head back to our hotel. The throbbing continued even with the ice pack.

Two young men, who had been in a different raft, sat in the seats in front of me. They kept turning around and looking at me. I was about to tell them in no uncertain terms to mind their own business when one spoke.

"Hi, I'm Pablo, and this is Diego; we are doctors from Argentina. We finished our medical training and are taking a holiday before we start our practice. When we stop, we'll look at your eye and see if you broke your nose if you like?"

My face flushed. I stuttered a bit, then, in a respectful tone, said, "Yes, thanks, that would be amazing, I'm Joyce, a nurse and am grateful for your help."

When we stopped, they examined my nose and eye. Everything was in working order, but they confirmed I would have a black shiner.

The next morning, my eye was predictably black and blue when I met with members of the local Canadian Physicians for Aid and Relief (CPAR) group working in Uganda. I had arranged to visit their office in northern Uganda to learn firsthand about their projects and to teach a program in quality management.

CPAR and WaterCAN provided safe water wells in northern Uganda's vulnerable communities. Through this project, they aimed to provide safe and clean water within a radius of 4,129 feet (1.5 kilometers) from homes. This distance was considered an easy walking distance for people to carry their water. Women, young boys, and girls use five-gallon (19-liter) jerry cans to collect the water. Often women must make as many as five trips a day, returning with the full water cans on their heads. These wells soon became bustling commerce centers and local meeting places.

I visited one of the wells where the water caretaker was now growing tobacco and bananas to sell to those who came for water. He had also planted the tops of pineapples to start his plantation.

We were ready to leave the wellsite when one of the women who came for water each day asked for my empty plastic water bottle. Her lips curled up in a bit of a smile as she turned it over and over in her hand. I could almost see her racing thoughts; how was she planning to use the bottle? Then, she gave a little curtsy, the way African women did, and laughed, stroking the bottle while gripping it tightly.

The primary purpose of my visit was to present a two-day workshop to the CPAR staff on quality improvement and problem-solving techniques. Using the lessons I had delivered in Egypt, Saudi Arabia, and other countries with the World Health Organization, I told stories about other people's experiences and successes, then asked them to solve their problems working as a team.

My lessons were direct and simple. The class was developing new skills to use in their day-to-day work and also at home. All team members, including supervisory staff, participated, ensuring everyone would use the same techniques. After the group shared their projects, we celebrated with cake and sodas. I smiled at their accomplishments, but most of all at their demonstrated feelings of success and satisfaction.

The next day I was offered a ride back to Kampala by Charles, a local friend and supporter of CPAR. As we drove along, the conversation turned to the Lord's Resistance Army (LRA). I had read news stories about the LRA and how they were kidnapping children, forcing them into their army, the boys to fight, and the girls as sex slaves, wives, and cooks. I was uncomfortable as he began to talk. I felt deep grief and despair in his voice.

He spoke in a low measured tone as if he was pulling up feelings and thoughts he wanted to bury forever.

"I want to tell you this story. Because it needs to be told. For many years Joseph Kony's LRA has been forcibly kidnapping boys and girls in northern Uganda for their army. Then, three years ago, on October 9, 1996, rebels attacked St. Mary's College–Aboke, a boarding school, forcing one hundred and thirty-nine girls to line up along the wall. The prettiest girls stood at the front. My daughter was in that group. All the girls walked out and disappeared into the jungle that night."

He took a deep breath and continued. "An Italian nun, Sister Rachelle Fassera, the school's deputy headmistress, followed the girls and their captors. Through her skills, she was able to negotiate the release of one hundred and nine of them. Later she secured the release of more girls, but my daughter did not return."

Staring at the steering wheel, he whispered, "She is still there. I am told they move camp on a moment's notice if the scouts alert them the authorities are coming. Other girls have escaped and tell me she was with the head commander, has had two children, and will stay there. My heart shattered into a million pieces when this happened. To this day my daughter has not come home."

I held my breath, unsure of what to say to Charles. I felt physically nauseous. What comfort could I possibly offer this man? Even as a parent myself, I could not grasp the magnitude of his loss and suffering. I remained silent.

After a few minutes, he started again. "The captives face a difficult situation. Unfortunately, if a captive escapes or is rescued, either boys or girls, they are often disowned by their families and shunned by their communities. They are not welcome anywhere. They cannot go back to the LRA, or the LRA will kill them. The women cannot marry as the men think of them as dirty. Often, they are left to fend for themselves. Struggling with the psychological trauma of being kidnapped and then the shame brought by their families, their lives become unbearable."

He said, "One of the kidnapped girls told me when she returned home, her family shunned her. She told me, 'I must be strong to take care of my children, fathered by a commander, because my family rejects my children and me totally. So how will we survive?' She asked me. How? Fortunately, a nongovernmental organization gave her a sewing machine, and she was able to make a living," said Charles. "But her life and those of her children are not easy."

The conversation with Charles made a profound impact on me. We arrived in Kampala where he dropped me off at my hotel. I felt a bit of my heart stayed with him and his family as he drove away. He had touched me deeply. The way he accepted his daughter's fate was remarkable, but what other choice did he have?

Sleep did not come easily that night.

Uganda is a beautiful country, but the trip left me with a roller coaster of emotions. I had loved hiking into the jungle to find the gorillas, the rafting trip was thrilling, sharing my professional knowledge and skills with the CPAR staff was satisfying and fulfilling, but hearing aboutthe atrocities carried out by the LRA on the gentle people of Uganda was tragic and unfathomable.

Later that year, on March 3, 1999, as I traveled through Malawi, I stepped into my hotel's dining room. I stopped dead in my tracks, feeling an instant chill. The television was on and it showed images from the Abercrombie and Kent compound in Uganda, where I had stayed and hiked to find the gorillas. Approximately 200 rebels had attacked the compound, swarming out of the bushes, and kidnapping the tourists.

I stared at the TV and visualized the guards with their bows and arrows. They did not have a chance to protect the tourists.

Many years later I happened to meet one of the few survivors of that attack waiting for our plane to depart. On the day of the assault, she had just dressed except for her shoes when the rebels appeared. So her captors forced her to walk through the jungle on her bare feet.

"How could you walk through that dense bush in bare feet? The bush was so rough. It was an incredibly sharp and jagged path," I said, remembering the thorn that had pierced my skin on the hike back from seeing the gorillas.

"It took a few years for the feeling in the soles of my feet to return. Then one day, I realized I could feel them. I jumped for joy," she said.

"What happened to all the people?" I asked in hushed tones, as I tried to recall the newscast I had heard that night.

"Unfortunately, they killed most people, robbed us, and took our passports. My guide and I were allowed to leave after some time but were not sure why. As we left the captors' camp and walked away, we expected they would shoot us in our backs. Even now, five years later, this terrifying feeling continues to haunt me at night if I am walking outside, especially alone."

"I can't begin to imagine your experience and its lingering impact. I am truly so sorry. Did you happen to keep in touch with your guide?" I asked curiously.

"Yes, but I have not shared my story with the press, although many people have asked me to be on their shows. I'm slowly getting over the trauma," she said.

I hugged her as we parted. We never met or communicated again.

Chapter 28

My Memories and Thrill of a Zambian African Safari

After another IESC assignment in Zambia in 1999, I took advantage of booking a classic African safari in the Luangwa Rift Valley in the South Luangwa National Park. I loved this rugged, relatively unknown park. It was home to a high concentration of endangered mammals such as lions, leopards, hippos, and giraffes along with over forty bird species. It was an absolute must see for a nature lover like me.

The first morning our guide offered me some termite honey. I shook my head with a defiant no, ready to pass on his offer, but I succumbed to my curiosity and opened my mouth for a taste. The termite honey was thinner, but as sweet as the bee honey I usually put on my toast at home. I opened my mouth for more, but two tastes were the limit. We moved on.

There were few tourists at that time of year, so I had a direct view of the birds and animals when our group headed out on our first day safari. The animals appeared shy and disappeared as the Land Rover approached, a complete contrast to the animals in the more popular and tourist-crowded parks, who just stared and looked at you when you drove up and then returned to whatever they were doing.

Each evening our group gathered on the beach at sunset to enjoy the safari tradition of sundowner cocktails. As the majestic fiery red and golden orb of the sun slipped from the horizon, it left in its wake a sky painted in a kaleidoscope of glorious and ever-changing hues. It was enough to make anyone believe there is a God. The birds' calls would deepen with the gathering twilight, then suddenly hush fell as the jungle seemed to hold its collective breath. But not for long.

Moments later, the jungle would erupt with the sounds of the night. The insects became almost deafening, night birds sent out their greetings, and an occasional roar pierced the darkness as the lions and leopards readied for the night's hunt.

During our night safari, we used a bright spotlight fixed to our customized Jeep to spot a leopard stalking a herd of impala. We watched silently, holding our breaths, as the leopard deliberately circled the herd. Then with lightning speed, it made the kill. My stomach churned as I felt the cruelty and yet the grace of how one species survives by killing others. Ruthlessness and beauty are such strange bedfellows, yet nature in all her design is perfect, even if brutal at times.

My favorite time to walk along the riverbank was at six in the morning. Our group spotted eleven lionesses, on the opposite riverbank, starting to look for their food. They deliberately spread out, surrounding a herd of zebras who had come to the river for a drink. There was nothing like seeing these lionesses at eye level while walking. Peering through my binoculars, I realized they were huge, their muscles rippling under their fur as they moved. Their eyes were focused solely on the zebras standing at the edge of the herd. We had to move on and could not wait for the kill.

Walking further along the path, we watched with sheer delight as eight adult elephants sprayed their bodies with the river water. They were massive. Two baby elephants were being washed by their mothers. One young male threw up his trunk and flapped his ears.

He was the center of attention for a few minutes. We were so close we could see the wrinkles on the elephants' skin, and standing on the ground, I felt small, so tiny compared to the group's matriarch.

A group of warthogs scampered up the bank. I did not realize they could move so quickly. They looked so awkward with their short legs.

Hippos poked their heads out of the water, protecting their sensitive skin from the early morning sun. Finally, they submerged and were gone. Then in due time, they broke the surface again, curious to keep an eye on everything as they looked around.

Later we spotted one lioness with blood on her mouth and a cub tearing apart the carcass of a killed zebra. It was hard to look at, but I saw firsthand life and death in the jungle.

Life and death in the jungle on our safari in Zambia.

The staff served a delicious lunch of salad and fresh pineapple as we sat on the beach watching giraffes munching on leaves high in the trees before they headed off for an afternoon nap. The jungle was quiet in the midday sun, so we returned to our camp for our own siesta.

The quiet break gave me time to reflect on the creatures I was seeing, their lives and how blessed I was to be here to experience the jungle in the raw. I was beyond grateful for the opportunity to see these breathtakingly magnificent animals and birds up close in their habitat. To be privileged to feel and share the wildness of it all. The scents, the sounds, the colors were total sensory overload—majestic, humbling, extraordinary on every single level possible. Primordial. I loved it all with absolute passion and gratitude and was sad to say goodbye to the staff and the animals when the safari ended the next day.

I returned to the capital city of Zambia, Lusaka, a bustling commercial center. Entrepreneurs were selling intricately detailed animal ebony and stone carvings at the market. Their artisan skill was exceptional, but the weight of carvings and the cost of sending one home prevented me from making a purchase.

I took a trip to Victoria Falls, named after Queen Victoria in 1855 by David Livingstone, a British explorer. My guide told me in the dry season, people could walk across the river at the top of the falls, but now it was a high-water season. Mist spread for at least 31 miles (50 kilometers). The massive force of the high volume of water thundering over the falls meant rain poured down on the path where I stood. Luckily, I had the protection of a plastic rain-coat as I stood utterly mesmerized. My eyes were locked onto the crashing water as if I were in some sort of a trance, like staring into the depths of fire. I'm not sure how long I stood there, but it was probably close to thirty minutes.

Livingstone, a sleepy little tourist town in Zambia, was connected to the bustling city of Victoria Falls in Zimbabwe by the
Victoria Falls Bridge, built in 1905. I relived the passion of that
long-ago era by taking an eight-car train across the bridge, pulled
by a 1922 steam engine. The staff replicated those early days by
wearing white British uniforms with contrasting red sashes as they
served a delicious meal accompanied by champagne.

We chugged along the tracks and stopped to watch tourists
bungee jumping the 364 feet (111 meters) on the Zimbabwe side,
listening to their yells and squeals as they free-fell over the river.
That was one activity I refused to do. I knew the risks and didn't
want to develop a detached retina.

Later in the day, I attended a local cultural dance performance
at the Maramba Cultural Center in Livingstone, where some of
the dancers moved on stilts to the rhythm of a drum. Others wore
masks woven from the local plant material and painted black, with
a white tree-like design at the top and slits for their eyes. Their
long pants were made from pounded bark, painted with circles and
images of birds. One of the dancers wore a striped head mask and a
bodysuit under knee-length white shorts. Another was dressed in
a red and orange costume, noisemakers clanging against his calves
as he danced.

All the dancers moved quickly and smoothly to the rhythm of
the three drums. The drummers, dressed in red and black, moved
their hands rapidly, keeping the music's beat consistent for the
dancers. The local audience swayed to the drums' rhythm and
stuffed money into the performers' pockets, showing their support.

It was hard to choose a mask, but decisively I purchased a
black one with a leather shoulder cover, which now hangs in my
Canadian home. I liked this event because of the genuine joy it
brought to the local audience; it was not for tourists. The Zambian

people loved music and demonstrated their pride in embracing their heritage.

I ended my Zambian trip by taking one last look at the falls, flying above them in a micro-light plane, which was breathtaking.

My view of Victoria Falls was unbelievable from the micro-light airplane.

Chapter 29

Beginning My Climb on Mount Kilimanjaro, Tanzania, Part One

In July 1999, I went on a scuba diving trip in the Seychelles Islands. Afterward I flew to Tanzania. Tanzania is bordered by Uganda and Kenya to the north; Zambia, Malawi, and Mozambique to the south; Rwanda, Burundi, and the Democratic Republic of the Congo are neighbors to the west; and the Comoro Islands and the Indian Ocean lay to the east. The capital is Dodoma, and the national language is Swahili.

As we got closer to our destination our pilot announced, "On your left is Mount Kilimanjaro."

I stared at its majestic snow-covered peak. I was so excited. When I had been working in Riyadh, my friend Marg had climbed to the top. I remembered how proud she had been after her climb, how she had raved about the flora, fauna, and clear air.

I turned to my seatmate and said, "I'm going to climb that mountain next week."

He nodded and returned to his book.

My nose pressed against the window, I was mesmerized, looking at the snow-peaked mountain. I pictured myself reaching the summit. Maybe a plane would fly over while I was there; I'd wave even if no one saw me.

Kilimanjaro is one of the world's tallest walkable mountains, meaning you do not need mountaineering gear or oxygen to summit it, but everyone who reaches the summit works hard. Kilimanjaro rises above the Ngorongoro Crater in Tanzania's massive game-filled Great Rift Valley, and to climb it and reach one of its three summit points—Gilman's Point, Stella Point, and Uhuru Peak—you have to pass through five distinct climate zones beginning with cultivation, then rain forest, next moorland, then onto the alpine desert, and finally, the glacial arctic with snow.

I had set this as my authentic goal; no one pressured me except myself. That was the way I lived my life: challenges, goals, and accomplishments. To me, and only me, not reaching a goal was devastating, embarrassing, and felt like a failure. Instead, now I thrived on inner excitement, planning, execution, and evaluation.

I had trained for this next adventure by running on the beach in the Republic of Seychelles and climbing flights of stairs with my full backpack. I had brought along waterproof broken-in boots and roomy socks. My shirts and pants were made from moisture-wicking fabrics, absorbing the sweat to keep my skin dry. Five layers of clothing were folded into my backpack to protect me from the high-altitude cold.

Day One: Hiking from the Park Headquarters at the Marangu Gate to Mandara Hut

Zaynab, the knowledgeable and helpful general manager of Zara Tours, laid out my options for climbing Mount Kilimanjaro.

"Joyce, the two trekking paths have pros and cons. The first is called the Whiskey Route, where you sleep in tents. The second and easiest route is the Marangu Route, a six-day hike where you sleep in dormitory-type huts instead of tents."

"Okay, Zaynab, let's be smart about this," I said, smiling at her concern for me. "I'll be sixty-four years old in November, so I'll choose the easy one as I'll have a better chance to make it."

"We provide a guide, meals, and porters to carry your belongings. You only carry your day pack and remember to take your tip money with you for the porters as agreed in your signed document," Zaynab said.

"That sounds easy enough, but can I do it?" I asked.

That question was always haunting me, somewhere in the back of my brain. Can I do it? Should I do it? The answer rushed back at me. Yes, you can do this. And do this, you will!

Zaynab gave me a comforting hug and tapped my shoulder. "Think of the little train," she said. "I think I can, I think I can, I think I can."

Our group gathered at the gate for our briefing. Nickolaus, our head guide, said, "When climbing Kilimanjaro, each person must be aware of high-altitude sickness. We call it the barking dog at your neck. The signs and symptoms are difficulty sleeping, dizziness, fatigue, headaches, loss of appetite, nausea or vomiting, rapid pulse, and shortness of breath."

Nickolaus looked around to be sure everyone was listening.

"Listen up. There is no research to indicate who might suffer from this condition—fitness, age, and previous high-altitude experience are irrelevant. Altitude sickness is a life-or-death situation for many trekkers. If you have any symptoms, let me know immediately. Any questions? Hands up if you will tell me immediately."

He looked around. Everyone put up their hand.

Our group, two women from Norway in their twenties, a man from Wales in his forties, a man from Belgium in his late thirties, and I became quiet as this information sunk in.

"Let's register at the park gate now and begin," said Nickolaus.

We started our climb in the rich cultivated forest zone, the five of us, the porters, the assistant guide, and Nickolaus. The forest zone encircles the complete base of the mountain. The damp forest and the altitude create a broad band of clouds. The moss on the trees dripped with moisture from the high humidity and damp-ness. It was misty and a bit spooky.

Together Aagot and Martha, the women from Norway, and I walked along, and at noon, we stopped at a picnic table for lunch. I kicked off my boots and wiggled my toes. I took a deep breath of fresh air as I stretched my feet.

A stream ran along the path. Tall trees with broad trunks grew next to hefty tree ferns. Gray-green streamers of bearded lichen encircled the tree branches, and mosses and ferns encrusted other tree limbs. Moss-like plants carpeted the ground and wild orchids were hanging onto trees and blooming in the ground.

The three of us watched a group of black and white Colobus monkeys play in the trees. Three of them stopped on a branch and stared back at us. It reminded me of the old proverb "See no evil, speak no evil, and hear no evil." I laughed and wondered if I could train the monkeys to hold that pose, the first with his forepaws over his eyes, the second with his forepaws across his mouth, and the third with his forepaws covering his ears.

They moved and my attention turned to two other monkeys, dark gray and black with long slender tails. I pulled out my binocu-lars and shared them with the others, as we watched the monkeys jump from limb to limb.

Our four-and-a-half-hour walk along the forest trail ended when we reached 8,946 feet (2,727 meters) altitude and settled into the Mandara Hut with its peaked roof. I felt powerful. I massaged my feet. My boots had felt comfortable, and I had no red marks anywhere.

One of the other hikers had blistered his foot and didn't have any soft skin plasters to protect the area during tomorrow's hike. I was happy to have several in my first aid kit and gave him one.

We devoured our dinner of rice, meat, bread, and an orange, then shared our stories and headed off to bed.

I snuggled down into my sleeping bag on a lower bunk, secured my eye mask, and popped in my earplugs to drown out the loud snoring working its way through the paper-thin walls from the room next door. Then, fortunately, sleep came quickly.

Day Two: Mandara Hut Trek to Horombo Hut

The next day started with a hearty breakfast and a briefing. I packed up my gear, refilled my water platypus, and tucked my lunch in my day pack. The bright sun was beginning to filter through the forest canopy, making me feel lighter and calm.

As we began our trek, we took a short fifteen-minute detour to clamber up to the rim of Maundi Crater, an inactive volcano.

From there we got our first glimpse of the imposing Mount Kilimanjaro. I stared up in awe and said to Aagot, "The mountain seems so large and far away; I find it hard to believe I will climb to the top. I can feel a kind of powerful magnetic pull from the mountain, but from here it still seems rather invincible."

We returned to the path and quickly had to step aside. A young man, I'm guessing in his thirties, wrapped in blankets and strapped onto a trolley, was being rolled down the bumpy trail by porters. He likely had altitude sickness. I bowed my head as he passed. I swallowed hard and looked away. Despite being a nurse who had worked in numerous settings, many of them dangerous, I felt shaken because next time the person could be me on that stretcher.

As we walked along, we left the tropical trees and the streamers of bearded lichen behind and moved to the flat heath and moorland terrain zone, where the low shrubs replaced the trees. The climate was incredible. The sky was clear except for mist and fog at the forest boundary. As we hit an altitude of 9,843 feet (3,000 meters) the sunshine became intense.

"Hey, Martha, just a reminder it's time to reapply our sunblock," I yelled as I threw my day pack on the ground and pulled out a tube of the thick, white ointment. "It's zinc oxide and protects from both UVA and UVB rays; it's also sweatproof. Do you need some?"

"No thanks, Joyce. I have some. But thanks for the reminder."

"Darn, I must have missed the back of my neck this morning; it feels tender. One of my friends, who climbed Kili a couple of years ago advised me to apply zinc oxide even to the inside edges of my nostrils; she ended up with a terrible sunburn there. Insane, isn't it?" I laughed thinking how I must look, zinc oxide on my lips, under my eyes, around my ears and up my nose.

Thousands of black safari ants marched across our path, following each other as if a sergeant major were leading the line. They were on a mission and determined—nothing got in their way—they went over, under, or across whatever was in their path. Their tenacity knew no bounds. I was counting on my own tenacity to see me to the top of Kilimanjaro.

Birds were more common now than yesterday, and I heard a couple of them chirping. I saw two small brown birds, probably the streaky seedeater from the finch family. One bird was eating fruit and worked hard to break the outer skin of a red berry. The bird sang a sweet melody, ate three berries, then flew away.

We walked until noon and stopped for lunch on a flat rock. The chicken sandwich and apple were both tasty and I drank lots of water. In the afternoon the terrain turned to the heath zone with its large fragrant bushes of giant heather, about 10 feet (3 meters) wide, covered with beautiful yellow everlasting flowers, prickly and stiff. They contrasted sharply with the fresh green cypress bushes and brown soil, also in the heath zone.

Aagot, Martha, and I often stopped to drink water. We were consuming at least four to five liters per day. The only problem was we needed to pee constantly. A large dramatic, blue-black raven with a white-triangle area below its neck and on its back glared accusingly at us as we searched for a secluded bush, which was getting more difficult at higher altitudes. Soon, there were no bushes to hide behind.

We entered the moorland area with its clusters of giant lobelias and senecios, giant succulent rosette plants endemic to this area. Senecios can grow over 6.5 feet (2 meters) tall. Midway up the stem it breaks out in branches, with the dead leaves forming the base and the bright green leaves creating a hat-like formation on top. The stem acts as a reservoir for the water needed for the sizable cabbage-like rosette of leaves. The thick leaf buds protect the plant from subzero temperatures by forming an insulating mass for the delicate central growing shoot.

Mount Kilimanjaro has a species found only on the mountain, the *Senecios Kilimanjaro*. They were clumped together along the path and scattered throughout the area. Many other beautiful flowers grew close to the ground.

Birds were scarcer now, but I caught a glimpse of the alpine chat, a small brown bird with white side feathers in its tail.

The path was often steep and wet, especially in the rain forest. It was slow going at times. We stopped now and then for a short rest and to drink more water.

Finally, after six and a half hours, we came to the Horombo Hut at 12,204 feet (3,720 meters). I was more tired than the previous day but still moving along reasonably well, keeping up with the younger ladies.

After dinner, we chatted with other groups hiking up the mountain; the hut was crowded.

I was in bed early and grabbed the bottom bunk. I slept reasonably well, except for a loud snorer in the bed next to me. I wanted to throw something at him but didn't. My earplugs just didn't do their job that night.

Day Three: Acclimatization at Horombo Hut

Our group stayed at Horombo Hut to acclimatize our bodies to the high altitude. Experienced climbers knew that spending an extra day to allow the body to adjust, taking short climbs to a higher altitude and coming back down, was the best way to prepare for the final climb.

The A-frame huts were made of wood, with stacked bunk beds tightly placed along the walls. Meals were served on a specific schedule, and we arrived on time to get our share of the chicken, potatoes, carrots, and fruit.

Mount Kilimanjaro hovered in the background. Again, it still looked exceptionally high, and I wondered if I would make it to the top. The closer the time came for summiting, the more nervous I felt, but I often thought of the little train: I think I can.

Martha, Aagot, and I walked up the trail to the Saddle from Horombo Hut via the Zebra Rock near the end of the moorland zone. The Zebra Rock at 13,123 feet (4,000 meters) altitude got its name because of its black and white vertical bands, caused by water seeping down the rock face from above and leaving light encrustations on the dark lava rock. We devoured our lunch here and took a little rest. Another alpine chat pecked on the ground nearby and paid no attention to us.

Colossal groundsel plants, which grow in higher altitude zones of mountain groups near the equator in Africa, were all around us. They had sizable flower-like rosettes, and their stems split into two or three branches, almost looking like candelabras. Some plants were as tall as telephone poles. I couldn't keep my eyes off them as they were spectacular. There were so many in this area—an artist's paradise.

Before heading down, we took photos of the three of us with Kilimanjaro in the background. We returned to our Horombo Hut and talked with the others who had walked different trails to acclimatize their bodies. We were glad to see our cooks had a tasty hot dinner of ground meat, vegetables, and cookies ready when we returned. The food disappeared quickly.

After dinner, our group gathered for photos. We would start our final climb tomorrow night. We chatted about how we felt; some of us were unsure, but most thought we would ace the climb. I was especially conscious of my age and feeling a bit pressured after one member of the group complained he would have to wait for the "old Biddy." Fortunately, Nickolaus was going to split us into two smaller groups and the complainer would be in the other group.

Nickolaus encouraged us to get some sleep, so I climbed into my lower bunk, curled up in the fetal position, tossed and turned for an hour before falling into a deep sleep. Thank goodness the heavy snorers were somewhere else.

Chapter 30

Continuing My Climb on Mount Kilimanjaro, Part Two

Day Four: Trek to Kibo Hut before Heading to the Summit

After breakfast, we packed up and walked over flat rocky ground.

"Keep a steady slow pace, Joyce. It will take us two to three hours to get to the Kibo Hut," said Nickolaus.

Aagot, Martha, and I ate our lunch. We were drinking lots of water to keep us hydrated so we needed to pee often, which presented challenges. The flat rocky ground was devoid of shrubs, no place to hide, no privacy. We finally gave up and did our business.

During the trek we arrived at the Highland Desert, transitioning from 13,123 to 16,403 feet (4,000 to 5,000 meters). With temperatures reaching 104°F (40°C) during the day and zero degrees at night, the alpine zone was summer every day and winter every night with intense radiation and high evaporation.

We stopped at what looked like a moonscape, a bleak view of the Saddle, strewn with boulders and lava gravel, between the peaks of Mount Kilimanjaro and Mount Mawenzi. Now we were at 14,416 feet (4,394 meters), and each additional meter meant I was closer to my goal.

Finally, we had climbed to 15,583 feet (4,750 meters) and reached Kibo Hut. I turned to stare at the mountain. I would start to walk up Mount Kilimanjaro tonight. The peak looked awfully far away and the trail zigzagged up the enormously looking steep slope at what seemed to be a 90-degree angle. Again, I felt the collective energy of Aagot and Martha who spurred me on.

I turned to them and said, "I am so grateful for your friendship and support and for being my walking companions."

We were so happy to be together. My mind was joyous. The view was spectacular; it was worth each step I took and every sore muscle I had.

We all took a few pictures and felt the brisk, frigid air swirl as the sun set. We devoured a large serving of meat stew with pasta, vegetables, and bread, which was flavorful and filling.

Another group was at the hut so there were twelve excited climbers in our cabin, which made it hard to rest, let alone sleep. I stretched out in bed from 7:30 p.m. until 11:00 p.m. and tried to sleep without success. The adrenaline was racing throughout my body. Now was time to pack my personal belongings into the bag left at the hut, which I would pick up the following day.

Day Five: Beginning the Night Ascent

We divided our group into two sections, the slow and the fast groups. The sky was dark at 11:30 p.m. when Nickolaus set our slow group's pace. I followed him, then Martha, and Aagot followed me. Martha kept nipping at my heels until I mentioned this to Nickolaus.

"Martha, slow down," said Nickolaus in a commanding tone. "You will burn yourself out walking too fast. I set the pace."

At 12:15 a.m., as Day Four turned into Day Five, we started to climb up a steep slope. Our goal was to reach the top in time to see the sunrise.

"Pole, pole, pole," Nickolaus said over and over, keeping us in a steady rhythm just like the metronome when I practiced piano as a child. In Swahili, the native Tanzania language, *pole* means slowly,

slowly, slowly. Nickolaus was patient and knew how fast we needed to walk to see the sunrise. Other groups passed us, and I wondered why we were slow.

"Most likely, you will see them sitting at the side of the path further up the mountain," said Nickolaus in a hushed tone. Only the three of us heard him.

Martha still pushed to go faster. She moved forward, almost touching me. I felt pressured to move more quickly, but Nickolaus set the pace.

"Nickolaus, let's have Martha walk behind you," I suggested.

"No," he said quietly, "I want you behind me, then I know we are all together. This is extremely important, especially if the full moon slides behind the clouds."

After we seemed to settle into a steady rhythm, I relaxed, moved quickly, took deeper breaths, and savored the moments. Soon enough we passed the climbers, who had quickly moved ahead earlier, resting at the side of the trail. We heard later many of them didn't make it to the top. It reminded me of the children's story about the tortoise and the hare where the tortoise won the race.

We reached a sign pointing to Gilman's Point, still five hours away, and took a photo of the three of us, Martha, Aagot, and me, standing next to it.

"Only five hours, I can do it," I said to Nickolaus, feeling motivated and smiling as I nodded my head and continued the climb.

The full moon lit our way and soon the stars joined in as they began to twinkle. I felt them speak to me: "Joyce, look here, see me." Everywhere I looked, it was as if a fairy had sprinkled glitter on a black background, then tried to attach even more glitter. The twinkling stars were intense and helped to light our way. The only black sky I could see was the size of a postage stamp. I saw millions of stars in the sky, brighter than those I had seen in the desert, and even more brilliant when I looked at them through my binoculars.

"Would you like to use them, Aagot?" I asked as I handed her my binoculars.

"Wow, what an awesome sight. How could you ever explain this to someone who hasn't seen it firsthand? How do I possibly describe this and do it justice?" said Aagot.

"You're right. How could you ever describe all this," I said, throwing my arms wide and circling around. "I'm so glad the three of us are climbing together, and during a full moon. It was a brilliant choice. Climbing Kilimanjaro is a dream come true and making two new friends is definitely an added bonus. Let's try to keep in touch over the coming years."

We rested for ten minutes, then moved on at our same steady pace. Midway through our climb, clouds obscured the moon and the stars. I turned on my battery-powered headlamp to see the rough, irregular path before me. It was pitch black out now, but a bit warmer.

As we reached 16,404 feet (5,000 meters), we walked through an area that had less than 4 inches (100 millimeters) of snow a year. We knew there would be little atmospheric protection from the sun's radiation during the day, so sunscreen at sunrise would be essential.

The climb became more formidable as the night wore on, and after five and a half hours, we celebrated when we reached Gilman's Point, on the Crater Rim. Thankfully we had time to sit and take a few deep breaths as the sky seamlessly slid from night to day. Slowly the sun's rays streaked with lemon yellow and red, peaked over the horizon, followed by the massive explosion of the full sun, so bright I shielded my eyes. The sky turned from red to orange to cerulean blue, clouds appeared everywhere as if by magic.

The sun's rays lit up the Gilman's Point sign.

YOU ARE NOW AT
GILMAN'S POINT, 5,756 METERS (18,885 FEET)
TANZANIA,
WELCOME AND CONGRATULATIONS.

Both groups began taking pictures. I gave a thumbs-up. The sunrise was illuminating the whole mountain and washing it with a pale, yellow hue. I had made it to Gilman's Point, one of the three official summit points on the mountain, but now we were going to push on for another hour or so to our final destination, Uhuru Peak.

Summiting Mount Kilimanjaro, Part Three

To get to Uhuru Peak we had to walk around the rim of the crater. I looked across the crater and saw the peak of the mountain. My gosh, we had climbed above the clouds. The Southern Ice Field was all around us on the high cliffs, with its layers of snow and ice packed tightly together, streaked with dirt. The scene reminded me of the Columbia Ice Fields in Banff National Park in Canada, halfway around the world.

Getting to Gilman's Point was only part of the challenge. The most strenuous part was ahead—walking at an even higher altitude with the wind whipping around us.

We were off, and after seeing the sunrise, I couldn't contain my joy and began to run. This was a critical mistake. The air was even thinner now and running consumed my body's reserve oxygen. I never regained that energy in my body, and I struggled during the last part of the climb, passing Stella Point at 18,885 feet (5,756 meters), and on to Uhuru Peak.

"You're so stupid," I kept repeating in my mind as I took tiny steps toward the peak. My day pack became heavier and heavier.

Others in our group quickly went on ahead as I plodded on. I fell farther and farther behind. My heartbeat was rapid, but steady, and I was still breathless. Nickolaus soon appeared at my side, and we walked together. His steady reassuring "pole, pole, pole" kept my mind and body going. His being there gave me the strength, power, and desire to keep taking one more step forward. I would have turned back if he hadn't been with me. When he left me to find the others from our group, I felt alone and deserted.

When I finally reached Uhuru Peak an hour later, I was utterly exhausted. I waited my turn to have my picture taken at the sign. This added another twenty minutes at high altitude and more time keeping my team waiting. I knew I had to begin descending as soon as possible. My own group had left long ago. I was alone at the top, and I felt it acutely.

My turn for the photo finally came:

CONGRATULATIONS, YOU ARE NOW AT
UHURU PEAK, TANZANIA, 5895 M. AMSL
(ABOVE MEAN SEA LEVEL)
5895 METERS (19,341 FEET)
AFRICA'S HIGHEST POINT
ONE OF THE WORLD'S LARGEST VOLCANOES

I stood there, as proud as a lioness who had just killed her prey. The sun was bright, the sky clear, but the wind was still brisk. I grew an inch or two after my photo. I reminded myself to absorb the spectacular view and remember I had accomplished my goal.

Yay! I did it! I reached my goal! Uhuru Peak, Mount Kilimanjaro.

Finally, I walked down as fast as possible to catch up with the others. I was the last to arrive and received some annoyed looks from several of our group who wanted to return to the Kibo Hut to pick up their supplies before heading on to Horombo Hut for the night. I didn't blame them; I wanted to do the same.

We gathered back at Gilman's Point before heading down. The weather changed quickly. A thick fog was rolling in; I couldn't see anything except what was immediately in front of me.

As we passed William's Point, hailstones the size of small golf balls began bouncing off my body. There was no place to get cover. The hailstones pounded against my head like sledgehammers. I pulled up the hood on my jacket, looking for some padding, but it didn't help much.

The hail obscured the trail, and I slipped on a rock, recovered, and moved on. When the hail finally stopped and began to melt, the smaller pieces of volcanic rock shifted as I descended, making it harder to increase my speed.

It was getting steep, and I sank into the wet slurry of rock and ash, up to my ankles. Fortunately, I had covers on my boots, so the smaller rocks didn't slip inside. But I hadn't tightened my boots enough and the pressure created on my big toes during the descent was beginning to cause a problem as they were continually smashed up against the tips of my boots. Weeks later I was in excruciating pain after both big toenails came off from the damage to the nail beds.

By the time I reached the Kibo Hut late in the morning, plenty of snow had covered the ground. I picked up my belongings I had left there before the summit and continued to the Horombo Hut. This part of the walk was flat, but I was exhausted. It was raining, and my rubber poncho felt like the heavy lead protective shield used in X-ray departments.

Nickolaus was keeping his eye on me, dropping back to walk with me, but long conversations were sparse because of my nonexistent local dialect and lack of energy to talk and walk.

I could barely keep putting one foot in front of the other. I was alone; Martha and Aagot had gone with the rest of our group. My posture slumped, and I shuffled along. I turned and gazed back up at the mountain. It was hard for me to believe I had made it to the top. It looked so hard to get there, and it was. I rubbed my temples looking for magic energy. It never came.

With several more hours to walk, I tried to focus on the area's natural beauty, scanning the sky and listening for chirping birds, but there were none. Where would my energy come from to hike to the hut?

I said out loud, "I think I can, I think I can, I think I can," over and over until I got a rhythm. The story of the little train was my boost of energy and motivation. I struggled alone to keep a steady walking pace.

I staggered into Horombo Hut about 1:30 in the afternoon. I had been on the move since 11:30 the previous night and I had been looking forward to a comfy bed. But when I arrived, I found there were no more beds, none of the younger climbers offered to give me theirs. I was disappointed and realized how much they resented my slowness and how out of place I felt in the group.

So much for chivalry by the younger generation. My bed was going to be a mattress on the floor. Although this was not the first time I'd slept on the floor, a real bed, especially after my climb, would have been heavenly.

Suddenly there was mutiny in the ranks. Tipping the porters was customary and part of the agreement, which we all signed before starting the climb. But now most of the climbers were refusing to pay up. My lips pressed together, my jaw got tight, and my voice rose. One man from Europe was leading the rebellion. Others supported him. I was upset as the porters worked hard for the climbers who used their services.

One male climber was so blatantly rude. I tried to convince him to add money for the tip, but he refused. Everyone had agreed to pay before the trip. He made nasty remarks such as I was too old, too slow, and got preferential treatment as the guide spent too much time with me. We collected what we could from those who didn't refuse to donate. My heart ached. I felt strongly that people who did not contribute should carry their bags, full stop. When we gave the money to the porters, I saw the disappointed looks on their faces.

Day Six: Horombo Hut to Moshi and a Hot Shower

The following day after a sound sleep, I awoke with joy in my heart. I knew today the trek would end and I would soon be on my way to a hot shower at my hotel in Moshi.

The path down to the gate seemed shorter. With a bounce in my step, I watched the Colobus monkeys with their stark white facial fur contrasting against the black fur around their eyes, nose, and mouth. Black fur also covered their bodies except for a white stripe on their back and tail. One mother was carrying a baby whose fur was all white. My eyes followed her as she glided among the trees— her long tail providing needed security as they swung from branch to branch.

"Aagot, there's those monkeys again: See no evil, speak no evil, and hear no evil. Have you ever heard about them in Norway?"

"Yes," Aagot said, "my mother used to tell me that when I was a little girl." We both broke out laughing.

Aagot, Martha, and I had reformed our group. I couldn't take time to stop and enjoy the fauna as much on the way down as I did on the way up, but it was just as beautiful. Again, I felt the pressure to keep up with the group.

Nickolaus walked beside me again on the way down. "Nickolaus, do many climbers refuse to tip the porters after the climb? I have to say I am so sorry and ashamed of the members of our group who refused to contribute even though they were told this was part of the payment in our documents. Does this happen often?"

Nickolaus studied my facial expression and after too long a pause, he said in English, "Unfortunately, it happens too often. The porters get a small wage. They depend on tips to look after their families. Some groups are generous. Others treat the porters terribly in the way they talk to them. I can tell after the first day about how much they will receive in tips."

"I am sorry to hear that, Nickolaus. I feel angry, disappointed, and the porters should be rewarded for their work."

But I cheered up when we arrived back at the gate and I received my certificate:

This is to certify Ms. Joyce Perrin has
successfully climbed Mount Kilimanjaro,
the highest peak in Africa, right to the Summit—
Uhuru Peak—5895 meters.
Date: August 15, 1999, Time 8:30 a.m. Age 63
Certificate number: 4164/99

With one last look at the park gate, I climbed on the bus to go to Moshi, where on arrival I checked into my room and stood under a warm shower for a long time. It felt like a massage on my sore muscles. As the water splashed over me, I thought about the trip, my efforts, and how happy I was to have made it to the top. The sad part was how some of the climbers treated the porters.

Later, we enjoyed a celebration dinner with the group. Zaynab gave us each a T-shirt embossed with "I have climbed Mt Kilimanjaro." The dinner was tasty, the refreshing Kilimanjaro Premium Lager slid down my throat smoothly. We chit-chatted throughout the evening, and I admitted it was one of the most challenging and soul-searching experiences I had encountered so far, yet it also scored off the scale for an exhilarating and rewarding adventure.

The trip was a trifecta of the mind, body, and soul. I was immensely proud of myself as I headed off to sleep in a comfortable bed.

Chapter 32

I Accepted More WHO Assignments and Experienced New Adventures

In September 1999 again I accepted World Health Organization assignments to work with the Ministries of Health of Lebanon, on the Mediterranean Sea, where I also presented a paper at the WHO conference. Again, hugs and greetings from old friends filled my heart.

"Yes, we are implementing your recommendations and your consultation was helpful," said one official. I smiled.

My next WHO assignment took me to the Palestinian territories, Gaza and the West Bank. After I finished that assignment, I toured Israel. I loved floating in the buoyant water of the Dead Sea, then slapping the famous black mud over my body. After rinsing it off, my skin was as smooth as silk.

Soon I was in Jaipur, India, and celebrated Diwali, the Hindu festival of lights. Hindus often painted rangoli, white and reddish-brown designs on the street, as well as on their front doors. These designs wash away during the rainy season. Small oil candles in clay diyas or holders were placed around their houses and on fences, giving the illusion of a warm bright glow of stars in the night sky. The loud bangs of firecrackers filled the air.

A trip to India would not be complete without embracing the grandeur of the Taj Mahal at sunrise. I stood mesmerized as dawn broke and the sun's rays splashed on the magnificence of the inlaid marble building. The detail and the carving workmanship were remarkable.

Wanting to explore more remote areas in India, I signed up for a three-day camel safari. I rode the most uncomfortable camel in this desolate desert area in northern India. Villagers greeted me with friendly smiles. I sipped tea with the men and women, who were wearing traditional clothes typical of this region. Like I did with children worldwide, I connected with the younger villagers with a warm smile, a laugh and a hug and became the center of attention when I passed out Canadian flag pins.

In crowded cities I watched in surprise as trains sped past, men hanging out of the car doors and on the back of the train.

The river Ganges beckoned. I explored the area and watched fully clothed Hindus wading into the holy river. This ritual is believed to promote salvation from the life and death process of life. Several bathers mentioned they believed the waters washed away their sins. Some devotees stayed longer than others, but all appeared relaxed as they waded out of the water.

Before the end of the year, I returned to Saudi Arabia for a WHO assignment with senior officials from the Ministry of Health. Smiles went from ear to ear as I reconnected with my Saudi friends. Of course, I could not resist buying more gold jewelry at the souks.

Christmas was about family, so I headed back to North America where I spent time with my children and their families.

Mom and I took advantage of a five-week vacation in the Bahamas. What a joy to be with her, sitting on the beach and soaking in the warm ocean waters.

People's hearts warmed to Mom as new friends welcomed us. We toured the local rum plant and enjoyed rum and Coke during our stay.

After visiting the Bahamas, I had a fantastic time in my hometown of Edmonton, Alberta, connecting with friends at my Westglen High School reunion. I was glad we had our name tags on with our maiden and married names. Together again, we friends flipped through yearbooks, commenting on the crazy clothes we wore as well as laughing at our hairstyles. As the former head cheerleader, I gathered our old team, and we called out a few of our yells. No routines, though; our bodies were not made for them now.

In 2000, Mom was now ninety-five years old and we headed for Dover, England, to embark on an eighteen-day cruise to the Faroe Islands, Iceland, and crossed the Atlantic to Norway's Spitsbergen and the Norway fjords and returned to Dover.

We rented a wheelchair for the trip so Mom could see the port sites. The staff were always ready to carry her down the steps in her wheelchair so we could depart with others and go on the daytrips.

We experienced the midnight sun. It was strange seeing the long shadows on the boat deck at 1:00 in the morning.

When Mom saw a photo of the young Roald Amundsen in Spitsbergen, Norway, before he became the first man to reach the South Pole, she said, "I met him several times when I was young because he wanted to go to the North Pole, and learned from Canadian Eskimos how to survive in the Arctic, as well as find the Northwest Passage. He needed to get permission to go to the Arctic from my father, who served in the Canadian government. My father invited him to dinner several times, and he was so interesting to talk with."

Although I was never able to confirm the dinner event, the Roald Amundsen expert on the boat concluded it was entirely possible. The timing was right.

On the ship, passengers were challenged to submerge into the cold arctic water in the onboard pool to earn an arctic solar plunge certificate. I was in and out quickly.

After the cruise, Mom returned to Canada and I stayed in England to visit friends and continue my travels.

One of my most profound deeply personal experiences was attending the Oberammergau Passion Play in Germany. The play has been performed every ten years since 1680, honoring a promise made during the Black Plague. It tells the story of the last days of Christ's life. I felt renewed.

My next stop was Scotland, where I visited the Orkneys and identified grave headstones of my ancestors and traced my family heritage from Scotland to the Orkney Islands, and to Canada.

I stayed with friends I had met on my travels. Bob introduced me as his friend Joyce, a nomad, whose job was to explore the world. I had never thought of my life as an explorer, but he was right. I clapped my hands as I threw them in the air.

In Edinburgh, I attended the Royal Edinburgh Military Tattoo, a festival with hundreds of pipers from all parts of the world. It was outstanding and such a remarkable experience to be there. Returning to Canada I visited family and prepared for my assignment in Guyana.

Chapter 33

I Struggled with Challenges Promoting Change in Healthcare Delivery in the Co-operative Republic of Guyana

A dinner conversation in Cairo, Egypt, in 1999 led me to volunteer with the United Nations Development Program (UNDP) in Guyana. During dinner I shared my experiences with Marie, a UNDP manager representative.

"You know, Marie, I volunteered with the International Executive Service Corps (IESC) at a new eye hospital and felt so many rewards helping them set up their hospital systems. My expertise is in quality management and I prepared a manual for the World Health Organization."

"Do you have other plans after this project?" Marie had asked, studying me.

"Yes, I have committed to a couple of other assignments with the WHO, but we have not firmed the dates yet."

"Would you be interested in volunteering with the UNDP?" asked Marie, a hopeful sound to her voice. "We would love to sponsor you to have you share your healthcare expertise, and especially for you to adapt the WHO Total Quality Management Program for the Ministry of Health in Guyana."

And so, that was how I happened to be flying to Georgetown, Guyana, in September 2000, to introduce the WHO Total Quality

Management Program I had developed and would adapt for the Guyanese Health Care System.

Guyana is an English-speaking country located in the north-eastern region of South America on the North Atlantic seaboard. Only the size of the United Kingdom, Guyana is surrounded by Venezuela to the east, Brazil to the south, and Suriname to the west.

As my plane neared Georgetown, the capital, I viewed the emerald green rain forests and winding bands of sapphire rivers below me. The jungle looked dense, magical, and mysterious.

From the plane, I could see the country was wild, rugged, and sparsely populated. As we dropped lower, the ground became dotted with virgin rain forests and blackwater creeks that wound like snakes through the remote areas. Even though the country was in South America, its roots were more Caribbean in nature, culture, and population.

The plane landed on the tarmac, and I stepped into hot and humid weather. I had understood someone would meet me, but no one showed up. I was disappointed, and alarm bells started to ring in my ears. Were they expecting me? I felt lonely and unwelcome.

Fortunately, I connected with two Canadian tourists, Perry and Frank, who were staying at the same hotel, so we shared a taxi. I checked in, slept for a couple of hours, then called the UNDP office number I had been given and arranged for someone to pick me up at 11:00 a.m.

When I met the driver from the Ministry of Health, he was cold and abrupt, but I forced a smile. I tried to have a conversation, but his responses were dismissive, and he remained quiet. The silence was deafening. The tension in the car wrapped around me like a blanket. I became more concerned about this assignment. My efforts to be friendly fell flat. I could not understand the complete contrast between the way the WHO member countries had welcomed me when I started new assignments with how the Ministry of Health greeted their new members.

Then I met the man who was to be my boss at the ministry. He was as cold as a block of ice—aloof, detached, and uninterested sharing any information or any conversation or the details of my assignment. Instead, he shuffled papers, tried to show he was busy, and I was indeed an inconvenience and a nuisance.

I sat silently and waited.

Finally, he abruptly said, "Goodbye."

My mind swirled with his dismissal approach. Should I stay here for three months to work with an organization that did not appear to want me to develop the assigned new program or leave and start my journey in South America?

As I had taught many sessions on change management, I knew change was difficult. This was especially hard if others were fighting to keep the status quo. I had my work cut out for me.

I wondered whether I should call someone at the local UNDP office in Georgetown to find out what was going on.

At the hotel, I reviewed my UNDP volunteer assignment. Over the next three months I was to develop a sustainable quality improvement program, write a manual, educate at least sixty participants from all eight regions in Guyana through Train the Trainer sessions, and set a plan in place to maintain the progress in all parts of the country.

Clearly, I was on my own. There was no team or support staff. The lack of support from this ministry boss was a 180-degree contrast from previous WHO or IESC assignments. I knew the UNDP was funding the program for the benefit of the Guyana Ministry of Health, but which one of the two organizations mandated this program?

Now, I had to make a decision. I would see how the first few weeks went and then decide to stay or leave.

Thank goodness I got to hang out with Perry and Frank that evening. We devoured large, succulent prawns, washed down with a frosty cold beer at the Dublin Bar.

On Saturday, I awakened at 6:00 a.m., grabbed my laptop, and dialed into the relatively slow internet. Later in the day, internet access was minimal, so I opted to wander around the city with Perry and Frank, trying to get my bearings before returning to the hotel to get some shut-eye. We used this time to connect with other expatriates in Guyana who provided some advice on how to succeed in this country.

Still the question of whether to stay or to leave kept churning in my mind, just like the needle of a record stuck in a groove.

I went into the office each day, and at night I lugged my laptop home because it wasn't safe to leave it at work. One day at the market, a lady pulled me aside and said, "Don't carry your computer in a briefcase. It attracts too much attention. Instead, use a plaid plastic bag like the one I use to carry my fresh produce."

I said thank you with a big smile and gave her a hug.

I appreciated her advice and bought a red and blue plaid plastic bag with a zipper to close the top just like hers at a nearby stand.

The United Nations housing manager showed me several apartments. The first was in a grubby part of town, with a dirty cupboard door hanging by one hinge and garbage littering the unkempt lawn. I felt uncomfortable and knew I would never go out in this neighborhood alone at night. She showed me others in different parts of town, but I refused them. I made it clear to her I needed a clean apartment in a safe, comfortable area. This type of accommodation was essential to my mental health. Nothing happened.

Two weeks flew by, and it was time to move from the hotel to a permanent residence.

Fortunately, by taking the situation into my own hands, I found a fantastic apartment and became friends with the owners, Selina, Ovid, and their two boys, Chris and Roger. I credited Selina for supporting me during my stay in Guyana and for my survival. She took me by my hand and helped me understand the culture and how to navigate the systems.

My progress still seemed blocked at work; it took weeks for them to get me a proper desk, and while I waited for one to be delivered, I had to balance my computer on a metal stand, sitting perched on a stool. For a month I couldn't get an official key to the women's washroom in our department.

"Each department has a specific bathroom. Under no circumstances could a member of one department use another department's bathroom." The personnel manager was abundantly clear.

Usually, I could pick up a shared key from one of the offices, but one day the door to the office was locked. I had to desperately borrow a key from someone else. I even offered to pay for a key to the custodian of the key days before but was refused. Finally, after five weeks, I got my own key.

The daily power outages also presented a few challenges. I learned preparing documents for a meeting at the last minute did not work and planning took on a critical focus.

Thankfully I was making slight advancements on the implementation of my program, so I decided to stay.

In the cool of the evening, back at my apartment, relaxing over a beer with Selina and Ovid, I learned about the country's culture and history. Guyana developed much the same way as the other Caribbean islands, through occupation by British, French, and Dutch powers. For example, the Dutch built Georgetown's wide streets and set up a system of canals as the capital was below sea level.

One night Selina handed me a pamphlet outlining the mixture of the ethnic populations in the country. I read aloud from the pamphlet: "East Indian forty-five percent, African thirty-seven percent, mixed race twelve percent, and the rest is Amerindian."

"The Amerindians were native tribes of Guyana, some dating back 7,000 years. The Amerindian festival is in September, and I recommend you attend one weekend," Selina said.

"Oh definitely, it's an event I will visit. Thanks for the suggestion."

I cooked my own meals and enjoyed buying a wide array of fresh fruits and vegetables at the long-standing daily Bourda Market. The glossy bright green avocados, sun-colored mangos, papayas, passion fruit, pineapples, and the deep purple mangosteens with their sweet-sour flavor and juicy white pulp graced my table weekly.

Communication with my boss was still complicated; however, I was beginning to make progress. By this time, he realized I was not going to go away.

One weekend in September, I had a relaxing time at the Timberland Resort on the other side of the Demerara River. The resort was rustic, without electricity. After three weeks of getting acclimated to the humidity, the culture, and how work gets done in Guyana, I needed a rest. My body and mind were tired. I didn't realize how exhausted and stressed I was until I slept for hours in a hammock. It was a perfect time to be in the wild.

Tom, our guide, took guests on morning walks in the rain forest, where he shared his expertise, talking about the plants, animals, and birds as his sharp eyes scanned the foliage for something unique to show us. As a botanist, he identified mushrooms, fungi, and many different plants. We saw black spider monkeys with their small heads, long gangly limbs, and pink faces. The monkeys teased us by dropping fruits and nuts and seemed to want to connect with us as we watched. We also heard the red howler monkeys before we saw them. They were large and easy to spot with their red-orange-brown fur and beards. The locals called them baboons.

I floated in the Blackwater Creek and drifted along with the warm river current. The water soothed my muscles. At dinner, we tried eating pica or labba, called the royal rodent, because it was served to Queen Elizabeth II in 1985 in Belize. This wild forest animal looks like a small pig except it doesn't have a snout. The pinkish meat was smoked and tasted much like ham. Plantains, tomatoes, and fresh pineapple completed the tasty meal.

Back at work on Monday, I charted my work progress. As I continued to build relationships with the ministry staff, I grasped how their systems worked. Soon I noticed a difference in people's responses when I asked for help. I was ecstatic when the staff willingly stepped up to give me a hand. Eventually, we became a productive team. The challenge was to write a program, which addressed the needs and capabilities of the staff and the healthcare system.

To do this, I gathered information by visiting the hospitals and health centers. After discussing the issues with ministry officials, I soon had written, tested, and edited all the needed documents.

But I was beginning to panic again. The most troubling issue was getting approval to print enough copies for sixty people to start the Train the Trainer workshop in October. It was now the end of September, and the launch of the program was fast approaching. Trying to get the printing cost approved took every ounce of my well-honed skills and negotiating techniques, but I was unsuccessful.

This frustration was the straw about to break the camel's back. I mentioned to a secretary I was taking this critical issue up the organizational ladder to plead my case. The next day I heard the printer would have the documents ready for the opening session. I was ecstatic and ready for a relaxing weekend.

Chapter 34

How I Succeeded Building Trust with Management and Staff in Guyana, Then an All-Night Drive in a Truck Called Thunderstorm

Just like Selina had said, September was Guyana's Amerindian festival month, and local communities were celebrating their native heritage. On the last Saturday in September, I went to St. Cuthbert's Mission to attend their event, traveling in a bus along a paved road. Once the pavement ended, I and all the other passengers clambered aboard a four-wheel-drive truck.

Luckily, I secured a seat in the cab, along with the driver and an Amerindian man named Steve Cannon. Steve was the captain of a fishing boat and was returning to the mission to celebrate the festival with his family. With a warm grin and a twinkle in his eyes, he invited me to join him and his family for their celebrations. I was thrilled. I feel blessed and grateful when people welcome me with open arms.

The back of the truck was filled with cargo, most importantly, Steve's cases of beer. As many people as humanly possible climbed in the back to get a ride. For forty-five minutes the driver steered his truck through the sand and deep grooves in the road. I was concerned for the people sitting and standing in the back of the truck, but Steve assured me the Guyanese rode this way all the time.

Steve's family welcomed me with warm hugs, as if I was a long-lost relative. The air felt electrified with excitement. His family had hunted, killed, and cooked the pica but this time the meat had not been smoked, so it tasted more like beef rather than ham.

Also being served were tacoma worms sautéed in a tasty pepper-pot sauce. This dish had been prepared as a special treat for the celebration. Seven weeks before the event the men cut a palm tree and left it to rot. During the sixth week, they cut open the tree and removed the worms, which had been feasting on the tree's insides. As I ate the first one, I closed my eyes and gulped it down. It was tasty, so I popped more into my mouth. I liked the crunchy feeling of the outside of the worm; the inside had a mild garlicky taste, and the hot spicy sauce gave it a kick.

The women had made fresh cassava bread, cooking the pulp from the plant over a fire in a large round metal pan and then making the dough by mixing the cooked plant with a bit of water.

We topped off the meal with parakari or kari, a fermented bile-colored drink made from the cassava root. The smoky, bitter liquid slipped down my dry throat; my head started to buzz. Darn, no more for me I thought, I must travel home tonight.

After the meal I headed off to attend the festival. The women of the family pulled me along, their arms around my shoulders. I felt I was a member of this family, not a stranger from another country nor someone they met a few hours ago.

The Minister of Culture gave an inspiring speech, asking the community to donate money so they could continue to purchase authentic Amerindian drums for the local museum. He promoted the free violin lessons given to boys to encourage them to play the fiddle. Unfortunately, men had switched to playing the electric guitar instead and the traditional violin playing was being lost. To maintain the intricate basket weaving skills, he asked the women to teach their daughters to support this tradition.

Floodlights supplemented car headlights and the air was filled with music as dancing continued into the night. The time to leave came too soon. I said goodbye, with warm hugs for my new Guyanese friends. I wished I had decided to stay overnight to celebrate the following day as well.

The first Monday in October was the launch of my quality training program for the Guyana Ministry of Health. There was all the pomp and ceremony one could ever want at the official opening ceremonies; the Minister of Health, the director of Guyana's National Board of Standards, the hospital board chairman, and the chief medical officer of the Ministry of Health all attended.

After the opening ceremonies, I went to work. Ice-breaking activities set the tone as the first group of participants to take the Train the Trainer workshop worked diligently in small groups to practice the new skills I was teaching them. I was impressed by how quickly they grasped the new concepts. I was surprised and humbled when the participants presented me with a pair of hand-crafted Guyanese gold earrings at the end of the training sessions. The gift would have taken a big bite out of their wages.

They wrote and sang a song for me. I was sure they had done this on their own with no help from my boss. I was overwhelmed by their show of appreciation. As I hugged each person in thanks, I was filled with gratitude and happiness. Their responses made up for all my frustrations preparing the program. The stress was devastating at times. The workshop's positive outcome ensured a high acceptance of the program in the rest of the country as I got ready to hold more Train the Trainer workshops. The positive

workshop comments traveled fast, so I had no lack of participants in other areas.

That weekend, I celebrated with a trip to Kaieteur Falls, one of
the world's largest and most powerful single-drop waterfalls.

The plane landed on an airstrip at the top of the falls. The green
of the jungle contrasted sharply with the fast-moving river, which
cascaded over the bluff. The view took my breath away as I walked
along the bluff with a UNDP volunteer from Pakistan named Grace.
We compared the Kaieteur Falls, with its 822-foot (250-meter)
drop, to Canada's Niagara Falls, which is five times smaller. It was
Grace's dream to come to Canada, but sadly Canada's immigration
regulations were presenting challenges.

The morning at Kaieteur quickly passed. At noon, I flew to the
beautiful Orinduik Falls, where I changed into my bathing suit and
stood under the water, escaping from the hot and humid air and
being refreshed by the cold shower. I enjoyed a relaxing afternoon
in this most idyllic and picturesque setting.

One weekend, my Canadian expat friend Jane and I flew to
Karanambu Lodge (Ranch) in the remote Rupununi area in south-
western Guyana. The lodge was a paradise for nature lovers, and
the owner, Diane McTurk, had grown up there and now managed
it herself, raising cattle. But unfortunately, she could not make ends
meet just by raising cattle, so she turned to the tourism business,
promoting the preservation of wildlife and the savanna.

Diane was sixty-five years old, five feet ten inches tall, with gray-
ing blonde hair, well-tanned skin, and a thin frame. She had a regal
way about her and just oozed how to enjoy life. We ate, drank,
and laughed our way through the weekend as she spoke her mind
about politics, culture, and her farm and animals. Knowledge
flowed with every word she spoke. I absorbed it like a sponge.

Diane took us on a boat trip on the Rapununi River to see the giant black river otters, an endangered species. They are carnivores and a member of the weasel family. Diane stopped the boat and we climbed onto a bank as she called out to them by name. Several surfaced and came ashore to get the fish she was offering. They seemed to enjoy playing with Diane as she rubbed their stomachs and backs. We sat quietly and watched at a distance.

One night, Diane, Jane, and I took a canoe down the river to see the black caimans, the largest predator in the Amazon basin. They are like crocodiles; their eyes turn red when the beam from a flashlight shines on them. Two bright red eyes followed us as we paddled along. I was scared as I visualized a large mouth opening behind us.

I was distracted when a few foot-long leatherjack piranhas flung themselves into our boat. I flinched as one hit my knee, but I followed Diane's example, picking it up by the tail just long enough to throw it into the water. The caiman's red eyes disappeared immediately.

Instead of returning to Georgetown by plane, Jane and I took a Bedford truck, which the owner had named Thunderstorm. Our ride felt like a bucking bronco to me. The twenty-four-hour journey was one of the most dangerous trips I've ever taken. The road was unpredictable. Deep furrows ran through the dirt road, and it took the driver's assistant hours to remove and adjust the drive shaft each time we hit a rock or to allow the 4x4 wheels to make progress.

More disturbing was the assistant didn't help with the driving and the driver appeared to doze off to sleep from time to time. Sitting beside him in the cab, I had visions of the truck rolling down a cliff. During the night I kept talking to him to keep him alert; it became my full-time occupation. I was relieved to be back at my apartment at 5:30 a.m. I slept the rest of the morning before going to work in the late afternoon.

After the success of the first Train the Trainer workshop, arrangements for me to present my programs in other parts of the country soon became a reality. I flew to Mahdia, a remote area in the interior of Guyana, which turned out to be one of my most thought-provoking visits.

Mahdia was in the center of a dense jungle with an unbearably hot and humid climate. The gold mining town had a high AIDS population. Electric power was limited, only available from 6:00 a.m. to midnight, so radio contact was their only form of communication. If people needed medical assistance beyond rudimentary treatment, they would airlift them to Georgetown for care.

The only hospital had one physician, George, a divorced thirty-four-year-old Cuban man. The government had hired him through the Cuban embassy because no Guyanese physicians wanted to live here. George was gentle with delicate features, a ready smile, and embraced his life in this isolated, malaria-infested area. This was where I conducted my last workshop. I was glad to come because the hospital staff in this remote region were often left out of most in-service education. Their gratitude filled my heart.

I had mixed feelings as I began to wind down my volunteer assignment. The people who had become friends, especially Selena and Jane, had made my stay a happy one. But this was one of the most challenging assignments I had ever undertaken professionally.

I had traveled across Guyana, training fifty-eight members of the healthcare staff in quality improvement processes. These new Train the Trainers teams were remarkable and immediately began using the new tools to deliver more effective care. At the end of the day the teams were my reward, and I left Guyana with a feeling of deep satisfaction. I had helped one person at a time and then they had helped others.

Chapter 35

With Joy in My Heart: I Explored South America Using Basic Spanish

After finishing my contract in Guyana, I traveled with Selena's brother to Suriname, a country east of Guyana, on the Atlantic coast. Here I wandered along the docks, examining shark fins and other fish drying on wire tables, as the sellers got ready to ship them to Hong Kong. It was big business for the country. Cashews, my favorite nut, grew here. Family entrepreneurs sold small bags of the tasty nuts in the market.

Most houses were built with wood, with thatched roofs, and were raised off the ground. I loved hearing the chirps and songs of various colorful birds, often in cages by the front doors, welcoming visitors to people's homes.

After a brief visit to Guyana to say goodbye to Selena and her family, I headed to Caracas, Venezuela, to begin exploring every country in the South American continent as a solo traveler.

My first goal was to take a Spanish immersion class. Trying to be fluent in Arabic had taught me that learning languages was not easy, and Spanish was no exception. I immersed myself in the country by living with a family for a week as part of my class. Sleeping alone in the daughter's room, surrounded by Barbie dolls, brought back memories. I loved talking with the family in Spanish and learned more from them than in my class. After the course I felt more confident, and I was ready to hit the road.

Soon I traveled to Mérida in the Yucatan Peninsula between Mexico and Central America, a city known for my favorite food, ice cream. The Heladeria Coromoto ice cream parlor was in the *Guinness World Records* book for having the most ice cream flavors, 760 were listed on its sign; however, the parlor rotated flavors depending on the time of year. Sixty flavors were available, such as cornflakes, basil, beer, wine, avocado, salmon, and hamburger. I tasted several unique flavors and selected garlic. It was strange and my taste buds were totally confused. This cannot be ice cream. Not my favorite, but I could not let it go to waste, so I finished it.

I spent Christmas and New Year's in Mérida with new friends Carmen, her husband, and their two children who welcomed me to join them at their posada (home) as a homestay for the festive celebrations. We shared life stories, and I made lemon squares with fresh lemons and lemon zest. Sharing food was always a bonding event. Christmas meant a lot to me. I missed my family. These children reminded me of my grandchildren with their happy smiles. To celebrate the new year, we made an adult-sized scarecrow and lit it on fire to say goodbye to the old year. Then we made a younger scarecrow to welcome in the new year.

Next, I headed to Argentina because I wanted to attempt to summit Mount Aconcagua in the Andes. At 22,838 feet (6,961 meters) Aconcagua is one of the Seven Summits on the seven continents.

When I bought my gear for the twenty-one-day trip, I met Gabriela Furlotti, a knowledgeable clerk at a local store in Mendoza. Gabriela invited me to her grandmother's spacious home and large yard to have dinner with eleven family members. I appreciated their warm welcome being included with their family group. We devoured delicious beef roasted on the barbeque and outstanding wine produced by the famous Furlotti family winery, pioneers of Mendoza's now huge wine industry.

Gabriela and I enjoyed a swim in their spacious pool, and Gabriela painted my toenails in different colors. What fun. I felt young and ready with energy for the climb.

Our climbing group met in Mendoza and checked our supplies before starting our trek. Mount Aconcagua can be harsh, cold, and windy. The path was challenging, littered with stones and steep, rugged parts. Sometimes we had to cross rivers, and it was often hard to find a dry track. Hydration was essential. Our guide made sure we drank at least four to five liters of water a day.

Each day we walked and built our stamina.

By day eleven, our group of four male climbers in their forties and me at sixty-four had reached Nido de Condores, the Condors' Nest, at 17,552 feet (5,350 meters). I was pleased I made it this far. This was day twelve, my decision day. I had to decide if I wanted to continue or return to base camp. I listened to my body, and it told me it had had enough. Although sad, I respected its message.

Experiencing the outdoors, the spectacular views of the Andes from different altitudes, and allowing myself to try was a successful experience, but honestly, I was sad and disappointed. My descent was easy, and I waited for the only one in our group to make the summit, and then we headed back to Mendoza.

Happily, I reconnected with Gabriela in Mendoza, hugged goodbye, and headed to Santiago, Chile, by bus.

From Santiago I flew to Isla Robinson Crusoe, an island which is part of the Chilean Juan Fernandez archipelago. The island's population is about 700 people but visited by another 1,500 people each year. The island's terrain was brown, rugged, and flat. The cliffs were rocky and breathtaking. Knife-shaped peaks surrounded spectacular views of Cumberland Bay. I treasured the serenity of the land and found remote areas to hike, seemingly untouched by humanity. Birds nested on the cliffs; seals played along the coast.

One day, I donned a wet suit and swam with seals. Their big brown eyes seemed to say "hello." They were curious and came close, rubbing against my legs for a split second, then quickly made a 90-degree turn before disappearing. On another day, a group of us went with a guide who was spearfishing. The guide cooked the catch for our lunch, truly delicious fresh fish.

After flying back to Santiago, I caught a bus heading south along the Chilean coast. My goal was to reach Ushuaia, the capital of Tierra del Fuego, to catch a cruise to Antarctica.

Along the way I climbed to the top of a volcano. Steam and gaseous clouds rose up from the boiling lava, stinging my eyes and throat. I could not see any flames, but the gases were overwhelming. Crampons on the bottom of my shoes had helped me to climb up the icy slope. Coming down I took the fastest option and slid down the snow-covered trail, sitting on a piece of cardboard—laughing and smiling to the bottom.

Moving on, I saw a sign, White Water Rafting. I was first in line. Our team rafted on the Trancura River in Pucon, Chile. We had fun, dumped a few times, and soaked afterward in the thermal springs.

After a rest, we ran a smaller set of rapids hanging onto hydro-speed flutter boards. At one point, I was too close to a whirlpool. I hung onto my board and kicked with all my might to avoid being dragged into the swirl barely maneuvering my way around the rocks. When I finished and looked back, I realized how close I came to be lost forever. I felt my heart race.

Finally, I reached my destination Ushuaia, Argentina, and embarked on a cruise to Antarctica.

Chapter 36

Three Cheers I Made It: Reaching My Seventh Continent, Going to Extremes in Antarctica

Antarctica is the coldest, remotest, and wildest continent on Earth. Nearly all of its 14 million square kilometers are covered by ice all year, except for a small area at the coast in the summer.

It was February 2001. The wind blew relentlessly and the spray from the surf stung my face as our Zodiac boat took us from our ship to the Rosita Harbor to see young fur seals.

I was on a twenty-one-day cruise visiting the Arctic Peninsula, the Falkland Islands, and South Georgia. Our ship, the MV *Professor Multanovsky*, was a small Russian research vessel. It carried thirty-two passengers who ranged in age from twenty-three to over seventy. They came from Austria, Australia, Canada, New Zealand, the United Kingdom, and the United States. The captain and the Russian crew were easy to talk with, answered questions, and that passengers had access to the ship's bridge any time was a luxury and bonus. The atmosphere onboard the ship among passengers and staff was informal and friendly.

I had spent the first few days watching the waves from the decks, spotting the wildlife: albatrosses, penguins, whales, and seals. The albatrosses were giant. The length of their long, narrow wings was unimaginable: 9.8 feet to 14.7 feet (3 to 4.5 meters). They loved to glide behind the ship on its air currents.

Now the water in the harbor roiled with over 1,000 seals; they reminded me of salmon jumping up the rivers in British Columbia to lay their eggs. Fifty or so seals followed the Zodiac—their pale undersides showing when they rolled on their backs. Penguins also appeared and then quickly disappeared—their sleek bodies cutting through the water as they dove below.

On another Zodiac excursion we saw five killer whales or orcas breaking the surface in unison as if to salute us. They did this several times, emerging then diving. What a sight. Our Zodiac boat was about 164 feet (50 meters) away. I felt as if each one was looking at me straight in my eye. Finally, they gave me one last look, almost a nod, or a salute before they vanished.

Today was the day I had dreamed about for many years. Giving myself a tiny pinch, the ship docked at the Almirante Brown's Station, an Argentine research station on the coast and I disembarked. I was standing on my seventh continent, Antarctica. Now, I had visited all the world's continents. I stood for a moment, took a deep breath, threw my hands in the air in excitement, and let out a cheer, "I did it."

Later, we visited the Petzval Glacier, a magnificent river of ice, which extended into the mountain valley as far as the eye could see, making the Columbia Icefields in Canada seem insignificant.

Out in the cove two humpback whales caught my attention, noisily blowing air as they surfaced. They were massive. Humpbacks can grow to an average length of 49 feet (15 meters) and weigh 661,386 to 881,849 pounds (300,000 to 400,000 kilograms).

As we recounted the day's adventures at dinner, I celebrated my seven-continent accomplishment with my table mates and a bottle of champagne.

The days passed and soon we headed north. We landed at Port Lockroy on Goudier Island. Norwegian whalers had anchored here from 1911 to 1931. It had been the site of a British wartime mission in the 1940s before becoming a British scientific station which had been relocated in the early 1960s. In the mid-1990s a museum opened for visitors.

First, I heard the deafening noise, then scanned the area to see around 3,000 Gentoo penguin pairs gathered to breed at Port Lockroy. They return annually during the Antarctic summer between October and March.

Unfortunately, two natural predators of penguins, the skua birds and leopard seals, were also here. The skua bird is a predatory gull-like bird that steals the penguins' eggs. As I watched, the birds worked in pairs; one skua distracted the parent sitting on the nest while the other took the egg. It was true teamwork and devastating.

My eyes moved to the water as the leopard seal seized a penguin and threw it around until it died. Then the seal skinned the penguin by tossing the carcass from side to side. When the skin sloughed off, the seal would devour the penguin's insides.

I gasped. I watched both these events unfold and understood the animal food chain was relentless yet necessary.

Our ship cruised to South Georgia Island, showing off its magnificent landscapes of mountain glaciers and grassy meadows. The island had housed whaling and sealing stations in the early years, which were left to rust and deteriorate in the cold arctic weather.

Wildlife roamed everywhere including King and Macaroni penguins, and I saw several of the twenty-five species of breeding birds. The Norwegian whalers had introduced reindeer to South Georgia as a food source. They still roamed over part of the island.

Our next stop was the capital of the Falkland Islands, Stanley, where I visited their museum. I found a treasure, an 1877 ink bottle retrieved from an old sailing ship. The old bottles still contained ink and the labels were in pristine condition. I bought one for my son who loved treasures from the sea and was a commercial scuba diver.

At Volunteer Point near Stanley, we saw another large colony of King and Magellanic penguins.

The history, flora, and fauna of Antarctica had me in its grip, and as I disembarked at the end of the cruise, then and there, I promised myself to return to explore the Ross Sea on the continent's south coast.

It would be three years before I would return.

Chapter 37

Discovering the Wonders of the Ross Sea in Antarctica, My Favorite Place

In the three years since first cruising around the Antarctic peninsula, I traveled back to South America, exploring all the places I had missed on earlier trips. These adventures took me to Easter Island, La Paz in Bolivia, the Galapagos, and a trek along the Andean Mountains in Bolivia and Peru. Those were happy times exploring unique countries and testing my stamina on strenuous hikes.

In June 2003, I had returned to Canada to visit my mom and was distressed to find her weak. Almost ninety-eight, she was ready to say goodbye. Her sight had failed her, and her lifelong friends had died years ago. I was so grateful to hold her hand, give her hugs, and just be with her. During her failing days we talked a lot about our happy memories, our trips, and adventures. We laughed a lot together, but I cried a lot, alone.

My brother, sister, and I were with her when she died. The celebration of her life was attended by all the generations from our family. She touched many lives and hearts. In her honor, I authored her life story in the *Globe and Mail* Lives Lived section.

In late December 2003, I boarded the *Kapitan Khlebnikov*, a Russian icebreaker with two helicopters for a twenty-four-day expedition cruise. I was heading back to Antarctica and was ecstatic about the highlights we would be exploring: the Ross Ice Shelf, the Dry Valleys, McMurdo Station, Shackleton's and Scott's huts, Macquarie Island, and a helicopter ride around Mount Erebus. The trip would end in Hobart, Tasmania. What a way to welcome in the new year, 2004.

After the mandatory lifeboat drill, I headed to the bridge and met our Russian captain. He was friendly and welcomed us at any time. Using my binoculars I spotted albatrosses, petrels, sooty shearwater birds, and my first New Zealand fur seal as we headed out to sea.

The next day, we steamed toward Antarctica, but disembarked for a six-hour walking tour around Enderby Island, called the Galapagos of the Southern Ocean. All passengers had vacuumed our clothes and our backpacks so we wouldn't bring any unwanted pollen or bacteria onto the island. This is the way New Zealand kept their islands from becoming contaminated. Yellow-eyed penguins waddled along the shore, and large pieces of southern bull kelp washed up on the beach.

Two male Hooker sea lions staged a fight on the beach, exposing their sharp and dangerous teeth. It was mating season and males were asserting their dominance. The males can weigh between 701 and 903 pounds (318 to 410 kilograms) and grow to 6.5 feet to 10.5 feet (1.98 to 3.25 meters) in length. The younger male sea lions tried hard to show who was boss, but the older and larger males stood their ground.

Trudi, the ship's artist in residence, gave sketching tips to those who wanted to draw. I used black ink pens to draw sketches to capture what I was seeing at many different locations during our trip.

We ate lunch in what the locals called the Enchanted Forest. Short dead trees were all around us, rising out of lush green ground cover. The trunks and branches of the trees were twisted and misshapen. The branches looked like fingers reaching to the sky. It was foreboding, yet serene at the same time.

The next day we landed on Campbell Island. The wind was fierce. We climbed to the top of a hill hoping for an expansive view, but the weather didn't cooperate, so we returned to the ship. A relaxing nap was in order after fresh air and exercise.

It was New Year's Eve and we rang in 2004 with a scrumptious meal and champagne at midnight. In the early morning we crossed the polar front, the biological boundary of Antarctica waters. Now, I was in the land of the midnight sun.

On New Year's Day I celebrated stepping foot onto the Antarctic Continent for the second time in my life when we disembarked at Cape Adare. The sea had calmed to a perfect glassy surface and reflected the dramatic iceberg cliffs that rose to 4,921 feet (1,499 meters) before me. A pod of about twenty orcas swam past. It was breathtaking and I felt as if they were welcoming me to their home.

Ridley Beach was a seething mass of Adelie penguins. The noise was deafening as each bird tried to find a place to land. The sight was astonishing. How did the pairs find each other in this crowd? Research showed they find their partner acoustically. We returned to the ship around midnight, although the sun still shone brightly.

The next afternoon we boarded Zodiacs and headed to Cape Washington to see Emperor penguins nesting on the sea ice. The regal Emperor penguins are my favorite species. I could not get enough of them. We quietly shuffled along the snow-covered ice for a closer look. Three thousand tall and stately penguins, adults and chicks, were all around us. The chicks looked like fluffy gray balls. They had hatched from their eggs and were now in creches being guarded by small groups of adults while other adults were in the sea feeding. When the chicks were strong enough, they would make the long walk to the water to begin their own adult lives.

I sat with Emperor penguins, "Come a little closer, my dear."

I wanted to stay out as long as possible and was one of the last passengers to board the ship.

In the morning a pod of orcas swam along the edge of the ice, a positive omen, as passengers waited to ride in the helicopter to the McMurdo Dry Valleys. For me, viewing the mummified seals was the highlight of this trip and the reason I chose a ship with helicopters. The only way to view these mummified seals was to fly to this area.

Our aircraft landed not far from the Canada Glacier, a glacial desert, discovered and named in the early 1900s during the Terra Nova Expedition led by Robert Scott. Seeing the bodies of crabeater seals, mummified and preserved by the 200-mile-an-hour (322-kilometer-an-hour) katabatic winds was a highlight of this trip. Researchers believed for thousands of years young crabeater seals moved inland, confused and thinking they were heading out to sea but instead traveling for up to forty miles on sharp stones.

When they eventually died, the winds dried and preserved them for us to see. I was amazed at their pristine condition. I had spent many hours studying Egyptian mummies in the Cairo Museum. These specimens were just as interesting.

After our excursion the staff served our lunch on the boat deck. We dined with sea birds flying around the hull of the boat as their voices pierced the stillness. It was a warm day and the Antarctic sun was intense. I took off my jacket, but sunglasses were a must.

Later, we stopped at Cape Evans to visit Scott's hut. I had researched Scott's life. The hut was filled with supplies, cans, bottles, scales, and buckets, left as if to expect the original party to return at any moment. Scott had made this his last stop before his momentous journey to the South Pole. A wooden cross propped up by stones reminded everyone of his ill-fated trek.

During a visit to Scott's cabin, I sketched this. Imagine if these walls were able to tell their stories.

Our adventures continued every day with something new. I took a helicopter ride to the top of Mount Erebus, 12,500 feet (3,810 meters), the only active volcano in Antarctica.

On another day the captain positioned the boat for those who wanted to take a swim in the icy Antarctic waters. Having done the polar plunge on my previous trip, I passed on this opportunity. Once was enough. But I heartily cheered on the brave souls who jumped in, a rope tied around their waist in case of an emergency. After submerging and returning to the boat, each brave jumper guzzled a shot of vodka, then ran to get into dry clothing as we applauded. Two Adelie penguins seemed to cheer our jumpers on as they waddled along, moving their flippers.

The next evening our boat cruised past the massive iceberg, B15-K, one of the icebergs that had calved from the first B-15 iceberg, which had itself broken off from the Ross Ice Shelf in 2000. B-15 was the largest iceberg ever recorded, 170 miles (273 kilometers) long and 25 miles (40 kilometers) wide, and 4,250 square miles or (11,007 square kilometers), nearly the size of Connecticut.

We could see the B15-K iceberg while we dined. After our meal, we grabbed our warm jackets, boots, and mittens and boarded the helicopter to land on top of the B15-K iceberg. Ice chips floated in our glasses of champagne served as the midnight sun shone on a bar made from blocks of the iceberg's ice.

I wandered around the top of the iceberg, sipping on my beverage and swallowing the billion-year-old water as the ice melted. The sheer incredibleness of the moment was not lost on me. The whole scene was fantastic. I raised my glass in a silent toast to all the explorers of the world.

The next day we stopped at Terra Nova Bay to visit the Italian research station where staff treated us to a tour, including delicious wine and Italian chocolates. During the winter season they maintained the station remotely through the internet.

We reboarded after our tour, and I watched from the bridge as our captain maneuvered the ship's massive bow to crush the pack ice surrounding the research station port, producing a pathway for the boats to dock. The staff were grateful and cheered us as we departed, sounding our horn and heading toward open water.

We headed to the inhospitable Balleny Islands, and true to its reputation, the weather prevented us from landing. Fortunately, we were able to tour in the Zodiacs on the calm side of the islands to see some Chinstrap penguins and Adelie penguin colonies perched along the ridge.

We all like to eat well and the meals on board the ship were delicious—traditional Russian dishes with a variety of flavors taken from other countries such as those in Europe, Asia, and the Middle East.

One night the chef prepared an authentic six-course Russian dinner. The bartender served shots of Russian vodka that was smooth with a tinge of a vanilla aftertaste.

The female servers were dressed in white blouses; elaborate floral designs were cross-stitched onto the long sleeves. Bright red flowers were also embroidered on their skirts and unique Russian hats were on their heads. Each one wore a different national dress depicting their specific part of the country.

The meal started with an appetizer of chilled Russian sevruga malossol caviar and smoked pike, served on a blini, and smetana with all the classical trimmings. It was sublime. Next up was pelmeni, traditional Russian dumplings, filled with minced meat and garlic. We made room for the next course by meandering over to the salad buffet to select fresh, crisp lettuce and other salad ingredients.

The staff served our soup, borshch Moskovsky, with considerable fanfare. Marinated cabbage, carrots, tomatoes, onions, bell peppers, and beetroot filled the bowl. It was tasty, but I missed the familiar sour cream on top.

As a palate cleanser, the staff served a yabloko (apple) sherbet, refined with vodka. I certainly enjoyed this treat.

We were then offered a choice of beef or salmon. I chose Russian kuli bijak, grilled salmon steak with beetroot and glazed potato balls, and lime sour cream. The salmon melted in my mouth. It was grilled perfectly, and the lime sour cream added a tangy flavor.

We finished with our dessert: bezes and morozhenoe, meringue cookies, and white Russian ice cream.

The staff sang Russian songs as many of us gathered in the bar to finish off a truly wonderful evening.

Later that night, we cruised toward Macquarie Island. Unfortunately, the weather gods were not with us as we heaved and fought our way through twenty-three-foot waves. Fortunately, my stomach handled the ship's pitch and rolls with ease.

Calm returned and the next day we landed on the black sand beach of Macquarie Island. We noted the King penguins were carefully guarding their young. Some penguins were in the process of their first-year molt, having shed half their brown feathers before growing the beautiful orange, black, and gray adult plumage.

The next couple of sea days were windy as we headed to our final destination, Tasmania. I took advantage of the time to catch up on my sleep and record more stories in my diary. I had tried to talk to everyone on the ship, sharing information, and learning more about their lifestyle.

Many memories crowded my mind—the stark whiteness of snow-covered mountains, the antics of playful seals, strutting penguins, and the effortless gliding of orcas. I felt sad as I said goodbye to my new friends, but I would take my memories with me.

Chapter 38

Investigating Down Under, the Unique Australian Continent

Hobart, the capital of the Australian island state of Tasmania, felt like a small town when I disembarked from the Antarctic cruise. In my sixty-eighth year I spent six months exploring the wonderful continent of Australia, focusing on this island and its unique topography. Throughout my travels friendly people chatted with me as I told them about Canada. They shared Australian stories, and their Aussie accent made me smile.

I joined a five-day Tasmanian tour, the day after my arrival, and the guide drove us 130 miles (209 kilometers) to climb Cradle Mountain. When we arrived, I saw tall 300- to 400-year-old trees. Tree huggers had pitched a tent in the treetops in an attempt to stop loggers from cutting the forest down.

"We are determined to save these trees," they yelled from their high perch.

The hike up the mountain was tough. As we neared the top, I dropped to all fours, forced to use my hands and feet to climb over the rough and large boulders. I wished I had had gloves with me. This part tested my determination and sapped my energy. But despite being the oldest in the group, I summited the mountain and gave myself a pat on the back, smiling as others shared my success. The panoramic views of the tall forests were memorable with deep blue lake waters contrasting against the green foliage.

Each day of the tour was different. At the St. Helens Wildlife Park I stared at a ferocious, but lovable animal, the Tasmanian Devil. It took my breath away. A wildlife ranger held what looked like a small black fox. I stepped back and stiffened when it viciously bared its sharp white teeth and let out a spine-tingling screech. It looked ready to bite me.

"Pet him, he likes it," the ranger said.

Gingerly, I got closer and stretched out my hand. I touched its black fur, its body and its eyes softened. It seemed to like my touch, so I relaxed too.

My next joyous animal experience was to pet and feed a kangaroo, with a baby in her pouch. I was almost knocked over as the baby joey jumped out of the pouch and bounded across the ground.

At the end of the tour, I took the ferry to Melbourne to visit my dear friends Lois and Bruce. We had met in Scotland four years earlier. Their smiles and welcoming hugs when I stepped off the ferry made me feel as if we had been together just days ago.

Bruce was active in a Rotary Club, and we joined other members in a 4x4 caravan to the Glenelg. This expansive beach is near Adelaide east of Melbourne. Our group drove along the famous sandy beach. The surf was remarkable and enormous. World-class surfers were riding the waves.

Someone had parked a car on the beach and left it while they went for a swim. The tide was now coming in and water was lapping at its back wheels. Men with bulging muscles began pushing the car away from the incoming tide, but the car hardly moved. Calls for help went out to other swimmers, and more muscle arrived as did the owner. Now they were using shovels and wire mesh, placed under the back wheels, as the car moved inches at a time toward safety. The waves were relentless, dissolving the sand just as quickly as the helpers tried to pack it under the wheels. Finally, the car was moved to dry land, and I saw it drive off the beach. Experienced members of our caravan knew all too well how easily situations like this happened and how everyone pitched in to help.

Driving on the sand at a beach near Adelaide with our 4x4s where I noted the car tracks in the sand near the water.

I rested on a rock in the bush after a walk on the beach.

Australian crab dinner at the beach. Fresh and delicious.

That night we enjoyed a crab dinner. It was sad to leave Lois and Bruce, but our friendship deepened, and we connect frequently to this day.

My next stop was Hahndorf to stay with Bob and Mary, whom I had met earlier in my travels. Australia is known for its sheep stations, and they welcomed me to theirs. Hundreds of sheep were grazing in the fields as sheep dogs expertly rounded up the flock, herding them toward a gate in the yard. The dogs' skill and speed made me think they earned their keep. No sheep were left behind.

Sheep moved through the gate while being rounded up by the sheep dogs.

Bob showed me how he sheared his sheep. I watched him wrangle the wiggling sheep, holding it in place with one hand and managing the shears with the other. It was hard physical work and clearly a one-man operation. At this time of year, they just sheared around the sheep's anus to prevent infection.

One evening we enjoyed a tasty dinner of mutton, barbequed over an open spit. Fresh garden vegetables, casseroles, and home-made bread rolls filled the table as everyone brought their favorite dishes. Desserts are my downfall, and I greedily enjoyed my favor-ite, a peach pavlova. I laughed a lot about family tales, a perfect evening. I felt relaxed and enjoyed life on a sheep farm.

Moving on to Sydney, I wanted a bit of culture and attended a performance of *The Merry Widow*, an operetta by Franz Lehár, at the famous Sydney Opera House. It was awe-inspiring with amaz-ing acoustics and an impressive performance.

The next day I climbed the Sydney Harbour Bridge, the longest single-span bridge in the world when first built in 1932. The tour company issued us jumpsuits. I secured my belongings in my locker, including my rings, earrings, and wallet, to ensure that nothing dropped onto the road below. Soon I tightened a wide belt around my waist. Using a clip that hung from my belt, the tour guide secured me to a metal rod, which ran along the bridge. The clip slid along the rod as I stepped forward.

At first, I took tiny steps and tightly held onto the handrails. My knuckles were white and my heart beat wildly. Then slowly my breathing relaxed as we moved toward the top of the arch. I fo-cused on the spectacular view of the city, the Opera House, and the ocean below. The day was perfect, the wind blew softly, and the sun shone brightly. I had the climb of my life!

Moving north to Brisbane I visited the Lone Pine Koala Sanctuary. As a child, my stuffed Koala had been my favorite cuddling toy. Here I held a plump, fluffy, gentle breathing Koala, the size of a three-month-old baby. It reached out its tiny forelegs and held onto my blouse. I wrapped my arms around its soft fur and snuggled its body to my chest. Childhood memories brought me pleasure.

After a fantastic swim in the Great Barrier Reef, the world's largest coral reef off the coast of Australia, I visited the Alice Springs School of the Air in the Australian outback. It was before the internet was widely used so teachers broadcast lessons to students over a high frequency radio. These children, aged four to thirteen years old, lived on cattle stations, in roadhouses, in Aboriginal communities, and in national parks.

I sat outside the sound-proof room and watched as the teacher spoke into the microphone, leading her class. She was excellent. When the children got older, they attended boarding schools for the rest of their schooling and then went on to higher education.

That evening at the Sounds of Starlight Theatre I heard a new sound. Andrew Langford played Aboriginal music on a didgeridoo—an instrument made from a long eucalyptus tree trunk hollowed out by termites.

Australian didgeridoos, which I tried to play without much success while I was in the Australian Outback.

Andrew was a professional. The deep mesmerizing low rhythmic tones were different from anything I had ever heard before. Afterward he asked if I wanted to play a didgeridoo. Andrew had made it look so easy. I blew my hardest, but I could only make a pathetic honk. It was a bit embarrassing, but I laughed at myself. Andrew showed me different horns, each carved with Australian pictures. They were uniquely designed, an amazing souvenir, but sadly I had to pass.

Driving north from Alice Springs, I took a bus along a one-lane highway used by the truck trains or road trains, a true Australia icon. Here tough Aussie drivers battled scorching heat, fires, red dust, single-lane roads, and phenomenal distances. The truckers pulled four trailers at a time and delivered gasoline, food supplies, and other freight across the outback. Everyone knew the massive trucks had the right of way and did not stop for anything or anyone.

Our bus driver announced there was a road train heading toward us. He slowed down and desperately searched for a spot to carefully pull off the road. Sitting at the front I had a clear view out the windshield and saw the road train. It was moving so fast it seemed we would not be able to find an exit place in time. Sweat beaded my brow and I held my breath as I watched it get closer. I knew it wouldn't be able to stop and would demolish anything in its way. Thankfully our experienced bus driver pulled off in time, and we safely watched the road train pass.

Changing to the next bus at the town of Katherine, I now headed west toward the coast along Highway 1. This was my chance to swim with the largest known fish species in the world, a whale shark. These gentle giants are omnivores that feed on plankton but are classified as sharks. They are the size of a school bus or Sherman tank. They move through the water usually at a rate of three miles (four kilometers) per hour. Blue gray in color, they are identified by white spots on their backs. Each whale shark's spot pattern is unique, like a giraffe's individual spots.

Joining a tour group, I excitedly donned my bathing suit, life jacket, goggles, and fins and headed out in a sightseeing boat to an area where the whale sharks had been spotted. We jumped in the water, watching and waiting for the whale shark to pass. Other boats were there too. Our group was only allowed to stay to watch the whale shark pass by three times before tourists in another boat took their turn.

On the first pass, I was upright, submerged, treading water breathing through my snorkel when I saw the whale shark coming toward me. It was massive. My pulse raced as it opened its mouth, and my mind went blank. I stared in shock. Its forty-foot body softly swam by me and was gone in seconds.

On the second pass, I was better prepared and swam alongside this giant. The water propelled by its movement swirled against my body. I studied its spots and then stopped, watching as it swam away into the distance.

The third pass was the best and I swam alongside it for a longer time, working hard to keep up. Soon it picked up speed and I was left behind. This was a once-in-a-lifetime experience.

Australia brought joy to my heart as I reconnected with friends and learned about the unique vistas of this continent. Memories are vivid and friendships remain to this day.

Chapter 39

I Felt Like a True Explorer along the Silk Road, then Explored Mongolia, Russia, Finland, and Estonia

After Australia, I stopped in Singapore, then visited a family in Seoul, South Korea. The family was part of the Servas International Organization, where hosts in the country invite approved members to stay with their family for two nights as an opportunity to learn about life in their culture and country.

I stopped first in Seoul, where I stayed with a family with two children. Ari, the mother, taught me how to make kimchi, the fermented napa cabbage common in Korea; this process is similar to making dill pickles. It took a few tastes to learn to like it but soon I was a fan. It was a warm and friendly experience dining and living with the family.

Korean food at my homestay in Seoul, South Korea. It took a couple of meals to get used to the taste, but I soon loved the new flavors of the delicious food.

Homestays always brought me joy playing with the children and being part of the family.

When I left families I stayed with, or friends I made, I would give them a candle as a small gift as well as this poem:

YOU HAVE TOUCHED MY LIFE

You have touched my life in many ways—
Your smile, your laugh, throughout the days.
Your thoughtful ways, which showed you cared,
The times together we have shared.

Through my travels that's how we met,
Chatting and sightseeing; we were set
To build a friendship over the years
Our times together were filled with cheers.

My dear friend you're my inspiration
I send my love with much admiration
You were especially kind to me,
Thanks for your smiles and hospitality.

I am pleased that we have met
And shared a wee bit of time, and yet
The hours speed by much too fast,
Our thoughts and photos will have to last.

Until we meet one more time
And we can share more memories fine.
This candle is a gift from me to you.
This is what I ask you to do.
Strike a match and light the flame
From time to time, I'll do the same.
Even though we are apart,
Our happy memories are in my heart.
It's a pleasure—that's all I'll say:
May God bless you each and every day.

With hugs and happy memories,
Joyce

One day I went to the beach. And the number of umbrellas ready for people to descend on the beach was more than I had ever seen. I noticed the McDonald's advertisement.

Beach umbrellas ready for the day, many people were already in the water.

In 2004 the next adventure was an extensive three-month overland trip on a large truck equipped with holding tanks for our drinking water, tents, cooking supplies, and spacious areas for passengers to spread out in the truck. We traveled along the old Silk Road where traders moved products from China to the Middle East and vice versa.

Our stops included Turkey, Georgia, Azerbaijan, Turkmenistan, Uzbekistan, and Kyrgyzstan, then finished in China. Leaving the truck in China, I traveled with a group through part of Mongolia, then solo through other parts of Mongolia, Russia, Finland, and Estonia. I spent hours planning this trip and organizing the details, including reviewing average temperatures, money conversion, travelers' alerts, and the history of the countries.

I was excited. The Silk Road had deep meaning after living in Saudi Arabia, a major stop on the route. Our starting spot was Istanbul where the city straddles two continents—which two? A difficult trivia question.

No matter what country I visit, part of my life's mission is participating in local traditions and cultural activities, and eating and drinking.

Arriving in Istanbul two days before the overland tour gave me a chance to revisit my favorite places: the pancake restaurant, the grand bazaar, and the whirling dervishes as they spin in their trance.

The following day I returned to the Süleymaniye Hamam, a well-known Turkish bath built in 1557. After the traditional scrub I wondered if I had any skin left, and the steam bath was so hot, I felt I was melting. During the massage I heard a few snaps in my back, bones going back into place. That night I slept soundly.

Excitement filled the air as our group shared our backgrounds and goals for the trip. Russ and Mack, our leaders, quickly went over the details of our journey and their expectations of the seven participants, two women and five men. Our trip was divided into five segments, and passengers would leave or join at each point. A man from New Zealand and I had booked the entire trip.

We started in Istanbul where we clambered aboard our comfortable overland truck. Our plan was to stay in hotels most nights and tent occasionally.

We left Turkey, but to our surprise the weather changed to snow in Georgia. I froze. There was no heater in the truck, so we snuggled into our sleeping bags.

Chris, our guide, asked the manager at a ski hill in the Caucasus Mountains to open the ski lifts for us to enjoy skiing on this sunny day. What a thrill. I was able to add this skiing experience to those in Europe and North America.

Arriving in Georgia, we were greeted with a new snowfall, and took advantage of skiing on the sparkling fresh snow.
It was a glorious and unexpected adventure.

Several of us clamped on old-style skis and had fantastic runs down the mountain on fresh snow. What an energetic experience.

We moved through Georgia and stopped in Gori to visit Stalin's museum, an exciting way to learn Russian history.

In the historic city of Tbilisi, in Georgia, I learned how it controlled the Silk Road years ago because of its geographic location. In the afternoon we visited a carpet shop where young girls wove exquisite silk on silk carpets. Their tiny fingers hand-tied the knots. They worked between school classes and smiled at us as we watched.

In Tbilisi, where merchants displayed their handcrafted carpets for sale over the cars to catch visitors' eyes. The rugs were outstanding in design and texture, and I would have loved to have bought one, but I had previously shipped carpets home while in Saudi Arabia.

Georgia has some of the world's best long-standing wineries so wine flowed easily with our meals. A treat for a wine lover like me.

We drove across the border to Azerbaijan where the country has had a history of multiple countries dominating their area. In Baku, Azerbaijan, we dined in a fourteenth-century building housing a restaurant that oozed with ambiance and where we devoured traditional rice with saffron, cumin, apricots, and lamb.

Splurged at dinner in Azerbaijan where delicious food was uniquely presented, and the belly dancers added to the evening's atmosphere.

Belly dancers and singers accompanied by violin musicians entertained us for the evening. The music got my adrenaline going, but unfortunately there was no dance floor to swing and sway.

Driving beside the Caspian Sea the next day, we saw several brides wearing white gowns and grooms in dark suits having their pictures taken. Then they paraded in a cart pulled by a pony around the area where men played an accordion, a drum, and a tambourine to serenade the couples. Families and friends were dressed in black and celebrated by dancing in the streets.

We then crossed the Caspian Sea into Turkmenistan and headed to Uzbekistan and drove along the Gobustan plain in the Greater Caucasus Range. Here we examined Stone Age carvings dating about 5,000 to 8,000 years ago of animals and men wearing hunter's clothing and women emphasizing their busts and thighs. Carved animals were deer, goats, lions, horses, and birds. I was amazed how similar cave or stone drawings are worldwide, such as in Africa.

Petroglyphs of an animal in Stone Age carvings in the Caucasus Range in Uzbekistan.

In Uzbekistan, we toured Khiva and Bukhara. Our group took a three-day camel safari through the Kyzylkum Desert, meaning red sand, and slept in a yurt, a portable round tent covered with felt. The skies were clear and sparkling stars filled the night sky. Then still in Uzbekistan we headed to Tashkent.

Soon we traveled through the mountain kingdom of Kyrgyzstan. Because I am always interested in healthcare, I visited the hospital and the nurse in charge gave me a tour. She lamented the operating rooms were on the second floor, but the building did not have an elevator. That is a challenge for staff. Also, what can she do when there are no supplies?

We talked about hospital issues, and I shared some of my experiences. I felt a bond with her as we hugged as I understood her difficulties.

In the afternoon I ducked into a tea house during a downpour and sipped tasty green tea and delicious shortbread-like cookies. The ambiance was friendly, the owner spoke a bit of English, and I smiled a lot.

The spectacular Fergana Range was a perfect spot to enjoy camping for the night.

This is how we set up our tents for the night during our overland truck tour, where I traveled from Istanbul to China on the Silk Road. Our truck was comfortable and spacious, with clear views of the topography.

Another night we had a homestay with a family. I loved these experiences. I enjoyed our limited conversations, but sign language worked well. The food was prepared with loving care. We were served cereals, vegetables, and fruits—all local foods of the area.

Moving on we drove through the Ala Archa Gorge National Park in Kyrgyzstan, an alpine setting with mountains, glaciers, spectacular views, and vistas. I wanted to stay and soak in the atmosphere and solitude, but we kept traveling.

Crossing high passes, we entered China at the end of the Silk Road. Parts of the area seemed desolate; we saw few cars on the road.

We drove on one of the world's most famous roads, the Karakoram Highway, which took many lives and twenty years to build.

One day we experienced a sandstorm when we crossed the Taklamakan Desert. The vision was so poor, we had to stop. The next day we saw women sweeping the roads using branches of trees tied together as brooms. It was a difficult job, and the wind was relentless as more sand appeared. We were fortunate to catch a window into this part of the Chinese world.

In a remote part of China our guide took us to a community in the mountains and we stopped at some shops with secondhand jewelry. I spotted a gold ball watch on a chain and fell in love with it and intended to buy it after our hike. At the top of our trek I had my palm read by a monk. He told me I was going to lose my photos but not to worry, because I would get them back. When I returned to buy the watch, I learned it had been sold to someone else on the trip. I was disappointed and I learned a lesson: if you want something, buy it then, do not wait.

The Kashgar Sunday Market was the week's highlight, with all the smells, the crowds, and the noise. The city's history emphasizes its importance in the Silk Road and its history. Historically, the city's importance grew when the Great Wall of China was extended.

The last part of our trip included examining the famous Terracotta Warriors in Xi'An built in 246 BC to guard Qin Shi Huang's tomb. Along with a guide I walked beside the warrior statues. Based on the analysis and the research of each warriors' ears, no two warriors had similar ears. This finding confirmed that each statue was likely based on an individual warrior. They were taller than my five-feet-two-inch height, and the details of their body and facial expressions were incredibly realistic. I felt like I was living long ago and could have a conversation with one of the warriors. His life story would be fascinating,

Our next historical adventure was trekking along the Great Wall of China's strenuous 6.2-mile (10-kilometer) hike, which was a fantastic experience. I saw original tiles on the trail, which had been in place for thousands of years. This section of the wall had never been repaired. The Great Wall of China is a series of walls that were built to protect the northern area of China. Walking was difficult. Fortunately, I carried water with electrolytes to drink on the way. Unfortunately, some teammates did not prepare well for the walk. I gave a teammate a bottle of water and half my electrolytes, but I could have used them later myself.

The views were stunning, looking at the valleys and vistas with a 360-degree span of hills and forests. I sauntered to enjoy the scenery and when I arrived at the end, I smiled and murmured to myself, well done, Joyce. It was a historic walk; one I will never forget.

It was a remarkable three-month overland trip to see this part of the world especially in areas hard to travel solo. The thrill was the adventure, which left me with memories of extraordinary times.

Years later in Colombia I connected with Russ, one of our overland guides, when I lived in Panama. Friends remain friends no matter where they end up all over the world.

After mailing a package of souvenirs and treasures home for safekeeping, I traveled to Mongolia. Here Mongolia touched me through its friendly people.

One day I was entering a building when someone unzipped my backpack on the top and removed my purse with all my pictures from my three-month overland trip. I was taking them to be transferred to a DVD. I was devastated.

I sat on the floor and as tears came to my eyes, a young man who had seen what happened came to my rescue. The thief discarded my purse because it did not have money. My helper brought the purse with the slides back to me with all my photos intact. I was so grateful; he received a substantial reward. Once again strangers came to my rescue. It was only then I remembered what the monk had told me about losing my photos when he read my palm in China.

In Mongolia, I was fascinated by the young boys who rode horses bareback during long races. They were proud of their skills, and the crowd cheered them throughout the race. One afternoon I went horseback riding.

I enjoyed riding in Mongolia with a gentle Mongolian horse along desolate areas. I loved the feeling of trotting and galloping during the ride. My horse was shorter and stockier than horses I rode in Canada.

Throughout history the Mongols made felt, used for yurts, clothing, ropes, and blankets as they still do today. For food, the tasty Mongolian tsuivan noodles, vegetables, and meat including beef, camel, horse, sheep, and mutton, made a delicious meal. We downed it with instant coffee.

On the tour I lived in a yurt and was surprised how warm it was in the cool of the evening.

This yurt has a decorated wooden door along with the pipe that allows smoke to escape. Some of the yurts have wooden flooring. They are warm in the winter and the felt repels the rain very well.

The remote Mongolian areas were sparsely populated as the Mongols move their yurt from the plains in the winter to the mountains in the summer.

Saying goodbye to Mongolia in Ulan Bator, I took the Trans-Siberian Railway north, then west with stops in different Russian cities along the route to Moscow.

I took the Russian local train from Mongolia to Moscow.
We stopped at different cities where I stayed a few days and
explored the area. I continued my journey by catching another
train going west and made several stops, where I enjoyed
homestays with Russian families.

Of course, the language was a barrier, but when I met the families where I had a homestay, I always had a smile, and with limited conversation, we managed. Cell phones were not common then so instant translation was not available. I would stay in the city for two or three days and then catch the next train west. I repeated the process until I arrived in St. Petersburg.

On the local Russian train, I had a bunk bed as did three others, usually men. I learned to put my luggage under the bed of the person across from me so I could keep an eye on it rather than under my bed. Usually, we would share our meals by buying them at the train stations. The Russians were hospitable and generous. We always managed a conversation one way or another.

At one overnight stop my guide took me to Ekaterinburg where the Obelisk in Ekaterinburg in the Ural Mountains showed the dividing line between Europe and Asia.

I had one foot in Asia and one foot in Europe in front of the Obelisk in Ekaterinburg in the Ural Mountains. It reminded me of the equator, the imaginary line dividing me in half in Uganda.

During one part of the train journey, I shared a room with a Russian graduate student who was studying in the United States and was returning home to Moscow for a holiday. We never stopped talking. I asked him about Putin, the newly appointed leader of the country with his background in the Komitet Gosudarstvennoy Bezopasnosti, the KGB (in English, the Committee for State Security, Foreign Intelligence and Domestic Security agency in the Soviet Union). He expressed major concerns about Putin's leadership. We shared our meals, which he ordered, always tasty and filling and included vodka of course.

Staying at a homestay in St. Petersburg, I was fascinated by the art and other treasures in all the museums and was absorbed with the displayed artifacts from its worldwide collection.

My homestay room at one of the stops in Russia. The bed was comfortable and the pillows were soft. The tapestry hanging on the wall behind the bed was handmade by a family member.

Morning breakfasts at a homestay in Russia. Blini, like pancakes, were served with sour cream and jam. Delicious.

In St. Petersburg, I spent three days of my thirty-day Russian visa at the Hermitage Museum, viewing its vast collection of world-renowned pieces of art, one of the largest painting collections in the world.

Unfortunately, only nine of the Faberge Egg collection made for the last two Romanov czars were on display. They were encrusted with gems and decorated with pictures of the Russian Imperial family. They took my breath away as I studied the details of each egg. While I stared at them, I thought about the history of the czars and those who were killed long ago. A new Faberge Museum was built in 2013; I wish I could see them now.

Watching ballet performances was such a pleasure. I saw two performances; one was *Swan Lake*. On other days I toured Russia's magnificent churches and enjoyed walking alone around the city streets.

Moving on to Moscow, I explored the unique, beautiful works of art in each Moscow subway station. Many of the stations had huge chandeliers and elaborate finishes; the floors looked as if they were scrubbed each night. They looked more like museums than subway stations. I stopped at each station, examined the tiles and artwork, and then went to the next.

At one station, I was so engrossed in the tiles I got myself twisted around and could not figure out the correct way I should go as my subway map was only in Russian. The Russian letters were hard to read and did not look like English letters.

I started looking at people and smiling with my map in my hand and said clearly, "Does anyone speak English?" I wore a big smile and sported my Canadian flag pin on the collar of my blouse. In seconds a couple of men and a woman in their early twenties came to my rescue. They turned me around and pointed me in the right direction. Before we went our separate ways, we spent time practicing their English. First, I would ask a question, then they would ask me about my life and what kind of a house I lived in in Canada.

For me, it's the personal connections I make getting to know others. It always starts with a smile, then a question, a nod, and communication.

Canadians love hockey and I was no exception, so I cheered for one of the Russian hockey teams in the large Moscow arena. I loved sharing this experience with Russians. A lady spoke to me in English and shared her family pictures and we cheered for her team. One thing is for sure, no matter where you are in the world, fans cheer loudly for their team.

Cathedral of St. Basil the Blessed, Moscow, is fascinating and the stunning colors certainly meet their visual objective of symbolizing both a town and heaven.

I left Russia, traveled through Estonia and Finland, then returned to Canada.

After this marvelous experience reliving history along the Silk Road, then enjoying Mongolia and Russian culture, I was ready to rest and relax in Canada with my family.

Chapter 40

Investigating the Sights and Sounds in Mexico and Countries in Central America

After another brief rest in Canada, I continued to explore events or countries I missed. But now in my seventy-third year I was ready to look for a place to settle for a while.

With the world map spread out on the table in Pickering, Canada, while visiting my son and his family, my eyes focused on Central America. By March 2007, I was ready to explore Mexico and Central America and then stop traveling and living out of a suitcase.

I wanted to get to know people on a more permanent basis. My soul needed some roots, shallow ones for just a few years, as my family wanted me to return to Canada. I felt a deep desire to help and connect with others on a personal basis. I felt a push and pull. Canada was a wonderful place to live, but the thought of cold weather and snow sent shivers down my back.

I planned to resettle in Canada when I was eighty years old. But, for now, my mission was clear: to visit Central American countries to find a warm country to temporarily call home.

The organizers of the notable Toronto Travel Show invited me to share my experiences crisscrossing the world as an older single female world traveler. The show promoted travel and vacation destinations where participants shared unique slide and film presentations during the show. Experienced travelers shared their travel stories.

At this event, I had the opportunity to model Canadian-made Tilley clothing. They are known the world over for their indestructible and waterproof Tilley hats. It has a secure pocket built into the top of the hat where you can store credit cards and cash. I have worn mine all over the world.

I heard that a traveler once had told the Tilley organization that an elephant in a zoo had eaten his hat. Wonders of all wonders, he retrieved it none the worse for wear. My hat protected me from sun, rain, and insects during my travels, especially when walking in the jungle. It prevented bugs burrowing into my scalp and laying eggs. Unfortunately many travelers are unaware of the importance of an essential head covering. I also wore their clothing with secret pockets securely hidden inside the outer pockets and Velcro secured them closed.

The sound of the Velcro opening always alerted the wearer if someone was trying to open the pocket. More than once, this saved the day as little hands from children who befriended me tried to get what was in my pockets. The clothing was comfortable to wear and dried overnight, even in the hot and humid tropics. It always looked presentable, and wrinkles shook out as I walked. My audience roared as I shared some of my experiences, especially when I had ants in my pants.

My plans clicked when I learned about living in Panama while speaking at the Toronto Travel Show. It became one of the countries I wanted to explore. I would travel south via California, Mexico, then Central America, finishing in Panama, and consider the possibility of calling this country home for a few years.

My friend Gale and I wanted to see the Grand Canyon, so we decided to deliver someone else's car to California and see some sites on the way. Gale and I took turns driving, so we covered the miles comfortably by switching regularly. All went well with the driving on the famous Route 66 until the higher elevation caused the weather to change and required us to drive on ice-covered roads, which sent cars into the ditch.

Trees glistened with ice, which forced us to take refuge at 10:30 a.m. in a Best Western Motel for the night.

Feeling hungry, we stopped at a local café where two characters—the sheriff packing lead and another man with a handlebar mustache and large potbelly, wearing a cowboy hat—introduced us to the locals. They were true Western cowboys with their cowboy boots. We eavesdropped on their conversation; we chuckled hearing their drawl. They were like characters straight out of a central casting agency for Western movies.

By evening one-half inch of ice covered our car and the trees were glistening. It was a magical, surreal, and slightly eerie sight. Luckily the hotel had a generator as the local power was out. We learned from the local TV station to put a newspaper over our windshield and the other windows. The newspaper acted as insulation so the ice formed on the paper. It was an easy way to clear our windows the next day.

The trip's highlight was our visit to the Grand Canyon and our private airplane trip over this fantastic natural scenery. After the plane trip, Gale returned home, and I dropped off the car. Then solo, I visited a cousin in California and another in Mexico, where we reminisced about growing up together in the summers at our lake home at Kapasiwin Beach in Canada. Family memories were unique and special.

Mexico looked like an attractive place to settle, but I crossed it off my list due to the lack of safe drinking water. So instead, wanting to explore Central America, I joined a small group tour leaving from Mexico City to investigate the Mayan and Aztec cultures. During our time together, we climbed many of the ruins and marveled at their builders' abilities while we traveled along the Yucatan Peninsula.

In Belize, a small Central American country, formerly British and still part of the Commonwealth, we explored several small islands called cayes. Here I enjoyed a couple of spectacular scuba dives. The visibility was clear to 100 feet (30.5 meters) or more, and the marine and coral life was an explosion of color and formation. The sheer magnitude of life was at once awesome, its beauty exquisite. I could see why Belize was considered a world-class dive destination, as I drifted silently in and among the Mesoamerican Reef, the largest barrier reef in the Western Hemisphere. It touches the coasts of Mexico, Belize, Guatemala, and Honduras. It's a dreamscape of unfathomable delights.

We arrived in Guatemala, the country with the largest population in Central America, combining the history of Indians both in language and culture. It was Holy Week, the day before Good Friday. The community planned a processional path with sand spread over the sparkling clean cobblestone roads to ensure they were level.

We skipped El Salvador because of difficult roads and our group moved on to Roatan Island in Honduras, formerly British Honduras.

Shipwrecks peppered the Roatan waters due to famous pirates' wars of long ago, and storms, gales, and hurricanes.

We moved on; our next stop was Nicaragua. We viewed the smoking cone of one of their highest and most active of twenty volcanoes, San Cristobal. Primary cloud forests often covered the volcanoes and promoted unique biodiversity and the rare beauty of nature. Small-scale coffee plantations abounded. The aroma of hand-rolled Cuban cigars floated through the markets, which offered unique handicrafts such as their famous colorful hammocks, traditional clothes, fine ceramics, and, of course, cigars.

Costa Rica is located along the Ring of Fire, sporting over 200 active volcanoes. I chose to give my legs a workout climbing one of them. It was tough at the top because of inhaling the volcanic gas, which burned my throat and nostrils. I tried wearing a mask around my face, but that didn't help much. Nevertheless, the 360-degree view was spectacular and made the effort worthwhile.

At this time, I had explored all the Central American countries I wanted and headed to Panama. I had not yet found the country where I wanted to settle. The decision weighed heavily on my mind. I loved the hot and humid climate in Central America, and I felt at home. Maybe Panama would be it. If not, perhaps Canada would beckon me home.

Chapter 41

Panama, A Place to Hang My Hat, for Now

It was May Day 2007 when our group arrived in Panama. The thought of settling there was becoming more appealing as each day passed. Panama met my six criteria: a warm climate, safe drinking water, a stable currency (US dollars), a country able to generate income from the Panama Canal, and a sizable English-speaking expatriate community. It was also within a one-day flight back to Canada should my family need me.

As our tour continued, I looked at Panama through a different lens as I stared at the famous canal, an extraordinary feat of human engineering. Without question, the Panama Canal is twentieth-century man's domination over nature. However, nature definitely fought back with the tens of thousands of deaths it took to complete the construction of "The Unconstructable!" And once achieved, by the audacious raising of one ocean, by a staggering 85 feet (25.9 meters) through the jungle, to meet another—a dream once considered impossible, the passage between the Pacific and Atlantic Oceans, became a commercial reality. The engineering giants of the twentieth century took their place in history.

The high-rise apartment buildings along Panama City's waterfront felt like home, reminding me of a condo I had owned in Toronto years before overlooking Lake Ontario and where I'd enjoyed watching many sailboat races during the summer months.

The feel and energy of Panama City inspired me. The hot and humid climate was comfortable and ideal for me. With the large English-speaking expatriate community in the town and my basic Spanish-speaking skills, I felt comfortable.

The city was cosmopolitan; it was vibrant, electric. It was alive. Yes, I can settle here, I thought to myself. Panama was known as the Crossroads of the World, so what better place could there possibly be for a traveler such as myself? Yes, Panama seemed like a perfect place to hang my hat for a while.

Here was an amazing opportunity to meet people from numerous countries and cultures, each with their own story and adventures to tell. I decided to stay in Panama and explore the country in more depth. After much deliberation, Panama became my new home. I rented an apartment, settled in, and learned to find my way around my newly adopted country.

One thing I had learned traveling around the world and living in many countries was expats readily open themselves up to others. They understand many of the emotions of loneliness and frustration of not understanding a language or culture. With expats, there's a natural connection, and everyone has a story to share, positive, negative, and always different. though at the same time equally familiar.

By this time, I had passed my original goal of experiencing and connecting with people in well over one hundred countries, but there were always more countries to see. So I planned my last trip to encompass Ukraine, Montenegro, Croatia, Moldova, and Crimea. After, I would revisit Italy, especially Sicily, Rome, and Venice, and wanted to watch the beautiful and famous white Lipizzaner Stallions in Vienna perform. So, after this trip, I would have explored 156 countries.

The last and only other adventure I had on my to-do list was taking an icebreaker to discover the Northwest Passage in the Arctic. Unfortunately, ice prevented the passage of commercial tourist ships, so I had to wait.

In Panama City, I settled down and made my nest in the city's center after securing my Panama residency and embracing my newly adopted country.

The climate had two seasons: the dry season and the rainy season. The dry season was from mid-December through mid-April and the rainy season was from mid-April to mid-December. It rains for an hour or so a day in the rainy season, and sometimes water comes down in a deluge causing flooding in streets and cars to stall. High humidity levels occur in the rainy season and high temperatures are between 85 to 95°F (29 to 35°C) during the dry season.

Sitting on my balcony early one morning, wearing a flowing sundress reaching down to my ankles, I watched transfixed as flocks of colorful parakeets flew darting and squawking in joyous chorus to greet the new day. Then at dawn, as the sleeping city was beginning to stretch itself awake, I watched in silent wonder the ever-shifting pastel colors as the sun rose in the sky inch by inch.

It was my favorite time of day when life was beginning to move. It happened at every sunrise. I looked at my watch and smiled right on the minute at 6:00 a.m. I loved this way to start my day as I inhaled the aroma of freshly ground Colombian coffee and wrapped my hands around my warm mug.

Also, I would head to our pool in the building for my morning swim. What a joy to do laps and swim as I planned my day.

In the evening, also from my balcony, I could hear and see fireworks displays, especially during New Year's Eve and in June, the month of many weddings. In addition, Panamanians offered impressive fireworks after dark on holidays. So, parades, sports, and any reason to celebrate were always fun. Fireworks brought me to my balcony, often with a glass of wine to sip while watching these spectacular displays.

Most Sundays, I was up early to go birdwatching with the Panama Audubon Society in the Metropolitan Natural Park in the city. Panama is on the flyway for birds moving from North America to South America or vice versa during the change of seasons. Taking part in bird species counts and learning about many different birds was such a positive experience. It was a thrill for me to add the names of new sightings to my worldwide list of birds. As a bonus, we would see brown monkeys climbing in the treetops and hear their loud chatter as we wandered along the paths.

Panama life was full of social activities, dining out, going to the beach, and making new friends through being part of expatriate activities and club activities. Embassy functions were always a delight.

Alison, Susie, and I started a little writing club called the Secret Writers Society Panama Chapter (SWSPC) to get the creative juices moving. Alison was a former model and New York entertainment publicist, and Susie was a teacher. We met at the social activities in Panama and found out the three of us enjoyed writing. Unfortunately, our group did not last long.

Each week I had mind-stimulating activities. One of my book clubs got together at different members' homes and discussed a book of our choice, while at my second book club, we read the same book and shared our impressions of the story. I was never at a loss for a friend to call or something to do.

My neighbor from Colombia became a dear friend. We often enjoyed my favorite dish: ceviche, raw seafood mixed with vegetables purchased from the fresh fish market. Of course, fish was a popular meal and jumbo shrimp were on the top of my list.

The weather was warm, clothes were easy to wear, and there was no need to change seasonal wardrobes as we did living in Canada. Life was relaxed, people were friendly, and there was always something to do. There was a feeling of inclusion in activities. I never felt lonely.

Friends were generous. One offered me the opportunity to stay at her home next to the Pacific Ocean, where I could hear the lapping of the ocean as I fell into a deep slumber. It was a wonderful oasis, a chance to catch my breath from my busy life in the city. I loved the seclusion and opportunity to lounge by the beach, read, and sleep. After waking up early, it was a joy to walk on the beach as my toes curled into the fresh wet sand as the tide came in or went out. Some days the water was calm, other days rough, but it didn't matter. The salt air, the seagulls wandering the beach were joys which filled my soul. I treasured the solitude, especially the early morning walks, looking for different shells. Something is relaxing about an early morning walk and listening to the rhythm of the lapping waves.

In the city morning coffee was a pleasure when I often met my friend Dorothy, a Canadian nurse. One morning I felt particularly in need of Dorothy's advice.

"Dorothy, I had a tough situation the other day at the hospital while I was with Linda. Her husband was dying. He died quietly, just stopped breathing while we were sitting by his bed."

None of the staff caring for her husband had indicated his death was so close; she was not prepared.

Dorothy let out a sigh and said, "I am caring for a dying patient with severe pain at home and cannot get the needed narcotic pain medication for my patient. Not all physicians seeing patients at home can order narcotic analgesics. I don't know what to do about that either."

We both had an aha moment and realized the need for an organization to help expatriates learn how to handle the death and dying of a loved one in Panama.

"Dorothy, healthy expatriates come to live in Panama. Many people are retirees, and as the years tick by, their health changes from healthy and able to travel to becoming fragile and not able to return. Sometimes they can only fly home with a doctor or nurse, on a private plane, not on commercial airlines. The cost poses a significant financial burden for them and their families. They find themselves in a hospital situated in the country without the homecare resources available in North America. Can we do something?"

"Well, Joyce, it's definitely worth thinking about it," said Dorothy.

Dorothy and I were fortunate to learn about a program in Boquete, a community near the Costa Rican border. I visited their board and executive, where they shared their founding legal information. Dorothy was a trained hospice hospital nurse, and I had worked as a nurse in homecare. In addition, I had administrative experience as a chief executive officer of a hospital, as well as a nurse and an administrator of the Visiting Nurse Association. We recruited others interested in developing the program and each person brought their expertise.

After numerous difficulties and frustrations, in 2013, Dorothy and I cofounded the Panama Hospice and Respite Foundation with our lawyer's expert help. We quickly formed our team and started fundraising. The executive worked hard to open our bank account, develop a website, a public relations committee, a blood bank register, and promote our services on the local English radio program. We crafted and hosted training programs designed specifically for our volunteers to interact with patients using our hospice services.

We offered a course for Advanced Planning and Healthy Aging to create public awareness and raise funds for our programs. Soon we created a sister group in Coronado, a community on the Pacific coast, to assist those who lived there. We provided care and comfort to our patients and established a buddy system to ensure a specified contact person had access to essential documents and papers in a crisis.

Our Loan Cupboard offered the temporary use of equipment such as crutches, walkers, canes, wheelchairs, and bedside commodes to all Panamanians and expatriates. We needed consistency in both branches, so we established policies and procedures. We kept bedside notes, communicated with the medical staff, and kept a registry of nurses who provided care in the patient's home. We gave the families both emotional and physical support. Annually we held a fundraising conference to support our free services to both expatriates and Panamanians.

We helped many people and often Dorothy drove to patients in distant communities to provide care and act as a liaison with medical staff. We loaned out hospital beds, commodes, and other equipment so the patients could fulfill their wish and die at home.

We were touched when the family of one of our patients gave our hospice program the collection funds donated at her funeral. It was generosity from the community that kept us motivated to maintain the viable organization.

I remained president from its inception in 2013 until a few months before returning to live in Canada. Dorothy took over when I left.

There were many social activities to attend in Panama over the years. I was invited to numerous Canadian Embassy events, met interesting people who had come to Panama to visit or live, and when the Canadian Prime Minister visited, I was invited to have my picture taken with him. Connections with the Panamanian business community always provoked stimulating conversations.

I shared my experiences about the Panama Hospice and Respite Foundation and promoted our accomplishments.

Geographically, did you know Panama has a unique position in Central America and the world? You or I could watch the sunrise over the Atlantic Ocean and then drive to view the sunset over the Pacific Ocean in one day. Where else in the world can you do that? Panama is an unforgettable country.

People in Panama loved to entertain, and I was no exception. I joined the Panama Gourmet Cooking Club, where each team of two cooked different parts of the four-part meal—for example, appetizers, salads, main course, and dessert. We started with cocktails or wine and learned about pairing wine with each course of the meal. Each month we had a specific theme for the dinner, and many dishes were challenging to make. As a result, I always learned how to be a better chef. We laughed a lot, our evenings burst with happy memories of interesting stories and delicious meals.

While in Panama, true to form, I looked for ways to help others besides the hospice organization. I found my niche and loved coaching Spanish-speaking students to prepare for the English Scholastic Assessment Test (SAT) or the American College Test (ACT), the US university entrance exams. The energy of the students brought immense joy and fun to my life. One of the most memorable phone calls came from two students after completing their exams: "Joyce, we aced the exam, and thanks to you, we are on our way to university. We're going out to celebrate." I was excited and thrilled to hear their news. Their comments touched me deeply; they had worked hard.

During my years of living in Panama City, Panama, I had pondered about writing my travel stories. My big eightieth birthday was just a few months away. This birthday was my self-imposed deadline to begin my book.

Friends listened with interest and wonder as I shared my stories about traveling to 156 countries over twenty-three years and asked, "How did you keep motivated to continue to travel and explore the world?"

It was the path I chose at the fork in the road. My reward was the journey, as the road to my destinations kept me moving on to the next culture, then to the next. Yes, I was an energetic seventy-nine-year-old, former CEO of a hospital, with blonde hair and a slight build. That day in these early hours of the morning, I wanted to answer my own question: Why did I travel the world? Nothing came to mind, except I was a curious, modern-day explorer. I shifted from one hip to the other in my chair. My hands were on the keyboard, but they were still as my mind flooded back in time.

I looked at the sky and saw hundreds of black raptors gliding in the uplift of the wind. I sat quietly while the flashback of thousands of black wildebeests trudging in what seemed to be a single line on their way to the Zambezi River during their migration filled my mind.

The view was from a hot air balloon. The burst of the hot gas was deafening but forced the balloon to follow the animals below. They kept moving, keeping up with the beast in front of them one by one. It was as if someone had drawn a straight line and the animals followed it.

I was looking down on the herd and watched a lioness chase a young one, then ran after an old wildebeest. They were the ones that could not keep up. The lioness followed them, waiting for the kill. From above, I could watch the old wildebeests slowly fall behind. The balloon drifted above until I could only see a speck in the distance. I wondered whether the lioness made the kill. I will never know.

Wildebeests made the trek each year following the rain and thus their food. Trekking in July through October, the animals moved from Serengeti National Park in Tanzania clockwise to the Maasai Mara National Reserve in Kenya. Wildebeests, zebras, and antelopes made the journey. The lions followed their food.

Travel memories flooded my mind. Then my mind turned to my family. I began missing them more and more.

Medical issues reared their ugly head, causing severe left leg pain, forcing me to use a cane and then a walker. After injections in my spine and many hours of exercise, the pain disappeared. However, after complicated right cataract surgery, my vision was compromised and caused many problems and concerns and, ultimately, I became totally blind in my right eye.

On the celebration of my seventy-ninth birthday in November 2015, Panamanian friends held a marvelous party. Seventy-nine long-stemmed red roses filled a vase, their aroma filling the air. The party theme was travel, with balloons throughout the home marked with the names of some countries I had visited.

A dear friend produced a printed photo book highlighting my stay in Panama. Friends wrote comments in the blank areas alongside the photos. I blinked hard as I read the notes; they touched my heart. Comments like, "My dearest Joyce, your presence in Panama has placed a permanent glow in the lives of every person you have come in contact with—your smile and presence will always be remembered. Happy B-day." Another comment: "Dear Joyce, so happy we are to have met you in Panama. We've had so many connections, I wouldn't know where to begin—birding, brunch, dinner parties, at your place with friends. You are cherished. Cheers—xoxo." "To an exceptionally strong and beautiful hearted woman, God bless your life, Joyce, always." And so they continued.

They still bring a huge smile and a warm feeling to me when I savor their comments in my Panama memory book. My heart filled with happiness and my loving friends from Panama.

During the holiday season, I visited my son in Pickering, in the greater Toronto area, to look for accommodation to settle in Canada in June and say goodbye to Panama.

Change was in the air.

Chapter 42

I've Explored Our Wonderful World, Now Canada Is on My Mind

June 2016 rolled around, and I moved to Pickering, Ontario. Thanks to my son Bruce, my apartment was ready for me. There was food in the refrigerator and pantry, the kitchen was equipped, and there was basic furniture throughout to get me started. This allowed me to choose how I wanted to furnish my home.

I was excited to return to Canada, yet it was strange to be back. To experience the cooler weather, no daily swim, no Spanish conversations, and no tropical foods at the farmers' market. On the plus side I reconnected with family and friends. We reminisced and enjoyed catching up.

I thrived by spending hours at world-famous sites such as the Art Gallery of Ontario, the Aquarium, the Royal Ontario Museum, and the McMichael Art Gallery. I cheered loudly at both the Blue Jays baseball games and the Toronto Argos football games. I attended the Canadian National Exhibition, held on Toronto's famed waterfront. All these events brought back memories of Toronto's exceptional arts and cultural activities, which I missed while traveling.

Celebrating my birthday in November in Canada brought the thrill of my big eightieth birthday. But, over the years, I wondered if I would ever make this milestone and mused for a split second where I would be in my eighty-fifth year.

The night before my party, I pondered what the following years would bring. Where would I focus my time and energy without travel, hospice, or teaching students? How would I fill my time?

The most memorable experiences about my travel years were touching people's lives—the human connections. No matter where I was in the world, my encounters connected me with others, their countries, their cultures, their histories, their personal stories. That's what I treasured most about traveling. The sheer diversity of it all. The complex, wonderful, beautiful, at times tragic, shocking, and messy stuff that is simply being human. Humanity in its never-ceasing capacity to amaze.

People from all over the world affected my life profoundly and influenced my thinking. I absorbed the world's natural beauty, flora, and fauna, everything I saw, but it was the people I remember so vividly. Human connection is the soul of travel. Would people be as open here as when I traveled? I stared out the window: what is my goal, my purpose, how will I contribute?

My children, Betsy and Dan, arrived from the United States to join Bruce who lives close to me, for my eightieth birthday party. The warm feeling of pride, the deep-down joy as I looked at my three children as their lives unfolded in my mind. Each one had chosen their path as I had, and it is a wonderful feeling to look at each of them and be a proud mom. Then I thought of my love for my eleven grandchildren. How blessed I am and was proud of everyone's accomplishments—indeed, every mother's and grandmother's wish.

The day of the party arrived; what a privilege to share time with family and friends. Lots of smiles and hugs. I felt loved and was thrilled to see people I had not seen for years. Friends are friends; we just started where we left off years ago.

That evening after my guests had left and I had returned home, I thought about my adventures over the years, when I treasured the different celebrations in other countries. You cannot be in two places at the same time and we all make life choices.

The following week my world collapsed after a biopsy in my right breast. I was diagnosed with breast cancer. I had the C word. Having managed a cancer clinic, I understood the ramifications and the treatment. I would require a right mastectomy and chemotherapy. Why did this happen to me? My life changed at that second. I had a lot to learn about my diagnosis, and because cancer had spread to my lymph nodes, I understood the increased risk to my health.

At the same time, another medical issue surfaced. I needed a surgical cornea transplant in my right eye as my vision was getting worse. I changed from an active, healthy person to one struggling to get through the day. The November weather, with its gray tones, matched my feelings. Everywhere was overcast, especially inside. I was feeling depressed and didn't want my chemotherapy to interfere with my eye surgery. It was a juggling act planning my treatments.

My daughter, Betsy, a physician, came from Wisconsin to be with me during my mastectomy surgery. I felt relaxed having her beside me in the pre-surgery room and when the doctor gave me the injectable dye to track the cancer cells. During my first post-operative night, she stayed with me and was there to observe the home care nurse change the dressing. I felt blessed.

Home care nurses came daily at first to change the dressings and make sure the drainage tube was open. These were challenging days with my chemo treatment. I absorbed the details about my cancer treatment during the educational sessions at the Hearth Place Cancer Support Center that provided courses for newly diagnosed patients. Their exercise sessions helped me maintain my strength.

Getting to the clinic for treatments was an issue. I was fortunate that cancer volunteer drivers took me to my hospital appointments. Another person taking the classes took me to Hearth Place, or I took the bus, as I did not drive. I missed being independent and able to drive and go where I wanted when I wanted. I felt frustrated. It was a terrible time in my life. Distances where I lived were long, and how I missed the warm weather, my daily swim, and the short distance and frequent taxis in Panama.

After my mastectomy surgery, my recovery was smooth, but it took longer than I thought. Fortunately, I was in splendid health, except for my eye, but basically fit because of my daily swim in Panama. The days dragged by while being affected by chemo treatments given by excellent staff at the R. S. McLaughlin Durham Regional Cancer Centre I slept a lot. Energy escaped me; I had little and some days none. It was hard to adjust as I always had lots of get-up-and-go to accomplish my daily routine. Get it done was my motto, but now that wasn't happening. Daily chores were left undone, which bothered me, but I had to learn to let them wait. It was difficult and frustrating for me.

On the positive side I tolerated the chemotherapy treatments well. My family was my support system, and Cindy, my daughter-in-law, visited and brought me lunch during my chemo sessions. In addition, a dear family friend, Lois, kindly drove me to my Monday breast cancer educational sessions and treatments before or after we enjoyed a chat over our coffee that brightened my day.

My sofa became my day bed, warm blankets helped me stay cozy. All went well with support from my family, the R. S. McLaughlin Durham Regional Cancer Centre where I had my treatments, Hearth Place, a wonderful nonprofit, which provided programs for cancer patients, and the After-Breast-Cancer-Foundation founded by Alicia Vianga. While I worked through the treatment processes, my support system and educational sessions were critical to my mental and physical health. I used up boxes of tissues soaking up tears caused by frustration and worry.

Fortunately, I connected with the After-Breast-Cancer-Foundation, a national organization, which provided free prostheses for women who did not have insurance. Also, they offered pre-surgery mastectomy kits for women, so they would have the supplies they needed to be more comfortable immediately after surgery.

One unforgettable day I received an invitation to be featured in the 2018 After-Breast-Cancer Calendar as an Ambassador, or as I called myself a Calendar Pin-Up Girl at eighty. Our ambassadors' mission was to support those with breast cancer.

Being Queen for a Day was a fantastic and memorable experience. We arrived at the location and introduced ourselves to others. Immediately I found a chair with my name card and a fuchsia-colored satin wrap to wear while I was getting my hair and make-up done. I felt like a movie star. I had lost my hair because of my chemotherapy, but my new natural hair wig was easy for the stylist to give me a professional look. My pre-fitted gown was black with brilliant gold beads everywhere, with a large bracelet with black and gold stones and fabulous earrings, which finished the look.

I felt my body was trying to tell me something. Strange, I mused, what was happening to me? I had always been extremely healthy, hiking and exploring the four corners of the world, then just like that, when a baseball batter comes up to bat:

Strike one: right eye surgery that went horribly wrong in Panama, followed by two unsuccessful corneal transplants. Currently, I am totally blind in my right eye.

Strike two: breast cancer and a right mastectomy with lymph node involvement. Is the third pitch going to be another strike?

The third pitch: I hit a home run and became an After-Breast-Cancer Calendar Girl at eighty years old.

I was blessed!

I had my personal photographer, Cristine Sacco, owner of Boy, Girl Photography. We took photos in the Toronto Financial District, and I had someone carry the train of my dress. The photo opportunity was truly a once-in-a-lifetime experience. My picture and my quotation were printed on my 2018 calendar page, as follows:

*After my eighty years, I realized life is not a goal; it is a journey.
My positive attitude, courage, determination, patience, and a
little bit of curiosity are all necessary stepping-stones to an amazing
life adventure. So, never close your eyes to new challenges, no
matter how difficult they may seem.*

Chapter 43

Pondering My Journey with Thoughts to Share

There are many gems I've learned during my solo travels before the internet and cell phones. Many, many more experiences to tell, but there is no more room in this book to share them all.

I wished I had known the secrets before I began my journey. But, of course, if that were true, none of us adventurers would have ever left home. This is life.

New lessons keep coming regardless of age and how much you think you already know. It never stops—the learning. I think that's the point. To grow! Yes, to grow into the best versions of ourselves. And to that end, travel is universal in its teaching. To understand, to nurture compassion and empathy. Let go of the judgments or preconceived ideas you grew up with and within the time and place you were born.

Have the ability to embrace both the positive and the negative in any situation and come out unscathed.

Embrace the inherent positivity in people around the globe and find forgiveness for those who fall short.

While solving problems during travel, I developed stamina and new skills. Surviving uncontrollable difficult changes in situations, I became resilient. I learned to think of life in both physical health, relationships, and lessons learned when something goes wrong; my problem-solving skills improved. If I needed help, I had to ask and depend on others, often hard to do. Sometimes you are the problem-solver and you can do more than just survive, but take every opportunity to grow. The value of travel is it gives you an opportunity to not just survive but learn and embrace life. The value of travel gives you the ability to look at life in a broad way.

If the bus breaks down, you have learned skills to manage the situation and find a way to turn every circumstance into a success.

Life is a continuous learning experience, bringing new situations every day. I am eternally grateful to leave you with my adventures. Above all else, I made connections throughout the world, with everyone I met. And I hope I made as lasting an impression on others as they made on me, while I was making connections.

Acknowledgments

As a solo traveler, it was incredible how strangers befriended me as I moved from one country to another along my journey, exploring 156 countries. Although I traveled by myself, I never felt alone. I am grateful to all who touched my life and looked after me, supported me with a word or two, and a warm welcome. Others shared their stories and deepest dreams with kindness, smiles, and generosity. My journey would not be possible without their help. I thank each one deeply and think of you often.

Many years of my travel were before the development of the internet and cell phones as we know them today. Strangers were the glue that held my travels together. Their gold dust sprinkled during my trips brought joy, laughter, and friendships. I learned so much from them about their way of life, which only enriched mine. I thank you for all you did and for the journey we shared together for minutes, an hour, a day, or more.

This book would never have happened without my gran, my father's support, my mother's passion for travel and her belief in my book; Dan, Bruce, and Betsy, my children's encouragement, knowledge, and unfailing support, along with cheers of my eleven grandchildren who have heard many of the stories as they have drifted off to sleep. I visited my family and enjoyed giving talks and displaying my artifacts to my grandchildren's school classes.

Each class tested my memory and had interesting questions that kept me alert.

Without the support of my brother, Peter, and my sister, Marjorie, I could not have traveled for long periods as they supported Mom.

Many thanks to Katie Cronin-Wood and Alison Moore, my dear friends, who helped me tell my story with the passion of my life's journey, lived experiences, and to finish my book in my eighty-sixth year. Walter Kent, Lois McDonald, Wanda Strachan, and Heidi Stone supported me in their own way in my journey.

Thanks to my beta readers, Linda Babin, Jenny Casey, Debby Hammons, Jeanette Manning, Margaret Robb, Rick Pyves, and Deb Stratas, who added helpful comments and caught the details that were missed; Cristina Sacco, founder of Boy, Girl Photography Studio (www.boygirlphotography.com) my photographer for the After-Breast-Cancer Calendar shoot, who also generously took photos for promotional purposes.

And a special thanks and deep gratitude to my production team, Lisa K. Pelto, Concierge Marketing, Inc.

Over the past few years, my diploma in creative writing at Humber College, my Ink Sisters (you know who you are) and the Writers Community of Durham Region provided opportunities to learn and grow as a writer while struggling with my cancer, blind eye, and leg and hip problems. Everyone who shared the details and wise ways about the skill of writing, editing, and publishing a book deserves my thanks. There were so many friends who gave me encouragement and supported me throughout my journey, and I thank you. I am grateful.

To continue my life of learning and contributing to society, I have been active on the Executive Committee of the Writers' Community of Durham Region and was honored to receive the

2018 Ivy Berry Scholarship. Over the years, I have published travel articles in local newspapers and many professional articles in Canadian healthcare journals and The 50+ Worker Abroad by Joyce Perrin chapter published in *The BIG Guide to Living and Working Overseas*, 4th edition, 2004. I am also a contributing author to *The Game Changer: How to Win in Life by Doing Simple Actions* (2022).

At eighty-six years of age, I am grateful to continue paying it forward as a patient, family, and caregiver partner on the Executive Leadership Team, Collaboration Council, and other committees of the Durham Region Ontario Health Team.

With all the gratitude I could bring forth, I am thrilled to share this book with you, and I genuinely want to share more tales. I hope these stories and experiences reach others and move them forward on their path of empowerment, success, and most of all feeling the human connections while traveling.

I share these lessons I learned during my travels:
Life is a privilege, not a right!

- My life was richer, meeting fellow travelers. Some have become longtime friends, others I hope never to see again, but everyone added value to my life.
- Most people want to help, not harm me.
- Children about two years old are similar to others in the world. But after three years of age, their culture influences their unique differences.
- Traveling solo brought both fun and fear.
- Traveling solo taught me to trust and grow alone and cherish unique experiences.
- On this journey, I learned what was important to me and what was not.

- I did not need many material items to survive; I lived out of one suitcase for eighteen months.
- While traveling alone, I learned to ask a lot of questions and made new friends by sharing my life as they shared theirs.
- I learned to listen to my body to know what I could and could not do.
- Traveling with younger people was the best way to continue learning about what is happening in the world without social media.
- My next adventure often started with a conversation, an idea, and then grew into a trip.
- Globalization and technology have effected tremendous changes in cultures. And I experienced the changes firsthand.
- If you need help, all you have to do is ask.
- I learned I needed only a few items to survive when I traveled.
- I believe in positivity; it can change my day.
- Life goes on day by day like the ocean waves lapping at the beach. The tide comes in, and it goes out, like a barometer of our feelings, happiness, and sadness. The ebb and flow of the ocean could represent life in general, your life or my life.
- Whether I do anything differently or stay in my comfort zone, the days pass one by one, and they lead into months and years. So I choose to pay it forward by sharing my skills with others, embracing adventure and exploration.
- Everyone makes life choices. May you choose well.
- May you be happy with your choices as you look back on your life. However, you can always change your direction.

Discussion Topics for Readers and Book Clubs

1. When you read the book, how would you describe your feelings?
2. Did the story pull you into the book immediately?
3. Describe the ways you were able to connect with Joyce during her journey.
4. Name three countries in the world you would include on your to-see list.
5. How would you describe three favorite parts of the story?
6. Do you wish you could or would have done any of the activities Joyce did in her life?
7. Name the most unusual adventure Joyce experienced in her travels.
8. Were you surprised the way the story unfolded?
9. Thinking back, what is the essence of Joyce's story?
10. If a friend asked you to describe the story, what would you say?
11. What made you want to finish the book?
12. With whom would you like to share or recommend the book?
13. Would you like to read more stories authored by Joyce?

About the Author

Joyce Perrin penned stories when young, but what held her interest throughout life was the blue bound set of books at home called *Lands and People*, which had pictures and explained about countries around the world. She found herself imagining visiting new nations, talking to the people, tasting their foods, and learning about their culture.

In high school her interests included participating in sports such as senior basketball and figure skating, and she was head cheerleader for the senior boys' basketball games. Ultimately, teaching swimming and synchronized swimming were her passions. She competed in the Canadian synchronized swimming championships, swam for the University of Alberta and the Edmonton Aquadettes swim teams in individual, pairs, and team competitions, and won many prizes.

Joyce achieved the highest award in Girl Guiding, the Gold Cord, and represented Canada with ten others at an International Girl Guide camp in Sweden. At the camp she met Lady Olave Baden-Powell, the founder of the Girl Guide movement. Lady Baden-Powell was an inspiration to Joyce and during her lifetime was her role model. Her quote, "Happiness comes not from what we have but from what we give and what we share," has been a guiding light for Joyce.

Joyce married immediately after graduating from the University of Alberta with a BS in nursing. She worked in nursing administration with the Visiting Nurse Association. After her three children were in school, she attended graduate school and obtained her diploma in hospital administration and was appointed Chief Executive Officer of a Toronto hospital.

Life changed when Joyce and her husband went their separate ways, and after her three children were married, she was free from responsibilities for others. She resigned from her Canadian senior healthcare job to travel the world on her solo journey.

Now totally blind in one eye, and an eighty-six-year-old breast cancer survivor, she finished writing her book and finds herself giving support to other cancer survivors and has volunteered as a patient, family, and care partner with the local regional Durham Ontario Health Team since its inception.

After touring the seven continents Joyce settled in the Republic of Panama, where she cofounded the voluntary Panama Hospice and Respite Foundation. This organization helped Panamanians and expatriates maneuver through the healthcare system at the end of life.

She celebrates writing this book, hoping it inspires you to follow your passion no matter how long it takes.

Joyce makes her home in the greater Toronto area in Canada.

Contact Joyce here:
Email: joyce.perrin.author@gmail.com
Website: www.JoycePerrin.com

Made in the USA
Middletown, DE
09 April 2023

28452862R00213